The Domestic Life of a Medieval City

University of Nebraska Press: Lincoln and London

David Nicholas

The Domestic Life

of a Medieval City:

Women, Children,

and the Family in

Fourteenth-Century

GHENT

Copyright 1985 by
the University of Nebraska Press
All rights reserved
Manufactured in the United
States of America

Publication of this book
was assisted by a grant from the
National Endowment for the
Humanities, a federal agency
that supports the study of
fields such as history, philosophy,
literature, and languages.

The paper in this book meets the
guidelines for permanence
and durability of the Committee on
Production Guidelines for
Book Longevity of the Council on
Library Resources.

Library of Congress
Cataloging in Publication Data

Nicholas, David, 1939–
The domestic life of a medieval city.

Bibliography: p.
Includes index.
1. Family–Belgium–Ghent–History.
2. Belgium–History–To 1555.
3. Domestic relations–Belgium–
Ghent–History.   4. Children–
Belgium–Ghent–History.   I. Title.
HQ633.N53   1985
306.8'5'094931   84-22011
ISBN 0-8032-3310-8
(alk. paper)

For my mentor, Bryce Lyon

Contents

Preface

This book is the first of a projected two-volume study of the social and economic life of Ghent between the assumption of power by the guilds in 1302 and the accession of the duke of Burgundy as count of Flanders in 1384. These volumes represent nearly two decades of intellectual immersion in the archives of Ghent. I have incurred numerous obligations. I received microfilm grants from the American Philosophical Society in 1973 and 1978; a fellowship from the American Council of Learned Societies for the fall semester, 1978; a fellowship for Younger Scholars of the National Endowment for the Humanities for the academic year 1969–70; summer fellowships from the Research Council of the University of Nebraska–Lincoln in 1973, 1978, and 1983; and leaves of absence from the University of Nebraska–Lincoln for the spring semester 1978 and the fall semesters 1973 and 1984. Although some of these were awarded for projects that have resulted in other publications, each of them allowed me to devote time to examining the records of Ghent and thus contributed to the formulation of conclusions expressed in this volume.

I have received constant cooperation and assistance from my friends at the University of Ghent, particularly Professors Adriaan Verhulst and Walter Prevenier and Dr. M. Vandermaesen. The archivists and staff of the Rijksarchief te Gent have been extremely helpful, both in locating documents and in providing microfilm. I also thank the Archives Générales du Royaume, Brussels, for its cooperation.

The map accompanying this volume has been adapted from that of G. Des Marez, *Étude sur la Propriété foncière dans les villes du Moyen-Age et spécialement en Flandre* (Ghent: H. Engelcke, 1898).

The spellings used in the fourteenth-century Flemish texts have generally been retained for personal names and institutions (e.g., Heinric rather than Hendrik, *scepenen* rather than *schepenen*) except in cases where there is a commonly used English version (e.g., Bruges rather than Brugge).

My greatest obligation, however, is to the staff of the Stadsarchief te Gent. From the moment of my first arrival in the archive, in February 1966, the then archivist, Dr. Carlos Wyffels, and his staff, particularly Mme D. d'Hooghe-Floryn, showed remarkable patience and courtesy in introducing me to the wealth of the Ghent records. Dr. Johan Decavele, who became archivist shortly afterward, has been no less helpful. Nothing that I can say can express my gratitude adequately. I hope that the series of publications that this volume inaugurates will do so.

Introduction

The Subject
of the Inquiry

hent, in the county of Flanders, was the second largest city of Europe north of the Alps in the fourteenth century. Its population of some 60,000, even after the losses of the Black Death, placed it substantially behind Paris but made it half again as large as London and nearby Bruges.[1] Two primitive nuclei, an agrarian settlement near the Scheldt River on the eastern edge of the modern city and a merchant *Wik* outside the castle of the Flemish counts on the Leie River, had merged by the eleventh century and perhaps the late tenth.[2] The economic orientation was dual throughout the Middle Ages. The city is most famous for its textile industry, specializing in a fine export product.[3] Textile artisans constituted half to three-fifths of the work force of the city in the fourteenth century,[4] but the largest capital concentration in Ghent was in the hands of shipping magnates. Ghent had originated as an exchange point between grain-rich northern France and southern Flanders and the primarily pastoral and thinly settled Flemish coastal plain.[5] By the fourteenth century the city had a staple on all grain passing through Flanders on the Scheldt and Leie. The large industrial work force was itself a captive market, and the shippers also reexported large quantities of food.[6] Although Bruges, the western neighbor and frequent bitter rival of Ghent, is often considered a prototypical shipping center due to its spectacular involvement in the Italian, Hanse, and

English commerce,[7] while Ghent is seen as chiefly industrial, Ghent, in fact, had an immense shipping industry, concentrated on its two rivers and the northwestern markets which they provided. The shippers' staple and the industrial protectionism of the textile guilds led the city government to extend its influence throughout eastern Flanders and in periods of crisis over the entire county during the fourteenth century.[8]

Ghent was frequently racked by political upheavals during the fourteenth century, but historians have sometimes exaggerated the social or "class" character of these conflicts, particularly the dissension within the textile sector between the weavers and the more proletarian fullers.[9] Ghent had been ruled by a Francophile merchant patriciate in the thirteenth century.[10] This group was overthrown in 1302, when Ghent joined other Flemish communities in ejecting the despised French overlords of the Flemish counts. The composition of the two boards of *scepenen*, or city councillors, was changed, but not until much later were guilds or groups of guilds automatically assured of seats in the magistracy. The triumph of 1302 was temporary, for even by 1305 most of the patrician families had returned to the city and are found again in its government, although the composition of the ruling group remained broader than before 1302.[11] Between 1320 and 1338 Ghent was ruled by five captains, who overshadowed the still functioning *scepenen*.[12] During this period comes the first mention of a distinction that would later have a great impact on the political life of the city, among three "members": the fullers, who usually allied with the Francophile counts of Flanders; the weavers, who tended to be revolutionary and favored an English alliance; and the "small guilds," fifty-nine legally recognized corporations, most of whose members produced for or served a primarily local market. The small guilds were dominated by the shippers, the butchers and fishmongers, the carpenters or contractors, and the brewers. Together they constituted at least forty percent of the work force of the city and usually held the balance of power between the weavers and fullers. To this locally based group should also be added the numerous workers whose trade was not officially recognized by the guild organizations of the city.

Much of the turmoil in Ghent is due to the fact that while Flanders was a French crown fief and its counts generally loyal vassals, the economic interests of the city drew it toward an English alliance in a period of hostility between England and France, for the high-grade wool used in the export textiles for which Ghent was so justly famed came mainly from England. In 1337, when the English placed an embargo on their wool export to try to force Count Louis of Nevers to ally with them against the French, they caused considerable unemployment in Ghent.

Hence between 1338 and 1349, while Jacob Van Artevelde and his partisans dominated political life at Ghent, the city moved from a position of neutrality into an open alliance with the English. Although Van Artevelde is sometimes portrayed as a partisan of the weavers or even as a democratic reformer, his régime actually seems to have balanced the competing factions of the city very nicely.[13] But the English were unwilling or unable to be of much help after Van Artevelde was assassinated in 1345. In early 1349 Count Louis of Male, assisted by the French, installed a régime dominated by fullers and small guildsmen. The last adherents of the previous régime, including many weavers, were defeated in a pitched battle on the Friday Market. The weavers were excluded from participation in the city government, and many emigrated.

The weavers returned to power in 1359. Joining the small guilds, which were the great constant of the political life of Ghent, they in their turn permanently banned the fullers from public life. Another civil war erupted in 1379, this time over the attempt of Bruges, with the count's authorization, to channel into the Leie south of Ghent and so to divert directly to Bruges much of the grain trade that had made Ghent so prosperous. During this war the landholding *poorterij* became the third "member" in the city government. The uprising of 1379–85 may have caused more disruption in the city than any previous civil conflict. Population losses were heavy; some parts of rural Flanders only regained their prewar productivity in the fifteenth century.[14] The last independent count of Flanders died in 1384. His son-in-law and successor was Philip the Bold, duke of Burgundy, with whose accession the pretensions of Ghent to autonomy were curtailed, although that did not stop the city from making several fruitless uprisings in the fifteenth century.

The manuscript records of fourteenth-century Ghent are substantial. Information concerning the domestic life of the city comes largely from the registers of transactions before the two benches of the city council, the *scepenen* of the *Keure* and of *Gedele,* together with the *Zoendincboeken* (Atonement Books) kept by the *scepenen* of *Gedele* in their capacity as justices of the peace. The *Keure Jaarregisters* have gaps, but the other two series are continuous from 1349. These documents can be supplemented with other material, notably the city accounts, the accounts of the counts' bailiffs in Ghent, and occasional information from charters and rent books. Most of these records, notably the registers of the *scepenen* and the *Zoen-*

dincboeken, are kept in the Municipal Archive of Ghent. Most of the rest are in the State Archive of Ghent, but relevant documentation is found also in the General Archives of the Realm at Brussels, the Archives Départementales du Nord at Lille, and the archive of St. Jacob's Church in Ghent. The total constitutes a vast fund of hitherto untapped information on the situations of women, children, and the nuclear and extended families.

The purpose of this volume is to illustrate the extent to which legal norms conformed, or more often failed to conform, to actual practice in social relationships. The legal customs of Flanders were not uniform, and those of Ghent were only in the process of formation during the fourteenth century. Students of Roman law will note close correlations between the legal standing of women and children in Ghent and principles of classical jurisprudence. Yet these principles were as often honored in the breach as in the application. My intention is to show from the Ghent records how men, women, and children interacted within the family and how the family in its turn functioned as a social, economic, and defensive unit toward outsiders. Comparisons of the situation at Ghent with the findings of students of the European family during the early modern period will, I believe, demonstrate an essential continuity in the practical aspects of family life between the Middle Ages and the Industrial Revolution.

The Traditional Family and the Postindustrial Historian

We are mercifully far removed from the time when most serious historical writing about the Middle Ages was, as Joseph Ritson wrote in 1887, "consecrated to the crimes and follies of titled ruffians and sainted idiots."[15] Recent historiography has done much to rectify the neglect of women, children, and the family by traditional practitioners of the discipline. But while studies of the urban family in Italy have become de rigueur, most family research for medieval northern Europe has concentrated on the nobility. There have been some general treatments of medieval women, varying considerably in sophistication and emphasis.[16] These accounts have been based on narrative and statute evidence, and some have very colorful personality portrayals.[17] The doyenne of an earlier generation of medieval social historians, Eileen Power, recognized that while urban women in Italy seem to have been confined largely to a domestic role, their English and French contemporaries were active in many trades, particularly textiles and victualling, both independently and as helpmates or even substitutes for their husbands.[18] The French *Histoire Mondiale de la Femme* is noteworthy for its realistic portrayals of women of all social levels,[19] while the publications of the Société Jean Bodin take a characteristically juridical approach.[20] By far the most sophisticated of the surveys, basd on both original sources and the most recent scholarship, is the recent study of Shulamith Shahar, which is now available for English readers.[21]

Thus women have increasingly been the subjects of scholarly scrutiny. It is clear that while women in orders have received considerable treatment—certainly this is true for Ghent[22]—a vast body of material on women in the world awaits the attention of scholars. Since David Herlihy's early pioneering studies of the statistical evidence relating to women in Mediterranean Europe,[23] many scholars have devoted their attention to this problem.[24]

Students of the history of medieval women face the problem that most documents, particularly those of an official or public character, were written by men and reflect topics of concern to them. Thus women appear only incidentally. This problem is even more acute with the history of children in the Middle Ages. Most older accounts accepted uncritically the notion that children were mistreated by adults, who had little comprehension of them. Few today would maintain this extreme view.[25] Recent discussion of the problem has centered on the study of Philippe Ariès.[26] The theories of Ariès and some others who have approached the problem of premodern childhood and the family, notably Edward Shorter, seem rooted more in contemporary ideologies than in a desire for historical accuracy. Ariès argues that the Middle Ages knew no "concept of childhood." Children were treated as small adults, playing at least by age four the same games that adults played, and were generally considered part of the adult world. Children were not highly valued until the seventeenth century, which Ariès considers a great historical watershed. Adults kept a psychological distance from children because the danger of loss of a child was considerable in a period of high mortality rates; one could not afford to become too attached to one's offspring even if one were so inclined. But this had a positive side, for the "invention" of childhood in the seventeenth century also created a tyrannical family that deprived children of the freedom which they had enjoyed in "traditional Europe."

Totally apart from the question of whether the modern age has a generally accepted or applicable "concept of childhood," most historians have realized that Ariès's thesis simply does not fit the facts. But for all its faults, it did cause historians to begin to investigate childhood seriously. The collection of studies edited by Lloyd de Mause[27] is at a generally high level, but it is also interesting that while de Mause himself and the authors of the contributions dealing with childhood since the fifteenth century accept Ariès's views with only minor demurral, the two medievalists, Mary Martin McLaughlin and James Bruce Ross, do not use his conceptual framework. Their articles, although excellent, illustrate a serious problem faced by all historians of medieval childhood: most biographies and virtually all manuals of childrearing practice were written by or about clergymen, and both authors display a healthy skepticism of the typicality of such infancies as that of Guibert of Nogent. Ross's article on the middle-class child in Renaissance Italy finds that most children grew up in large extended families and were "lost" in a psychological sense in families often including an elderly father, a youthful but distant mother, a wetnurse, half siblings, and paternal bastards. Recent studies have confirmed this picture for the wealthy Italian urban child but not for the child of the artisan, who matured in an environment much more recognizably "modern."[28]

The literature on the premodern family is much larger than that on women and children. Recent scholarship has suffered from the concentration of family research in the Mediterranean area on the medieval and Renaissance cities, while that of northern Europe has focused on peasant families in England and France between the sixteenth and eighteenth centuries and on noble families in the eleventh and twelfth. Scholars have naturally noted tremendous differences but have failed to account for them by the great variations in time and place. The present study of the domestic life of Ghent, which to the best of my knowledge is the first book-length treatment of family structures in a medieval city of northern Europe, should at least bridge the gap and show that the current debate is not as incapable of resolution as now appears to be the case.

Several stimulating models of the origin and character of marriage and the family in traditional Europe have been suggested. It is not surprising that some cannot be recommended. In a work that has gained wide public acceptance, perhaps due to the highly visible endorsement given it by Ariès,[29] Edward Shorter sets out with admirable zeal to combat the Marxist view of nineteenth-century industrialization as an evil that destroyed the idyllic traditional family, but he quickly veers off into ahistorical distortions. Shorter inveighs against what he calls the "eternal constant" school, specifically Peter Laslett and Jean-Louis Flandrin, who portray social relationships in gradual evolution. Shorter insists that the eighteenth century witnessed a veritable revolution. Before this time the nuclear family was severely restricted by the clan and by its concern with its ancestors. Neither sexual attraction nor human affection was involved in premodern marriages, and even maternal love is not found before the eighteenth century. A cataclysmic onslaught of feeling thus ended the "structured, changeless, compact traditional order."

A work that invites comparison to Shorter's but lacks its often strident tone is the now classic study of Lawrence Stone.[30] This book has a wealth of detail that at times makes it very useful, but its analytical framework is that of Ariès and Shorter. The lineage, we find, was more important than the nuclear family in northern as well as southern Europe. Marriages were unemotional matters, and attitudes toward children were crass. The patriarch ruled with an iron fist, and kindred and parents, rather than individuals, chose marriage partners for the adult children in this "Open Lineage Family," which was gradually replaced from the early sixteenth century by that even greater evil, the "Restricted Patriarchal Nuclear Family."

Other recent syntheses, however, have presented ideas that warrant more serious discussion. Jack Goody, author and editor of numerous important contributions to the history of both the western and non-western family, points out in his most recent book[31] that endogamy within the extended family was normal in classical antiquity and remains so in the Moslem world, but this has not been true of the northern Mediterranean since the conversion to Christianity. The notoriously broad definitions of incest established by the medieval church were for Goody a conscious effort to make marriages harder to contract and thereby to hinder the production of children who could inherit property from their parents. The church put its authority behind customs facilitating alienation of property outside both the nuclear and extended families, notably to the church. The church also imposed restrictions not found in Roman law on the right of surviving spouses to dower. Together with the facts that most women outlived their husbands and that the church discouraged remarriage, this fostered the material interests of the church while imposing a revolutionary marriage structure upon the medieval West. Christianity had entered a Mediterranean type social structure characterized by loyalty to the nuclear family and the clan but had disrupted the family to further its own material interest. Goody also sees primogeniture not only as a means of keeping property within the nuclear family but also as a device for excluding the rights of collateral heirs and of the extended family, which no longer had to consent to alienations to the church. The emphasis that we find at Ghent on bilateral kinship and the strength of the nuclear family, but with an important role for the kindred, seems thus a reversion to an earlier social structure, with elements of the Mediterranean family combined with characteristics common to the primitive Germanic societies, which had bilateral inheritance and responsibility.

The computer-assisted analysis of the Florentine *catasto* of 1427 by David Herlihy and Christiane Klapisch-Zuber has led those scholars to a different model of the medieval family of the Mediterranean type that is not irreconcilable with Goody's.[32] Herlihy's earlier studies modified the view of Marc Bloch that a "progressive nuclearization" of the family since the time of the Germanic invasions meant that the clans had little weight by the late Middle Ages. Eleventh-century Italian families were consolidating their property, not dispersing it among family branches. Family bonds became looser from the mid-twelfth century only to become more cohesive again in the wake of the disasters of the late Middle Ages. There can thus be no question of a progressive and continuous evolution of extended into nuclear family, for both were important.[33] Most families reporting in the *catasto* of 1427 were single-generation nuclear families, and there were even many single-person households. The proportion of extended families is higher in rural Tuscany than in the cities. Within the cities the extended family is found most often among the wealthy, who had the most property to protect and were thus most careful to live in family complexes of houses and to exercise caution in contracting marriage alliances.

The extended patrilineal family was also very important at Genoa, particularly among the noble *alberghi,* which had both urban and rural branches. Yet even here the nuclear family was the norm among the artisans, for whom marriage created the essential economic partnership.[34] Throughout the Mediterranean basin family membership was strictly agnatic, without a trace of the bilaterality found at Ghent. Florentine women were often appreciably younger than their husbands, but both sexes married later than in nonwestern cultures, a characteristic which seems generally true of both the Mediterranean and northern family types. The length of apprenticeship and delayed emancipation due to the power of the paterfamilias meant that the young men were underoccupied and prone to violence in both the southern and northern cities. Comparatively few Tuscan widows remarried, for the ecclesiastical strictures against remarriage seem to have had greater impact in the South than in the North. Male domination of the family was absolute in all areas except childrearing. Women stayed at home. The situation at Ghent was markedly different. While men ruled in law, women played an important role in the economic, although not the political, life of the city.

Studies not undertaken from the demographic perspective have tended to uphold the Herlihy and Klapisch-Zuber model for the Italian urban family. Richard Goldthwaite has suggested that the new type of domestic architecture, centering on the *loggia,* associated with the Florentine Renaissance meant that the older custom of family blocs of houses was yielding in the fifteenth century to a modified triumph of the nuclear family.[35] Goldthwaite's conclusions have been criticized by F. W. Kent, whose work confirms the notion of the patrilineal extended family dominating Italy.[36] Kent emphasizes the efforts to keep property within the lineage through judicious wills and marriages; but since he is investigating wealthy and well-documented families, among whom family bonds were much stronger than among the less generously endowed, his conclusions probably cannot be generalized. Paolo Cammarosano has also emphasized the authority of the father and the strength of the agnatic kindred in urban Italy.[37] Patrilineal inheritance is found from the earliest period and continues to exclude female lines, although only among the wealthy were fathers able to limit the discretion of their adult sons or deprive them of property until just before the father's death. But Italian estates were partible equally among all sons, so that it was extremely difficult in practice to keep property within the same extended family.

Georges Duby has also established a model for the medieval marriage, but based on noble and royal marriage practices in France between 1000 and 1250.[38] Duby posits two "matrimonial moralities," the priestly and the knightly, which were initially in opposition but became reconciled during the twelfth century into the marriage ethic that is still recognized in western society. Marriage was still primarily a civil concern in the Carolingian age, for the theologians considered marriage to be at worst defilement and at best a poor substitute for celibacy. While Goody explains ecclesiastical restrictions as a device to facilitate the acquisition of property by the church, Duby sees the gradual sacramentalizing of marriage as the consequence of a laudable desire to provide a decent remedy for lust. Nobles who ignored the strictures of the clergy against repudiation of spouses, concubinage, and incest were acting in accordance with a changing aristocratic notion of kinship in the eleventh century, involving a shift from a concept of horizontal and bilateral grouping of two or three generations as the kin group to a strictly vertical and agnatic concept. This development weakened the positions of women and younger sons, who were often prevented by the power of the clan father from making a marriage, and of sons-in-law, who often found their wives' marriage portions limited to what had been their mothers' dowries. Ivo of Chartres provided the view of marriage that became the official position of the church and reconciled the priestly and knightly traditions: a priest was necessary for a valid marriage, but the consent of the contracting parties and not simply of their families was a prerequisite. The spouses had to be of the age of reason. The spiritual union preceded the carnal, while the woman, as the instigator of lewdness, was strictly subordinated to her husband. Above all, incest was defined as within the seventh degree, and marriage was made strictly monogamous.

Duby's model is more ingenious than convincing. The church was trying to regulate marriage practices long before it decided that marriage was a sacrament. Some cases that Duby cites prove that the ecclesiastical strictures had minimal effect in the real world, even after the supposed reconciliation of the two models in the twelfth century. And yet as a practical matter his position is not irreconcilable with Goody's; they differ in the motives assigned to the church but agree on what the church actually did.

The work of Peter Laslett and his research group at the University of Cambridge has inspired a second northern European model of the family. Laslett's views are shared generally by Emmanuel Le Roy Ladurie and Jean-Louis Flandrin. Laslett has been criticized, justly in my opinion, for taking a somewhat romantic view of the traditional family. Even the title of his best-known work betrays it as a lament for a bygone age.[39] The family is the *familia,* including household personnel as well as blood relations. Apprentices often helped to preserve the house by marrying their masters' widows or daughters. Although the family was essentially nuclear, old English society was an association of heads of families, not of individuals. When the factory came to outproduce the family, the family lost its importance to a mass society.

Laslett's other work is deeper. Following J. Hajnal,[40] he has suggested four characteristics of the western family, which is opposed to the Mediterranean model.[41] First, the family structure is essentially nuclear. Although the extended family is significant, it is less so than in the Mediterranean family. Flandrin has found that the extended family was powerful in seventeenth-century peasant society only if its members lived in proximity, usually in the same village, for distance eroded emotional bonds.[42] The western family is also characterized by a comparatively advanced age for childrearing mothers; a slight age gap between spouses, with many wives older than their husbands and marriages accordingly tending toward the companionate; and the presence of servants in many households. Although we have no reliable statistics on these points for fourteenth-century Ghent, the narrative and legal evidence clearly places Ghent within the western European family model.

Laslett has also concluded that the extended family is most often found in areas of impartible inheritance, and studies of English rural society place the western patterns there as early as the thirteenth century.[43] Le Roy Ladurie has pursued this theme in two articles based on the work of Jean Yver.[44] He finds that throughout the Middle Ages the most common form of handling the aspirations of daughters and some younger sons was to give them marriage portions, then to exclude them from the parental inheritance. But at the end of the Middle Ages and during the sixteenth century the "Parisian" or optative system came into use in parts of northern France and the Low Countries: the couple could return the marriage portion if they wished, then share equally with the siblings in dividing the parental estate. The earlier type was well suited to an agrarian society, for it kept the basic family property intact while compensating daughters and their husbands, whereas the newer system was more flexible and was usually found in cities. Ghent had the Parisian inheritance custom throughout the fourteenth century. Ghent and Flanders had rigidly partible inheritance for both rich and poor; although some Mediterranean customs make possible preferential treatment for certain heirs favored by the paterfamilias, children in our study were treated equitably.[45]

In other works Laslett elaborates on his theme that the "domestic group" was not larger and more complex before than after the Industrial Revolution.[46] Ghent shows a domination of the nuclear family, but the extended family intervened if the conjugal family was broken, generally by a death. Different branches or generations of the same family usually did not share a domicile. Those wealthy enough to afford them had complexes of houses with different residences for the several nuclear families comprising the extended group. But while residences were separated, the kindred had extremely important functions, and Ghent thus conforms more to Flandrin's notion of physical proximity leading to extended family interaction than to Laslett's suggestion of extremely weak extended families.

Our description of domestic life in Ghent during the fourteenth century will be closer to the model suggested by Laslett and Flandrin for the western family than to those of Duby for the nobility or of Goody and Herlihy and Klapisch-Zuber for the Mediterranean family. Flandrin's treatment has much to recommend it, but he bases his conclusions on a small number of persons about whom he has a great deal of information. We must derive a composite picture of the basic and generally applicable social norms of Ghent, for few individuals can be described with such detail as is possible for Flandrin's subjects. We cannot provide the wealth of information about human emotions and particularly about sexual practices that makes Flandrin's presentation so graphic, but we do have enough to suggest that life within the family in fourteenth-century Ghent, both relations between spouses and between parents and their children, was probably quite close to what he describes for seventeenth-century France. What Laslett saw as the norm in the sixteenth century, when his statistics begin, and what Flandrin considered startlingly new in the seventeenth, in each case based primarily on rural prototypes, must now be seen as the essential framework for family life in a very large and influential urban community during the late Middle Ages. The modern age seems less revolutionary as its medieval antecedents are explored.

Part One

*The Dragons
of the Distaff*

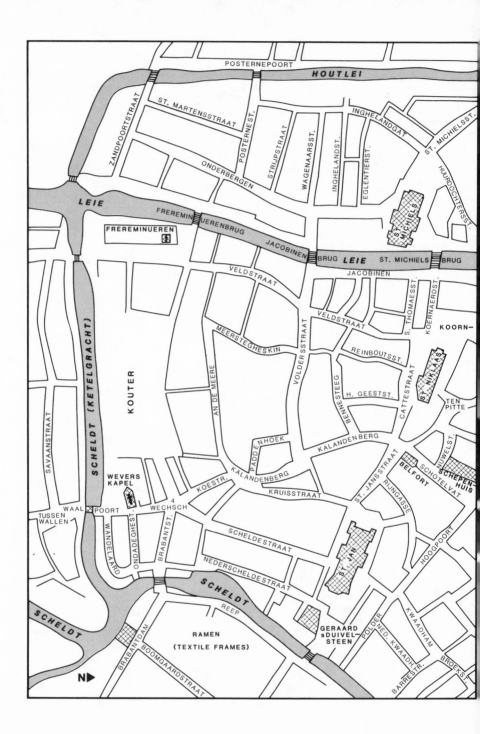

POSTERNEPOORT

HOUTLEI

ST. MARTENSSTRAAT

ZANDPOORTSTRAAT

ONDERBERGEN

POSTERNEST.

STRIJPSTRAAT

WAGENAARSST.

INGHELANDST.

INGHELANDGAT

EGLENTIERST.

ST. MICHIELSST.

HUUROCHTERSST.

ST. MICHIELS

LEIE

FREREMINUEREN

FREREMINUEREN

QUERENBRUG

JACOBINEN

BRUG LEIE ST. MICHIELS BRUG

JACOBINEN

VELDSTRAAT

VELDSTRAAT

S. THOMAESST.

KOERNAERDST.

KOORN-

MEERSTEGHESKIN

VOLDERSSTRAAT

REINBOUTSST.

CATTESTRAAT

ST. NIKLAAS

SCHELDT (KETELGRACHT)

KOUTER

AN DE MEERE

H. GEESTST.

BENNESTEEG

TEN PITTE

SAVAANSTRAAT

PADDENHOEK

KALANDENBERG

SUWELST.

SCHOTELVAT

SCHEPEN HUIS

WEVERS KAPEL

KOESTR.

KALANDENBERG

ST. JANSSTRAAT

RIJNGASSE

BELFORT

WAAL POORT

WECHSCH

KRUISSTRAAT

HOOGPOORT

TUSSEN WALLEN

WANDELAARD

ONDADEGHEST.

BRABANTST.

SCHELDESTRAAT

ST. JAN

NEDERSCHELDESTRAAT

KWAADHAM

SCHELDT

SCHELDT

REEP

GERAARD sDUIVEL- STEEN

POLDER

NED. KWAADH.

KWAADH.

N

RAMEN (TEXTILE FRAMES)

BRABANTDAM

BOOMGAARDSTRAAT

BARRESTR.

BROEKST.

14

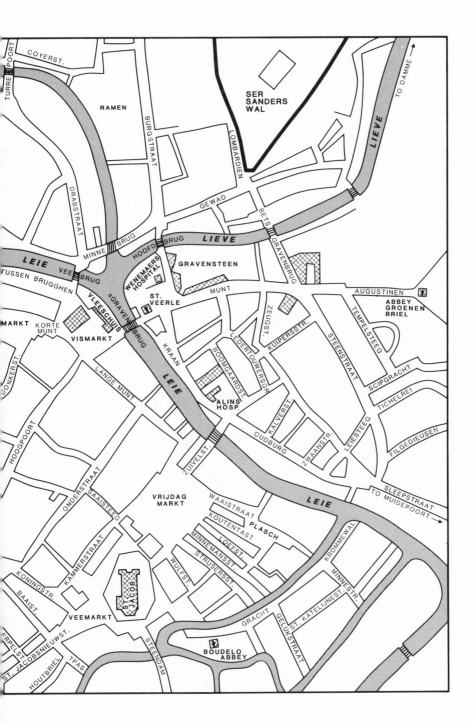

Chapter One

The Fruits of Frailty:
Violence and Marriage

The history of women and the family is in large measure a study of genealogy, which involves tracing personal and family names. The problem is serious enough for men, for whom the determinants were most frequently an occupation that became a family name and the compound names derived from "van" with a place. Since personal names tended to run in families and the overwhelming majority were the standard biblical or saints' names, it is sometimes impossible to determine even which generation is meant within the same family. There are exceptions, such as the surgeon Hector Van Nevele and his violent kinsman Ypocras. But persons of both sexes might even be called by different names under different circumstances: the guardian of Betkin Van Waes is called Jan Symoens in two texts, Jan Moenins in a third.[1]

But the issue is considerably more complicated with women. Females, particularly those of the lower classes, were sometimes called only by a personal name and an occupation or characteristic. One thinks, for example, of the married lady known as Lover Katie.[2] Although most legitimate daughters took their fathers' family names, some did not, and we find some legitimate daughters who assumed their mothers' maiden names. Illegitimate girls normally took their mothers' names, since they could not inherit from the father unless he acknowledged paternity; but if he did, they ordinarily took his name. Most women took their husbands' names upon marriage, but they might continue to use the maiden name, particularly if they owned substantial property or practiced a profession. Celie Amelakens, the prominent moneychanger who will be given detailed scrutiny below, used her husband's name but even after marriage she was occasionally called Rebbe, her maiden name. By contrast, Kateline Paridaen, the widow of Jan Van Libertsa, later married Jan Haec but continued to be called Paridaen. Kateline Van der Lake owed a debt under that name to her son Diederic but was being called Kateline Muloc, mother of Diederic Van der Lake, later in the same year.[3]

Most women had legal personalities only through male guardians.[4] The guardian's consent was implied even if he was not present to speak for her. The guardian of a single woman was normally her father, or failing him a brother or an uncle. Her husband assumed legal responsibility for her when she married. Widows who remarried were often called by the immediately previous husband's name, particularly if there were children of the prior marriage, but such women might also revert to using their maiden names. Husbands and wives are sometimes mentioned together in the same text without indication that they are married. Matheus de Backere is stated in 1370 to have become the guardian of the daughter of Wijvin de Roede. Nowhere is Wijvin called his wife, although they were married to each other by late 1361.[5]

For a woman who had no man to assist her in a city with a high crime rate[6] and loose sexual mores, life was dangerous. Under the circumstances it is perhaps surprising that women were as infrequently the victims of violent crime as seems to have been the case. Homicide was in principle a private matter to be settled between the clans, with the city government used only as an intermediary. The blood price paid for a murdered woman was normally only slightly lower than that paid for a man of the same social standing.[7] But as Table 1 shows, only twenty-six women were murdered in the thiry years between 1350 and 1380, and in only one year are there more than two cases. Only one woman was directly responsible for a homicide. There are two uxoricides, in 1364 and 1374. By contrast, 699 men were killed during this period, an average of twenty-three each year.

The picture changes when we deal with acts of petty violence and the use of foul language. Here women seem to have given as well as taken. Table 2 gives totals of the violent offenses punished by the magistrates at the regular trial days; homicides are excluded, since they were atoned by private composition and the blood price registered in the magistrates' book. The percentage of these crimes in which women were principals,

Table 1. Homicides at Ghent, 1350–1380

Fiscal Year	Homicides Atoned	Number of Women as Killers	Number of Women Killed
1350 (−51)	23	−	2
1351	27	−	−
1352	23	−	2
1353	19	−	−
1354	38	1	1
1355	24	−	1
1356	29	−	2
1357	42	−	5
1358	29	−	2
1359	43	−	1
1360	23	−	−
1361	20	−	−
1362	16	−	−
1363	28	−	2
1364	20	−	1
1365	17	−	−
1366	23	−	−
1367	20	−	1
1368	12	−	1
1369	39	−	−
1370	19	−	−
1371	20	−	1
1372	16	−	−
1373	18	−	−
1374	21	−	2
1375	24	−	1
1376	28	−	−
1377	21	−	−
1378	23	−	−
1379 (−80)[a]	19	−	1
TOTAL	725	1	26

[a]Partial year.   Source: SAG, Z 1350–1380.

Table 2. Violent Crimes Punished by *Scepenen*
of Ghent at Regular Trial Days, 1350–1379

Year	1	2	3	4	5	6	7	8	9
1350 (−1)	80	23	28.75%	17	2	2	2	–	0.00%
1351	102	26	25.49	17	2	2	2	3	15.79
1352	138	57	41.30	26	2	14	7	8	24.24
1353	117	58	49.57	36	2	9	4	7	17.50
1354	114	39	34.21	26	1	6	4	2	6.67
1355	92	27	29.34	14	2	4	4	3	16.67
1356	132	43	32.58	28	1	5	2	7	23.33
1357	142	28	19.72	17	2	–	1	13	76.47
1358	131	28	21.37	15	4	2	2	5	29.41
1359	155	39	25.16	25	3	3	2	6	22.22
1360	55	8	14.55	6	–	–	1	1	14.29
1361	132	35	26.52	26	2	3	2	2	7.14
1362	118	40	33.90	26	3	2	1	8	29.63
1363	152	41	26.97	23	5	4	1	8	33.33
1364	154	43	27.92	23	2	6	–	12	52.17
1365	194	59	30.41	30	6	10	4	9	26.47
1366	165	56	33.94	28	3	11	1	13	44.83
1367	160	35	21.88	25	4	1	1	4	15.38
1368	98	37	37.76	18	1	8	1	9	47.37
1369	170	49	28.82	31	2	9	–	7	22.59
1370	177	51	28.81	28	1	16	2	6	20.00
1371	145	54	37.24	35	4	6	–	9	25.71
1372	165	57	34.55	34	2	7	3	11	29.73
1373	183	50	27.32	32	4	2	1	11	33.33
1374	225	54	24.00	25	4	3	–	22	88.00
1375	220	63	28.64	33	3	5	6	16	41.03
1376	215	60	27.90	30	3	7	5	15	42.86
1377	250	55	22.00	31	8	1	1	14	43.75
1378 (−9)	187	67	35.83	39	6	10	–	12	30.77

Key to Column Numbers
1. Total offenses punished at regular trial days.
2. Total women involved as principals in the cases tabulated in column 1.
3. Column 2 as a percentage of column 1.
4. Women as victims of aggression from men *or* mutual aggression.
5. Women clearly aggressors against men.
6. Actionable language used by woman against man.
7. Actionable language used by man about woman.
8. Two or more women in violence or actionable language against each other.
9. Column 8 as a percentage of column 4 and column 7, indicating hostility between women as percentage of extent of hostility between men and women.

Source: SAG, Z 1350–1379.

either as victim or aggressor, is never lower than 14.55 percent and reaches a high point of 49.57 percent in 1353. The average for the twenty-nine-year period (since 1379–80 was a partial year for recordkeeping, it is excluded from the annual average) is 29.35 percent. Most of these, 58.03 percent, involve women as victims of aggression from men or are cases of mutual aggression; the two cannot be distinguished in cases where penalties were meted out to each party. The clear cases of female physical aggression against males are much less frequent. There are many cases of actionable language used by and about women. Column 9 shows that if we assume that most cases of "mutual aggression" were primarily male-inspired—and the other criminal records would certainly convey that impression—most violence and bad language for which women were responsible was directed at other women, not at men.[8]

Substantially the same picture is conveyed by the trimesterly accounts of the criminal jurisdiction of the count's bailiff at Ghent, which are recorded in Table 3. Women seem far less involved in violent crime than men except in one obviously atypical account. The cases of women assaulting men are statistically insignificant, and only in two accounts were more women victims of other females than of males.

The bailiffs' accounts list forty-three executions during these years. Six of the condemned were women. We are not given the crime of one, while the body of another was executed as judicial retribution for her suicide in 1376. The other four were burned as heretics in 1374. Two other women were acquitted of allegations of witchcraft in the 1370s. Mergriet, Pauwels Moer's wife, was allowed to pay a hefty fine and go free because several persons testified that she was innocent and that the whole rumor had been started by another woman who was jealous; indeed, she could not be guilty because she had a husband "and three or four lovely children." This action may have been retaliation, for in 1374 Amele sMoers was accused of "dirty work" by an unnamed sister, which in our documents can mean sister-in-law. The bailiff reserved the right to reopen each case if additional evidence could be found that would stand up in court, but nothing more is heard of the matter.[9]

Women, of course, faced very real dangers during childbirth, but the evidence from Ghent is inconclusive. Our best sources are the lists of property (*Staten van Goed*) compiled whenever either parent of a minor child died; for even if all property had come from the father's side, the mother's death gave her share of common property to the children. In most years the *staten* show more children inheriting from their fathers than from their

Table 3. Criminal Justice of the Bailiffs of Ghent, 1352–1379

Account Number	Year	1	2	3	4	5	6	7	8
1362	1352	20	–	–	1	5.00%	–	–	5.00%
1363	1364	19	4	21.05%	2	10.53	2	10.53	42.11
1364	1365	18	–	–	–	–	–	–	–
1365	1367	33	–	–	–	–	–	–	–
1366	1372	45	3	6.67	–	–	–	–	6.67
1367		36	–	–	–	–	–	–	–
1368	1373	59	3	5.08	2	3.39	–	–	8.47
1369		14	–	–	–	–	–	–	–
1370		51	2	3.92	2	3.92	–	–	7.84
2895	1374	38	3	7.89	–	–	1	2.63	10.53
1371		33	1	3.03	–	–	–	–	3.03
1372		16	2	12.50	–	–	–	–	12.50
1373	1375	50	–	–	–	–	3	6.00	6.00
1374		50	4	8.00	1	2.00	–	–	–
1375		60	2	3.33	–	–	–	–	3.33
1376	1376	56	2	3.57	–	–	1	1.79	5.36
1377		74	8	10.81	–	–	1	1.35	12.16
1378		70	4	5.71	1	1.43	1	1.43	8.57
1379	1377	65	4	7.69	1	1.53	–	–	9.23
1380		46	1	2.17	–	–	2	4.35	6.52
1381		65	1	1.53	–	–	–	–	1.53
1382	1378	45	1	2.22	–	–	–	–	2.22
1383		84	4	4.76	1	1.19	4	4.76	10.71
1384		93	8	8.60	2	2.15	–	–	10.75
1385	1379[a]	35	–	–	–	–	1	2.86	2.86
1386		32	3	9.38	–	–	–	–	9.38

Key to Column Headings
1. Total violent crimes handled.
2. Number of women who were victims of aggression from men.
3. Column 2 as a percentage of column 1.
4. Number of women who were aggressors against men.
5. Column 4 as a percentage of column 1.
6. Number of women who were aggressors against other women.
7. Column 6 as a percentage of column 1.
8. Total percentage of cases involving women, either as victim or as aggressor.

[a]The account for the third trimester of 1379 no longer exists.

Source: ARA, BR 1362–1386, 2895.

mothers, but there is little direct evidence of death during childbirth.[10] Difficult births could be as dangerous to the child as to the mother. First births tend to be more difficult than those following, and if most women who died did so while having their first child, and the child also died, no list of property would be provided for other siblings and hence no record would be left. It is nonetheless hard to believe that childbed mortality could have been as minimal at Ghent as the literal reading of the records suggests, for evidence from other cities shows considerable loss of life.

Women were also subjected to various forms of harassment, particularly during the confusion of the 1380s. The tribulations of the daughters of Everard Van den Spieghele provide an example, The elder daughter Josine had married the knight Willem Van Heyle, but his heirs refused to contribute to her support after he died, since apart from her dower on his estate this was the responsibility of her own kindred. She returned to her mother, who by now was guardian of her younger daughter Jehanekin. The mother had to support the girls from her own funds, and this included living with them outside Flanders during the entire civil war. Evidently Josine's problems were due in part to her mother's loaning the immense sum of 100 lb. gro. to the knight Colard Van den Clite shortly after her husband's death. Josine had died by early 1388, and her mother was at some pains to obtain her property, including this debt, for Jehanekin. She also had to honor a bequest to her late husband's bastard daughter. The mother was unable to prosecute her debt claims until it was safe for those opposed to the rebel régime to return, which despite the amnesty was several years after the war ended in 1385.[11]

Girls were also more likely than boys to be swindled by a guardian. Lisbette, daughter of Lauwereins Van Axel, was evidently orphaned in the plague of 1368–69. An original list of her property has not survived, but the heirs of her father's late wife, evidently the girl's stepmother, were contesting some dispositions that the father had made in 1367, in a record bound with the book of 1368–69. That document mentions children, and when a *staet* does survive for Lisbette, dated July 17, 1370, she had inherited from both parents, siblings, and an aunt. Since she had survived children of her father's two marriages, she was probably at least a teenager. Her guardian owed her money received from her rural rents in 1369, and in the following summer the magistrates accused him of mishandling her property, assessed punitive damages, and sent him on a pilgrimage. On August 5, 1371, the new guardians sold a number of household items and balanced the accounts. Lisbette was living with a female guardian by the following summer.[12]

Hence it is not surprising that most women married, even if they had their own incomes or practiced a trade. The sources do not permit us to ascertain clearly the normal marriage age for females. A betrothal during a girl's minority was not uncommon, but marriage was ordinarily deferred until the parties were of the age of consent, fifteen in the case of girls.[13] The marriage of underage girls was countenanced occasionally, although this required the magistrates' approval of a petition submitted by the kindred. One interesting case suggests that a teenage marriage was being allowed since the alternative was fornication, for it was countenanced for the honor of God "and the purity of the couple."[14]

Some informative cases have survived but may not be typical, for they concern the upper classes, whose members, eager to transmit property and forge political alliances, tended to marry earlier than lesser folk.[15] In 1375 Jan Van den Nuevile settled a maternal estate upon his daughter Lisbette, who is called the wife of Justaas Van Scoresse at the beginning of the text. Jan, however, states that if the marriage between his daughter and Justaas did not occur when she reached her majority, she would have an ordinary division of the maternal estate with her father. They were evidently married before she became of age, but the marriage was unconsummated, and Lisbette or her father on her behalf might renounce it when she reached maturity. Such an arrangement suggests that the marriage of minors was uncommon and unenforceable. Another case involving the nobility is the arrangement by kinsmen between Roger Van Veurhoute and Kateline, daughter of the late Olivier de Langhe of Assenede. Although the girl is not given a "kin" diminutive name, which would suggest a minor, she is awarded dower rights on the marriage settlement if she survives Roger, but only if she is eleven or more years old when he dies, suggesting that she would attain this age at some point in the relatively distant future. In 1351 Brandin Everbare was holding money belonging to the wife of Jan Van der Most, who was still a minor, and was to support her four years with the income of the money, which suggests that she may have been "married" only in the sense suggested by the Van Scoresse case.[16]

Unmarried persons of both sexes and of any age had to be emancipated from wardship before marriage. Adult women who were emancipated by the magistrates, normally with the consent of their kindreds, had the same legal standing as men.[17] But this is comparatively unusual, and single adult women were normally under the guardianship of their fathers or brothers, with tutelage reverting more generally to the kindred if the males of the conjugal family were dead or incompetent. The kindred could then appoint a guardian with the consent of the magistrates. Marriage, however, gave a new guardian to the women in the person of her husband and evidently released a man from wardship; a text of 1390 speaks of a person as "his own man, since he has married." Another test for men, although less invariably reliable, of emancipation is mastership in a guild. When the master baker Pauwels Blandewijn reneged on his pledge to marry Mergriet Van der Piet, she sued his evidently older brother Jan, but the action was quashed because as a master Pauwels was responsible for his own behavior.[18]

The kindred surrendered its rights of guardianship over a married female unless a separate suit was filed challenging her husband's competence. The jurisdiction of the husband even extended to his wife's relations with her own clan. In 1357 Pieter Van den Spieghele was withholding a sum from the paternal inheritance from his sister, although the lady had children and was in need, for her father had died after her husband left Flanders, and the brother feared that the husband would refuse to ratify the arrangement and on his own would demand her paternal inheritance from him. A father could not appoint his married daughter to transact business for him unless her husband consented. A woman whose marital status was in doubt had to find a man to act as her surety when she made a contract in the event that she turned out to be married and thus had no power to act on her own.[19] In a spectacular case the widow of Boudin de Beere had evidently returned to the house of her father, the prominent hosteller Simon Van der Zickelen, after her husband's death in 1383. His estate, however, was still being settled in the spring of 1387. In late March or early April of that year the lady made her father her proxy to manage her affairs while she was away, then eloped with Romboud Van der Elst. When her father discovered the deception, he renounced the proxy on grounds that he no longer had the authority to act for her, since she had a husband. Although Simon Van der Zickelen could not represent an obviously adult daughter, he and her clan and notably her mother were able to hand down and enforce punishment for Mergriet and her new husband. Simon was particularly concerned to clear himself of any liability on her behalf toward the clan of her first husband, and the last details of the de Beere estate were actually handled by Romboud Van der Elst and his wife.[20]

Although women ordinarily had only restricted disposition over their property, they controlled a great deal of wealth in Ghent during the fourteenth century, most of it in rural land, rents, or shares of urban real estate whose principal owner was a male; the land books of the city and of the various ecclesiastical landlords show very few women paying rent as heads of households. The custom of Ghent mandated absolutely partible inheritance without regard to sex or age, except in the case of fiefs, and thus was closer to the principles of Justinian's Code than to the customary law of most parts of northern Europe. But this in turn meant that women owned considerable property and explains the great care taken by wealthy kindreds to insure that their daughters married the right men; for although the husband's rights over his wife's property were not unlimited, the family could sustain severe losses through an unfortunate marriage.

Bequests were occasionally made to girls on condition of their remaining single.[21] This was rare, however, and most families provided dowries for their daughters. When this occurred, the other siblings were entitled to compensation, which normally took the form of the couple returning the marriage portion when one or both of the parents died or, at their option, of renouncing the estate.[22] Children were entitled to recover from a widowed parent the equivalent of a marriage portion already given to a sibling.[23]

Providing the dowry was the father's responsibility in principle, or failing him the other males of the family. Some fathers made dowries conditional upon the girl's good behavior, presumably meaning marrying a man of the father's choice. Even if another relative made the endowment, the father might have the right to determine whether the girl eventually got it. Marriage pledges had the binding force of a contract, much stronger than the modern engagement. Clans as well as individuals were being joined, and the more property was involved, the more potentially complicated matters became. Bond might be posted, to be forfeited by the party who withdrew from the arrangement. Some reluctant people were forced into marriage by their kinsmen. One interesting case involving an older couple rather than immature youths is the pledge of Daneel de Tolnere to pay an indemnity to the widow of Jan Van Laerne, the fiancée of his son Jan, and both parties provided surety to go through with the marriage. The father evidently saw a good match for his son and was forcing his hand. A man who married a lady who had broken a previous betrothal was legally bound to pay damages to the jilted man.[24]

Fewer marriage arrangements have been recorded in detail than one might expect, particularly since the dowry, as the wife's own property, was her safeguard if she was deprived of her husband's property or income. Most marriage gifts take a simple form: the couple are given cash or rents, sometimes land or other property, and frequently some furnishings. Some dowries had the form of a down payment with the rest due when one or both parents died. Another common form, particularly among aristocratic families, was for parents to pledge real estate but to reserve for themselves the exploitation of the properties for the parents' lifetimes, sometimes transferring half at the death of each parent. The young couple would receive an annuity until full management was conferred. Particularly in cases involving very young couples, the parents wanted to make certain that the children knew how to manage the property before surrendering it to them. The estate that a woman inherited from a deceased parent was normally considered the dowry, since it was her property even when under her husband's management. But some stepfathers also settled dowries on girls. The girl's parents sometimes agreed to support the newlyweds for a year or two. When Gerem Uten Hove agreed to marry the daughter of the physician Gelloet Speliaert, the girl's father negotiated with Gerem directly, although Gerem was still under the legal guardianship of his mother. She and his kindred consented. Gerem was to bring his entire paternal inheritance into the marriage. The couple would live with the bride's parents as long as either parent was alive. If they left, they would take only Gerem's property until one of the Speliaert parents had died, unless the separation was brought on by the older couple's actions. Such arrangements could last even after the younger couple had children.[25] Whether as part of a dowry or in a separate business arrangement, when Pieter Daens and his wife Lisbette Van Wondelgem bought a house in 1361, her relatives helped them pay for it. Some marriage pledges guaranteed a payment to the groom if his wife predeceased him, although this was unusual with first marriages, or to the bride or her heirs if the husband died first and there were no children. Premarital settlements were usually left unconditionally to the wife; but when Hugh Van der Eeken settled 12 lb. gr. on his fiancée if he died first and there were no children, the money was to be paid to her brother to be used for her, not to her directly. Other cases in which a settlement is to be paid to the bride's brother suggest that he had probably provided her dowry.[26]

In the fourteenth century as now most persons who lost a spouse, normally through death at that time, eventually remarried. The demographic records of Ghent are too imprecise to permit us to determine either the statistical incidence of remarriage or the rapidity with which it normally occurred. Orphans were to be assigned guardians within forty days of a parent's death, but the listing of property often follows much later, usually when the surviving parent remarries, and rarely does this occur at an interval shorter than two years.

But remarriage involved complications not present with first nuptials. Since a woman normally had a marriage gift from her family, which was her own property, her clan had a financial interest in the identity of a second husband. But no longer did her male kinsmen have an uncontested right to choose a husband for her. A widow received as her own property half of the common property that she had held with her late husband and dower rights, involving life usufruct, on half of the remaining half. Common property began from the time the marriage was contracted, not from the date of the ceremony. A text of 1379 refers to "debts belonging to the marriage contracted since the marriage was agreed upon between them."[27] Goody has distinguished a "community" system of inheritance, under which a widow would hold some property under a jointure, and a "lineage" system, under which the property is separated and returned to each set of kin when a marriage ends unless there are children.[28] Ghent has elements of both. The widow of a prominent man was thus a desirable commodity in the marriage market, and her late husband's relatives could be threatened if she married the "wrong" man. Her relations with her children could also be compromised, for her financial interests might not coincide with theirs. Zoetin Van Erdbuur, who sometimes acted as the proxy of her husband, Jan Van Longheville, in textile purchases, was the widow of Pieter Bailget. In the 1380s she and Van Longheville were living in three tenements on the Tichelrei that had belonged to Bailget in 1375.[29]

Adult children were keenly aware of the problem. Husbands and wives could not devise property upon each other during the marriage without the consent of the heirs of each. Without that consent spouses thus could not leave all common property to the survivor with the proviso that it would go to the heirs at the second death. An heir, usually a child, might agree provisionally to forego a division of the common property but reserve the right to an immediate division if the surviving parent wished to remarry. Particularly in cases of marriage late in life, it was common for one party, usually the man, to guarantee the spouse a set amount, usually in money, before the heirs of each began to divide the estate, but this also required the heirs' consent.[30]

Remarriage was thus common enough, with all its dangers, to cause many who perpetrated it to enter prenuptial agreements for the disposal of common property. But such arrangements might protect the mother against her child, particularly in view of her second husband's power over her. She could not even act as guardian or have physical custody of her children by the previous marriage without his consent. In 1378 Heinric Van Doinse was awarded restitution from his wife's mother and stepfather, who had appropriated properties that the girl's father had set aside as her marriage portion.[31] Some mothers clearly regretted the problems that their remarriages had caused for their children. By 1384 the two sons of the mercer Jan de Meyere had inherited a paternal estate that included half shares of two houses. In 1386, however, their mother and stepfather, who were already married when the *staet* was promulgated in 1384, separated, and the boys exchanged their share of one house with their mother in return for the entire house in which she was then living and in which they had half interest. When the older boy married in 1391, his mother promised that if she ever remarried again, her son would get an additional 15 lb. gr. beyond his marriage portion, and she gave the younger boy the same amount. Although the document places the initiative with the mother, it is likely that the sons did not want to be hurt again by having a stepfather, particularly one to whom their mother did not stay married, acquire rights over their paternal estate, rights which their mother was evidently compensating from her own property.[32]

Prudent mothers who were sufficiently desirable matches to gain concessions might extract property for their children from prospective second husbands. Lievin Van Drongen agreed that his wife's adult sons would receive all his property if he predeceased her; one suspects that the sons were to care for her in that event, although this is not stated. In July 1373 Jacob Van Huerne arranged his marriage with Mergriet Jours, widow of Ser Gerolf de Pape. Both parties were wealthy, but Jacob had to make special concessions to get her hand, for he admitted that "at the time of the marriage he had fewer chattels and furnishings than Mergriet." He accordingly willed her children 100 lb. gr. before he would have any rights on her estate when she died. He also pledged not to encumber or sell her property "unless from clear necessity."[33] Such stipulations could also protect the interests of a man marrying a woman less wealthy than he. Women who wanted to marry desirable men might also be ready to offer proprietary inducements. In 1379 Kateline Liefkind, who had an adult daughter who consented to the arrangement, pledged a bath house to Jan de Puut in the event that they married, and he was to have lifetime use of it if she pre-deceased him. One suspects from the language that they were business partners who planned a marriage of convenience. While the widow's rights of dower and the chances of remarriage made it difficult to keep large estates together, marriage and remarriage could also be used by the towns-men as well as the nobility to consolidate properties. The fortunes of the shipping houses of Mayhuus and Eeckaert were closely interwoven. In 1375 the children of Jan Mayhuus inherited from their mother a quarter interest in three-and-one-half houses at Damme, the outport of Bruges, where Ghent also maintained warehouses along the quay. Other members of the Mayhuus clan held half interest, and Heinric Eeckaert owned the final quarter.[34]

Similar to the practice of the husband in a late marriage making a cash gift to his wife-to-be was the custom of the groom's father, even in a youthful marriage, making a wedding gift to his son but providing that rights on it would descend to the son's wife, who could thus take it into a later marriage. Some cases thus show the practical impact that the claims of a second husband could have on the family of the first. Olivier, son of the Ghent noble Olivier Uten Hove, had been given substantial rents by his father, some payable when he married and some at the death of either parent. The son died, evidently in early 1374, owing debts to his father, for on July 19 the father sued Olivier's widow for the money. But she had already remarried, to Gerem Ser Sanders, and he in turn sued Olivier Uten Hove for the balance of the rents owed in the marriage contract. Ser Sanders and his wife were awarded half of the unpaid balance, but as late as 1387 they were still demanding arrears in court from the heirs of her by now deceased parents-in-law. All claims were finally settled in 1397 with a payment to the widow and her children by Ser Sanders, who by this time had also died. The language of the texts makes it clear that Gerem Ser Sanders and not his wife was the moving force behind these suits.[35] A marriage endowment could be used in ways which its donor could never foresee, for the widow's rights on her late husband's estate could create serious problems for his clan.

The problems involved in remarriage are also shown by the careers of the younger Jan de Cnoppere and his mother and widow. His father had died before 1367; in that year his widow remarried Goessin Borluut, who became guardian of her son. The boy was evidently very young, for he was still a ward in 1379. We next hear of Jan de Cnoppere on February 14, 1385, by which time he had been emancipated, married, died, and his widow had remarried and was disputing his estate with her late husband's mother, now herself again a widow. The mother responded by citing a receipt that her son had given her for all claims on his paternal estate, although she had been bound to continue to provide him with food and drink for a time. The magistrates awarded the daughter-in-law some compensation, but one suspects fortune-hunting here, for both the daughter-in-law and her new husband, the fishmonger Jan de Stoute, had remarried very hastily after the deaths of their respective previous spouses.[36] There could be problems even when the parties had the most honorable intentions. When the wife of Jacob Van Abbinsvoorde died, her share of their residence in the aristocratic Veldstraat was inherited by her son Jacob de Clerc, who was heavily in debt. His creditors took the occasion of the inheritance to seize his share of the house, and Van Abbinsvoorde had to buy out de Clerc's rights from them or risk being turned out of his own home.[37]

Simple prudence dictated measures to both parents and adult children that would place some constraint on the emotions. But those of mature years were no more immune than their offspring to the harmonies of the hormones. We have seen the problems which could result. In a case which did not turn out badly, Lievin de Maech, one of the wealthiest men in Ghent, was settling the estate of his late wife with her parents on May 12, 1371. A bare fifteen months later he was arranging his marriage to the daughter of the late wine merchant Simon Gommaer. With the consent of his brother and niece as heirs, he pledged her not only the enormous sum of 200 lb. gr. above her share of common property if she survived him, but an additional 100 lb. gr. to pay the bequests in her testament, which must have been enormous. On May 18, 1373, the lady declared to the *scepenen* that it was not proper for her husband's money to be used for her testament and accordingly renounced the 100 lb. gr., although she evidently kept the 200 lb. gr. jointure. She did this with her brother's consent, suggesting that she was not acting under her husband's pressure. The de Maech and Gommaer families were allies in clan feuds, that primordial social cement, earlier in 1372, when Simon Gommaer, evidently the lady's brother, and Lievin's brother, Laurens de Maech, stood surety for the party of Pieter Hoernic, killer of Jan Eelwoud. She was the widow of Jan Van der Meere, who had died by 1366. Her marriage to Lievin de Maech, clearly arranged by her paternal kin, was still flourishing in 1390, and her husband was frequently involved in the affairs of the Gommaer family.[38]

Most married couples of Ghent left no record of their feeling toward each other. We are on firmer ground discussing parental sentiment toward children. Marriage contracts involved the parties in a maelstrom of emotional, economic, and sexual bonds. Most marriages worked at least well enough to stay out of the courts. Inevitably, given the complexity of the marital relationship, some did not, and this is the group with which we must now deal.

Chapter Two

What Man Puts Asunder:
Domestic Violence
and Marital Separation

That the ordinary is not preserved well in the historical record poses severe problems to the historian who tries to reconstruct the history of women and the family in a medieval city. Only when there is conflict or some extraordinary circumstance does someone bother to write of it. Many have argued that marriage in the premodern world had little if anything to do with sexual attraction and that "romantic love" played a subsidiary role to property considerations in the arrangement and maintenance of marriages. There is an element of truth to this view for the upper classes, who had the most property to gain or lose, and most of our direct documentation for the internal workings of marriages comes from the propertied. We shall see that physical attraction knew no bounds of social class and that even among the urban aristocracy bastardy and concubinage were not uncommon. For the lower orders, whose property records we lack or who were less litigious about what they did have, a situation not unlike the contemporary was common. That we have more documentation of marital conflict than of concord proves nothing, for there was no reason for a record to be kept of relations between spouses unless a suit or public disturbance was at issue. When the conflict that brings the case into the historical record is of the couple against outsiders, affection between husband and wife is sometimes noted, but only infrequently, since most dealings with parties outside the family were conducted by the husband alone.

33

We have no way of measuring the extent of domestic violence statistically. Most violent deeds recorded at Ghent during the fourteenth century were perpetrated by males, as we have seen. But when a woman was attacked or her good name impugned, her husband frequently retaliated by beating up the culprit. This very attitude shows bonds of marital affection and the notion that the wife is to be defended. There are cases of wives surreptitiously sending goods to their exiled husbands. The extent of cooperation between husbands and wives in family businesses, which we shall examine separately, would not have been possible had couples not cared for each other. The *Zoendincboeken* furnish other sidelights, but all too infrequently. When the wife of Leins Lyen was ordered to do a pilgrimage in 1357, her husband went in her place. Wives occasionally tried to shield husbands who were being assaulted. When Jacob Van den Steene beat his stepmother, she forgave him, although only with her husband's consent, "out of love for her husband Wouter and their children."[1] When homicide was committed in the presence of the victim's parents, an extra penalty was assessed in honor of the parents. In what was admittedly an unusual case, since parents were normally not remembered in homicide atonements, a ruling of 1354 awarded 7 lb. gr. to the decedent's mother for the cost and pain "which our mother did and had with Jan her child, and he can never again [re]pay her, nor can she ever again find or see honor or profit through him."[2] A suit was filed in 1388 concerning the capture by opposing forces during the recent war of the wives of two burghers of Ghent. The husbands had tried to have the ladies exchanged for each other, but one had incurred considerable expense. Although the suit was disallowed, it shows that husbands were willing to go to some lengths to free their wives.[3]

The surviving records suggest remarkable stability of marriages in fourteenth-century Ghent. The *Staten van Goed,* which concern only property questions, mention only four separations during the 1350s, two of them in 1359. References continue to be fragmentary through the early 1380s, but between April 1385 and May 1390 there are sixteen, perhaps reflecting the strains of the recent war.[4] The books of the *scepenen* of the *Keure* show more separations, and these data are plotted on Graph 1. These are not new separations in each case, and the list is obviously incomplete, for only those who needed a written record of a property division would appear. The *Keure* books confirm the *Staten van Goed* in showing rarely more than two or three separations annually; but while the *Staten* references increase

Graph 1. References to Marital Separations, Jaarboeken Van de Keure

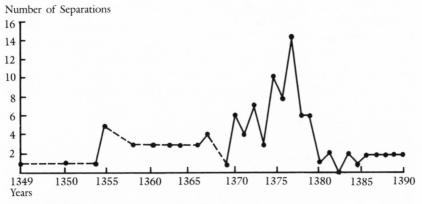

Number of Separations

Source: SAG, Registers of *scepenen* of the *Keure*.

from 1385, the *Keure* data, which are the more complete of the two, show that of 108 separations mentioned, fifty-nine come between 1371 and 1379, accounting for 54.63 percent of the total. The percentage is inaccurate, for only from the 1370s is there an unbroken series, and the totals would doubtless be higher if books had survived from the missing years. Even for the 1370s, however, there is an average of only 6.56 references each year to marital separations.

One would expect a low incidence of marital separation, since there could be no divorce according to the law of the medieval church unless an impediment could be found, and this was rare. In such cases the *scepenen* of Ghent would order the parties to provide a list of the property of each individual and of common property and to live on their own resources until a final settlement could be reached at the episcopal court at Tournai.[5] This subject has been explored by several scholars. Real life was greatly at variance with church law. Men and women loved, but also fought and fornicated with one another. When people could not live harmoniously under one roof, they had three options: keep fighting, which many did; cohabit with others outside marriage; and seek a separation through a church court, confirmed by the city government, involving division of bed, board, and property. Most probably took the first or second option. But there are some cases of formal separation, although its cost made this mainly the prerogative of the upper classes.

Although no statistics regarding marital separations can be reconstructed for Ghent at this time, a point of comparison can be a register of sentences of the official of Brussels from 1448 to 1459. It lists eighty-nine separations, fourteen of them for simple incompatibility. In another seventy-five incompatibility is cited along with other causes, most often adultery, sometimes physical cruelty, and occasionally impotence.[6] This is an average of only eight per year for the entire *officialité*, including Brussels and its environs, and it suggests that our figures for Ghent on Graph 1 may be reasonably accurate.

The standard form of initiating hostilities was for the wife to leave the husband's house, not vice versa, and presumably live on one of her own properties or return to her kindred.[7] The city magistrates for obvious reasons discouraged easy separation and preferred for couples to resolve their difficulties. A representative case illustrating both the problems involved and the attitude of the authorities is the action between Simon Spermaelge and his wife, who had been the widow of Jan Van Bursbeke. On April 20, 1352, the lady settled the estate of her late daughter and received half a house in the Oudburg. By early 1354 Spermaelge had ejected her from this property. She asked the *scepenen* to force him to take her back, for she wished to do for him as a "good wife should do for her legal husband." He refused to take her back, citing mismanagement of funds, clear proof that she and presumably most wives had some money to spend without recourse to a man, and also mentioning other reasons, which he did not care to specify. The council ordered him to take her back, since he was not claiming that the marriage was invalid, or failing that to arrange an equal division of the property which was in his possession, and she was to do the same. We do not know whether they resumed cohabitation, but Spermaelge was dead by November 25, 1355. According to law his heirs were awarded one-quarter interest in the half house in the Oudburg that his wife had from her daughter's estate, while the widow got the other three-quarters.[8] The magistrates clearly did not lack sympathy for the woman at the mercy of her husband, and the case shows well how a man could benefit by marrying a woman with property.

As one would expect from the gravity of the issues involved, most couples tried to reconcile their differences, and sometimes it worked. The furrier Jan Cant and his wife Kateline Van den Berghe had evidently separated before 1377, but "joined again in amity by common friends and for the support of both, they pledged to love and honor each other." Jan pledged to keep peace with his wife, not to mistreat her, and to live in their home practicing his trade. "If Jan gambled or drank immoderately or took his or his wife's jewels [household implements] from the house or mismanaged any property" and Kateline could prove it, he was to go to Tournai and arrange the separation previously agreed upon at his own cost. Common friends would then arrange a property division. Jan Cant evidently died in late 1382. The marriage had been childless, but the settlement with his heirs mentions the house where he and Kateline had been living when he died.[9] Clearly a wife had some recourse against a husband who drank, gambled, abused her, and wasted money.

Some marriages had mother-in-law problems. The mother's property interest probably led her to meddle in more cases than can be attested directly, and it was natural that mothers would usually take their children's side when marital problems already existed. When Lievin Van den Hecke took his wife Kateline Van den Bossche to court in 1374, her mother was mentioned in his suit. There had evidently been hostilities on both sides, for Lievin and his mother-in-law were ordered to leave each other alone in the future. Both Lievin and Kateline had taken property from the house and were ordered to return it, and Lievin was not to sell anything except for their common profit. Kateline, who may have worked outside the home as a domestic servant, evidently died in 1383, leaving a son in her husband's care.[10]

We cannot know how many couples lived apart without going to the trouble and expense of a formal separation, although this might be the only way to insure that neither would be liable for the debts of the other. Gillis Van Beversluus and his wife, for example, evidently lived apart and had separate debts from January 1, 1381, but they only formalized a separation on November 10, 1386.[11] Certainly the widespread concubinage suggests that informal separation was common.

A case illustrating the consequences for an estate of informal marital separation, together with the propensity of the shippers for violence, comes from the Bollin family, one of the most prominent of that guild. Jan Bollin had married Lisbette Walmare in 1359. In 1372 and 1376 he willed substantial properties to his maid, Aleit Van 'sHertogenbosch, and to his two children by her. She was then living in an apartment in the Bollin family complex near the Pasbrug, a section of town where many shippers lived. Bollin evidently died at the end of 1382, for a wardship was established for the children on January 21, 1383. But when the estate was settled the following October, several persons, claiming to be heirs of Bollin's wife, disputed the bequests to the bastards, amounting to most of his estate, on grounds that Bollin could not bind her half of common property. The city *exuwers,* who collected a tax on the property of persons who left the city, testified that Bollin's wife had left Ghent and had left no record of her destination with her neighbors; thus they wanted the tax on her property. Bollin's legitimate heirs claimed that the wife had stolen much of his money when she left and demanded its return before anyone could share Bollin's estate on her behalf.

Aleit Van 'sHertogenbosch, who clearly was a fast mover, was already the mother of another bastard, this one by Oliver Van den Eechoute, by July 1383. Further clarification was given in April 1385. Bollin's wife is now identified as the Lisbette Walmare to whom he had been married a quarter century earlier, and the men who earlier had claimed to be her heirs are now her proxies. She had some property at Bruges, where she had been residing, although so inconspicuously that her potential heirs had thought she was dead. She had been separated from her husband by mutual consent but without intervention of the ecclesiastical court, and she was ordered to divide this property with the Bollin family if she intended to share his estate as legal wife in Ghent. Lisbette Walmare was dead by August 1387, but the Bollin estate was still being contested in 1388.[12] Other businessmen of Ghent did considerable trade through Bruges and would naturally have contacts there. The mercer Jan Van Luevine in 1390 willed 12 lb. gr. to his bastard by Griele Scinkel of Bruges.[13]

A marital separation showing the impact of the prohibition of divorce upon illegitimacy, the precarious situation of women vis à vis men generally, particularly in connection with domestic service, and how family friendship could lead to unhappy marriages is shown by the case of the Platijns and the Overakkers. Lievin Van Overakker and Jan Platijns were sureties for each other under different circumstances in 1368 and 1371. In October 1373 Lievin Van Overakker and Kateline Platijns announced their separation. There is no further evidence of contact between the families. In 1380, however, Lievin Van Overakker willed money, chattels, and personal effects to Mergriet Van Paernackere and her two sons by him; he was still living with her, for if he had other children by her, they were to share in the bequest. He also willed 10 lb. gr. to a bastard daughter by a different mother. There evidently had been an impediment to the earlier separation between Lievin and Kateline Platijns, for a new decree was recorded on December 31, 1382; she may have needed the excuse of his bastards. Two months later she bought a house on the Houtbriel for 27 lb. gr., a price suggesting a substantial but not palatial residence; from the chronology one assumes that Lievin got their house, but we are not told where Kateline had been living since the first separation in 1373. In 1385 Lievin Van Overakker willed 10 lb. gr. to his daughter by a third mistress, Amelberghe Maelbroucs, and 6 lb. gr. to the girl's mother as compensation for loans and "services." The bequest was altered in 1390 to include two more daughters by Amelberghe. As a mistress Amelberghe evidently kept control over her funds, since she was making loans to him, a not uncommon arrangement; but it is clear that women were in an unenviable position in these circumstances, and whether she really had freedom of choice about the loan is doubtful.[14]

While most married men who fathered bastards did so at a decent interval after the separation, there were some who did not wait. Ser Lievin Wenemaer, scion of one of Ghent's most distinguished families, was already a city receiver by 1352. He must therefore have been at least in his sixties by the 1380s. Protesting that he was indeed master of his senses, perhaps to allay skepticism on the subject, he willed 6 lb. gr. each to his mistress and their bastard on August 12, 1382. On May 23, 1383, he was separated from his wife, Mergriet Dieregodgaf, "in table and bed until such time as God changes their hearts for the better." No restrictions were made on Lievin's right to dispose of his property, but Mergriet might do so during the separation, suggesting that she expected it to be temporary, only with the consent of her two uncles and her kindred generally. Since uncles are mentioned, rather than a brother, she was probably considerably younger than Ser Lievin. This was thus an informal separation, which could be reversed at the desire of the parties. Mergriet's legal standing was altered only in having her blood kinsmen, rather than her husband, acting as guardian.[15] A similar case of a man leaving his wife for a mistress, but in this case obtaining a separation at Tournai involves Wouter Coevoet, who was separated from Kateline de Backere in February 1390. In June 1389, "for alms and certain reasons," he had willed 6 lb. gr. to Kateline, identified as the daughter of Willem Bicke and thus probably a young woman, but the bequest would revert to his legitimate heirs if she died without having living children by him. This liaison may not have lasted long; on September 9, 1390, he acknowledged owing her 4 lb. gr. for a loan, but this document was to acquit each party of all other pledges, presumably including the bequest.[16] While husbands' infidelities seem to have caused more marital problems than wives', women strayed, too. In 1339 Lisbette de Broessche, wife of Jan de Wulf, acquitted him of all claims for common property but simultaneously pledged to the *scepenen* that she would have no more dealings with Jacob Van den Riede or others from whose society she or her friends might be subject to derision or defamation.[17]

Property was naturally a concern of all parties in marital separations. The wife's marriage portion was normally returned,[18] and each party received half of the couple's common property. But separation, in contrast to divorce, did not automatically end the rights of one party over the other's property, and thus most recorded separations contain renunciations. A typical case showing simple separation, together with the usual God-fearing rhetoric of the *scepenen,* was that of Jan Metsaert from Kateline de Caye. Each kept what was in his or her possession. Each might acquire or inherit property in the future without the other or the other's heirs having rights on it. But the wife might sell or encumber her land only with the consent of two men appointed her guardians; we are not told in this case whether they were her kinsmen. Her husband was to be notified of any transfer and would come at least as far as Ename (a town twenty-five kilometers south of Ghent) to go through the formalities and act as her husband to permit the transfer. This was to be annulled if either by the grace of God should remarry and thus "escape the clutches of the enemy."[19] The obvious assumption is that both would naturally fornicate during the separation. When the discords of Jan de Scuttere and his wife Mergriet de Meyere became a public nuisance, the *scepenen* divided their debts and ordered them to go to the ecclesiastical court if they wished to separate; meanwhile, they were admonished against violence in word and deed against each other. Mergriet died in 1353, and her husband claimed to be holder of her estate, but the heirs disputed it on grounds of an agreement during her lifetime. The *scepenen* investigated, but the issue was inconclusive. In a case showing the problems involved in some of these issues, Jan Van Buxstale and his wife Zoetin de Boem on May 13, 1374, announced a division of their assets with the consent of the court of Tournai. They made the usual renunciations of property subsequently acquired and of dower, and they even promised never to speak to each other again. Yet on September 23, 1375, Jan's heirs lost a suit to keep Zoetin from being holder of his estate, and in 1380 she even sold her dower rights on his estate to a third party.[20]

A marital dissolution of unusual complexity involved Kateline Mulaerts, sister of the lord of Eksaarde, north of Ghent, from Jan de Scouteete of Eksaarde. In January 1388 de Scouteete appointed his wife to manage his affairs, but the only action surviving in which she exercised this proxy was to fulfill a bequest by her own brother. De Scouteete refused to ratify a lease that she made in November and revoked the proxy. In general principle on March 27, 1389, and in more detail on May 26, 1389, a separation agreement was promulgated. Most provisions are standard, but each party also renounced dower if he or she predeceased the other. Acting as a couple and without mentioning the separation, they paid debts during the next several months. Further arbitration was necessary to untangle their financial affairs. When Kateline Mulaerts died in 1390, several of her clan renounced the estate.[21]

While in most cases we are simply given acquittals in the sources, the separation of Simon de Pape of Oosterzele and his wife Beatrise Zoete shows a strict physical division of common property. The marriage was of some duration, for they had a daughter old enough to be a nun and a son still a minor. There are two versions of the separation decree. In the earlier the couple evenly divided common property on their estate at Oosterzele, while the chattels went to their son. Beatrise was given dower on some of Simon's land, while he was awarded half of some properties that she had inherited from her mother. They divided joint debts. The later version is more precise and shows that the land given to Beatrise was the mirror image of what Simon received for his lifetime only, since it was essentially her property. To satisfy the rights of the husband on the wife's property, they were making a physical division of the fields of the estate.[22]

Marital separations thus might take several years to arrange. At least one case seems to have been timed to make it easier to divide assets.[23] Couples were very careful about alienating common property during negotiations leading to marital separation, for the magistrates prohibited alienation when they doubted the probity of either party. In January 1366 Daneel Uten Dale attempted homicide and was imprisoned awaiting trial. On June 2 his wife consented to the sale of common property to get bail money. She also pledged to pay all joint debts with common property if ordered to do so by three arbitrators, but this proviso was on grounds of the trouble between her and her husband. While one may grant that she may not have wanted him out of jail, she would have had legal difficulties in alienating common property without his consent during a separation proceeding.[24]

Once separated, the spouses could ordinarily make binding contracts without the presence of the other if there had been a renunciation. In a case of families in perhaps unhealthy friendship, Lisbette, daughter of the carpenter Jan Van Lovendegem, was married to Willem de Vroede by

March 1369; but her father then married a Lisbette de Vroede by October 1375, from whom he had separated by August 6, 1378. Jan evidently kept the house, for the term for joint debt was the day she left it. Two children were born during the brief marriage, and Lisbette had survived them and her husband by March 1386, when she renounced dower on their estates. She is still being identified as the wife of Jan Van Lovendeghem in 1390.[25]

The terms of the individual settlement determined survivors' rights, but both a church and a civil action were required for the marital break to be complete. On September 10, 1349, the *scepenen* of Ghent refused jurisdiction in a suit of Kateline de Valke against her husband Jan de Bels on grounds that they had been "separated in bed at the court of Tournai," but no property division is mentioned. In 1360 she sued Jan's heirs for half of his estate. When they cited, in turn, both the decree from Tournai and the fact that "since that time there had also been a division of property by her will and consent," the *scepenen* ruled the separation valid.[26]

Married couples fighting about money has a contemporary ring, and finances were a major source of conflict in fourteenth-century Ghent. While husbands seem to have handled the major transactions, they had to leave their wives enough to pay the butcher and the baker. Complaints about financial irresponsibility come from both sides but most often from the wife, who was less able to stop her husband from overspending and particularly from wasting property that she had brought into the marriage. Frivolous use of the wife's dowry was a great temptation.[27] Wives and children could stop fathers and husbands from alienating real estate under some circumstances. The city rent books contain occasional marginal notes limiting the paterfamilias' discretion in this way.[28] There are several separations in which the husband's right to create debts for which his wife would be liable is expressly ended, although the separation customarily terminated his right to consent to her alienation of her own funds.[29] Women had to pay their own costs of obtaining a separation, and even this could not be done without the husband's consent. Beatrise Blankaerts, wife and evidently business partner of the shipper Jan Tac, had to pay her half of the legal costs of separation or give her husband half the profits of a boat en route at the time of the decree. Nine years later she was still being called his wife but acted on her own recognizance as surety for another shipper, suggesting that she continued in the business.[30] There are also cases suggesting that the wife, rather than the husband, was wasting money. Simon Van den Pitte and his wife were married by January 1375. They moved to Bruges during the civil war after 1379 and separated there. While most language of the property division is standard, the wife was ordered to remove all encumbrances from her lands before Simon paid other debts insofar as he knew of them when they parted at Bruges. She was responsible for any debts of which he had been unaware at that time.[31]

Unless a married woman had property of her own that would provide her an income, she would tolerate considerable inconvenience in return for financial security. There was normally no annual payment of child support or alimony, and if the woman had no profession, she might be reduced to destitution even if she did get half the common property, particularly in view of the severe inflation in Flanders until 1389. Surprisingly few cases survive of women who tried to have property settlements revised in their favor, but in 1358 Kateline Van den Briele claimed that her estranged husband had concealed property when they had divided assets. The arbitrators rejected this claim, but on grounds of her poverty and to free her husband from further annoyance they awarded her another 10s. gr. in cash, a pittance. Their wish to help a man get rid of an aggravating female is painfully apparent. Another danger to the woman was the principle that when a challenge to a previous settlement was not sustained, the petitioner, who was usually the woman, had to pay the costs of both parties.[32]

Some settlements seem on the surface to favor the husband; but since he had extensive rights over his wife's property, he would naturally extract all the collateral compensation possible. On July 7, 1372, the dyer Clais Rabau and his wife Mergriet Ghiselins were ordered by arbitrators to seek a separation at Tournai. The decree was issued on August 28, 1372, showing that ratification could come quickly once the parties had agreed on an action. They had been married since at least November 1353. No children are mentioned, although a Clais, son of Clais Rabau, who is mentioned as an adult in 1366, may be a son of this pair or of the father by a previous marriage. Mergriet was to surrender all rights on property coming from Clais's side, on all that had been bought with common property, and on all dower rights. She would then pay him an additional 35s. gr. In return Clais simply surrendered rights on land coming from her side, which must have been considerable, for otherwise the arrangement is completely one-sided.[33]

A striking feature of most litigation over marital separation is the knowledge displayed by the wife. The husband was more likely than she to have access to the records, but the wives seem to have known when he was wasting money. Most were obviously mature women of judgment. We have seen cases attended by fiscal finagling on both sides, as parties collected debts and consolidated assets. In at least one case the wife took over the husband's business during a lengthy separation proceeding, although we are not told whether this was part of the formal arrangement between them. The moneylender Jan de Pottere was separated from his wife Aechte by 1362. He paid the tax levied by the city on his profession through the fiscal year 1365–66, but he thereupon disappears from the city accounts, and the tax is paid by Aechte de Pottere during each year except one for which an account has survived between 1366 and the fiscal year 1382–83. The amount paid varies but grew continuously until by the 1380s she was one of the most prominent moneylenders in Ghent. Her husband was alive at least until the summer of 1380; she was not taking over his profession as a widow. They did not bother to separate before the church court until 1374; the decree was reissued in 1378, evidently because one party had violated it. Beginning in February 1378, Aechte de Pottere had been in a flurry of activity, selling property, collecting debts, and making bequests, and this continued until the summer of 1380. The fiscal year 1380–81, which ended August 14, 1381, is the term of her inactivity as a moneylender. One suspects that she may have been planning an act of piety, such as a pilgrimage, rather than trying to keep money away from her estranged husband. She is known to have owned a house in the Kouterstraat during this year. She paid the tax as a moneylender in 1382–83, but she had died by July 16, 1384.[34]

The case of the tanner Jan de Costere and his wife Zoetin Van Eremboudegem suggests the separation of a couple who were active business partners. They evidently squabbled publicly. In April 1351 they appointed two receivers, including a cobbler who probably knew them professionally, to manage their business and specifically their leather, but there is no mention of formal separation at Tournai or division of property. Jan de Costere was murdered in 1353. His brother Jacob, also a tanner, pledged to respect his brother's agreement until Zoetin died, when her estate would be divided. Three weeks later Zoetin recorded a list of her property, and we hear nothing further of her.[35] Some wives objected when their husbands refused to involve them actively in their business dealings, even when there is no suggestion that the men had acted irresponsibly. Simon Van Coudenberghe and Clarissie Van den Pitte were married by early 1370. On February 27, 1378, she appeared before the *scepenen* to claim that she had told them frequently that because of the discords between her and her husband, he had seized all her property and its revenues, and she had nothing to live on. The *scepenen* agreed to a property division according to the terms of their separation at Tournai. We cannot evaluate the legitimacy of her grievances, although there is no prior record of her complaints before the magistrates. Van Coudenberghe's business dealings during the 1370s do not generally use the form of including his wife's name, and one suspects that he had merely acted as her husband and taken the incomes. The next years find Clarissie acting on her own, but she is still usually called the wife of Simon Van Coudenberghe. The party of Simon and his brother Jan assaulted Jan Van den Pitte, evidently Clarissie's kinsman, in 1386. Simon was settling with her heirs, who had renounced her estate, in the late 1380s. Although Clarissie had exercised freedom in commercial dealings after the separation, her husband had not renounced his rights on her estate.[36]

Some marital separations were "friendly" after a fashion. Clais Stuerkin was a widower in 1351. By 1363 he had separated from a second wife, by whom he had two sons. They divided their property into thirds, according to law, and agreed that each adult was to take custody of one child and live in the family home in alternate years. The second marriage was evidently of very short duration, for the older boy was still a minor in 1375. When Jan Bloume and Mergriet Van den Boemgaerde separated in 1373 after four years of marriage, they divided all property, but Jan pledged that he would compensate Mergriet or her heirs if his conscience ever told him that he had received more than she, a suggestion of good will not ordinarily found in these actions.[37]

But many separations seem to have been the occasions of physical violence. There is no way to measure the extent of petty household tyranny, for most cases of domestic squabbling did not come to the attention of the magistrates unless there had been a public disturbance. Jan de Maech was banished by the *scepenen* for killing his wife, but the count's court pardoned him in 1364 because he had made peace with her kin. The language suggests that he had intended to give her a thrashing but not to kill her. While marital violence was frowned upon, one cannot claim that it was generally punished with exemplary severity. Jan Aerdijns complained to the *scepenen* that his stepfather, Arend Van der Rijst, had mistreated his mother and had taken her property outside Flanders and squandered it. The magistrates told him to be nice to her, to treat her lovingly, and to post bond to manage her property and his business profitably. Despite the leniency of this ruling his behavior was so bad that he was in the amman's, normally a debtors' prison, for a time this year, apparently for fiscal mismanagement rather than for mistreating his wife. Arend Van der Rijst was a prominent man, evidently a wine merchant, which may have influenced the verdict. No less a person than Willem Van Artevelde stood surety for him.[38]

The accounts of the bailiff show occasional cases of wife beating, but there was a problem in getting victims to press charges against the man to whom one was inexorably bound in the sight of God. How many abused wives may have decided that a public complaint would make matters even worse cannot be estimated. In 1375 Lievin de Nayere was accused of beating his wife. Although her maid supported the allegation, the woman's kindred refused to press charges, and the matter was dropped. We are not told that the bailiff asked the victim directly. In 1377 Gillis Roetstoc was accused of injuring his spouse, but he was allowed to compose with the bailiff because she did not press charges and her life had not been in danger.[39]

Only two uxoricides are recorded in the *Zoendincboeken* during these years, but the nature of the crime in one case must be deduced by comparing the criminal record with other sources. In March 1364 Gerard Van Oestrem and his wife were heirs of Willem de Ledeghe and his wife. On June 9, 1364, Gerard paid 18 lb. gr. to atone the death of Mergriet de Ledeghe. The *montzoener,* the closest male relative and chief beneficiary of the blood price payments, which did not go to females, was Jan de Ledeghe, who agreed that the decedent's orphan would receive part of the payment, to revert to the mother's side if the child died. On July 19, 1364, Jan de Ledeghe as guardian of Merkin Van Oestrem acquitted Gerard Van Oestrem of the estate of the child's mother, Mergriet. It seems virtually certain that Gerard killed his wife and was acquitted of her estate by the woman's brother, who through generosity gave part of the blood price to the victim's daughter. Although the penalty is somewhat higher than is usually paid for killing women, that the deed is never called by its proper name suggests either a transparent cover-up or phenomenal callousness.[40]

Marriage is a serious business. Without great care it can become deadly serious. The marriage of Jan Van den Zande and Mergriet, daughter of Jan Van Coudenbrouc, illustrates this and a second characteristic found in our sample of cases, admittedly too small for valid statistics to be based upon it: most marital separations did not involve children. Most surviving cases are between couples married only a short time, or more frequently childless couples married between ten and twenty years. Both Jan Van den Zande and his wife, Mergriet, seem to have been less than pleasant folk, involved in brawls and bringing groundless civil suits against Mergriet's kin. On March 5, 1378, they divided their common property. Each got a house with brewery attached. The document concludes by noting that Jan had been injured while they were living together and that Mergriet had cared for him with common property, including paying the doctor's fees. She thus reserved the right to recover her share of these expenses. The reality behind this touching tale of a lady caring for a husband who was about to leave her is less edifying. In October 1378 Mergriet was fined severely and sent on processionals to the five parish churches of the city for hiring an assassin to try to murder her husband. One must assume that her complicity in the murder attempt was not known at the time of the separation. Such a "horrible and un-Christian deed," the magistrates piously intoned, can never be atoned adequately when committed against one's husband.[41] In point of fact the climate of violence was so pervasive in Ghent at this time that the *scepenen* in numerous other cases sustained the legal validity of collusive agreements to commit murder, but the fact that a wife tried to erase her husband made this one exceptional.

Another carving at the connubial couch involves Jan de Bleekere and his wife, Mergriet, daughter of Lievin Van Ghend. They were probably married by 1358. In 1362 Lievin Van Ghend tried to murder his son-in-law at the dinner table to which he had come in friendship. Jan de Bleekere acted as judge in his own case, awarded himself a hefty indemnity, and forbade Lievin ever again to enter his house without his permission or a court order. Lievin Van Ghend had died by the following August. Some amity had been restored between the clans by the late 1360s, but this may have ended when de Bleekere paid a large sum as damaged surety in a criminal case for Jan Van Ghend. Perhaps it was inevitable that Jan de Bleekere and his wife would separate, and the documents detailing this show the principles of property division clearly. They had received a decree from Tournai by June 6, 1373. He kept ownership of the lands that she had brought to him in marriage, but half the income was reserved to her for her lifetime. All other real estate was to be divided equally. Neither party was to occupy their house without the other's consent, but it would be rented for their joint profit. All property that each had taken from the house would be returned and divided equally. There were three children: each parent would support one, and they would support the third jointly, but we are not told where the third child would live. In August the city government ruled that each party would pay his or her own living expenses and legal fees from the time Mergriet had left the house, further indication that this was standard practice. Jan de Bleekere was a moneychanger, but his business was liquidated at this time and the assets divided with Mergriet, probably because he no longer had access to his house. Whether dissolution of the husband's business was ordinarily a feature of marital separation is impossible to say, although we have noted that Aechte de Pottere took over the moneychanging operations of her estranged husband. The de Bleekere establishment was on the Vismarkt, the financial center of Ghent, with other properties adjacent in the Korte Munt which were given to Mergriet in the final settlement. In 1378 the two parents accepted an inheritance on behalf of their children and secured it on their property without mentioning the separation, so it is at least possible that they had reconciled.[42]

The wrong marriage could involve a clan in the feuds of the in-laws, and this meant considerable physical danger. Quite naturally this sometimes found an outlet in physical violence between spouses or in-laws. In 1389 Willem Brunhals, noting the financial damage which the marriage of Clais, his son by a previous marriage, had done to him and his present wife, disinherited him and settled 86 lb. gr. in compensation on his daughter by the second marriage. Clais had apparently assaulted his mother-in-law, but since it had happened while he and his wife had lived together—they had separated during her pregnancy—the lady had to pay part of the fine to her own mother.[43] Clan violence complicated by business interests is found in the separation of Jan Van Everghem and Lisbette Eeckaerts, both of shipping families, in 1372. Relations between the clans had evidently been friendly through the 1360s, but on January 16, 1372, Jacob Eeckaert took responsibility for the life-threatening wounds and mutilation of Jan Van Everghem. The atonement was 24 lb. gr., more than was paid for most homicides. Not surprisingly, Van Everghem and his wife had separated at Tournai by August 4, 1372. We cannot know whether the disintegration of the marriage was the cause or consequence of other hostilities.[44] A brother might take his sister's part against her husband in other contexts. The prominent blue dyer Jan Van Libertsa was married to Zoetin de Pape by the mid-1360s. The couple and her brother Simon were frequent partners in business dealings through April 1379, but in February 1380 Simon de Pape took responsibility for a premeditated assault against Jan Van Libertsa. The deed was committed during legal truce, and Simon claimed to have been unaware of that fact, suggesting that he had been away, that Zoetin and her husband had had a sudden falling out but had been in truce, and that her brother took matters into his own hands when he returned without bothering to ascertain the circumstances.[45]

Several other cases of marital discord came to violence. In 1358 the *scepenen* declared a truce between Pieter Modde and his wife and admonished them to treat each other as they should according to the laws of holy church. When Willem Van Bassevelde was killed in 1352, his wife's kindred had to pay part of the blood price. Jacob Van den Driessche was sent on a pilgrimage in 1353 for misdeeds against his wife, mother-in-law, and others, but he was to leave only when his wife demanded it. She was evidently young, for she had still been a ward in 1352. She and Jacob were separated by 1361. Boudin de Moer was exiled beyond the Rhine for a year in 1362 unless his wife, whom he had attacked, remitted the punishment. The property division was stated by the *scepenen* to be effective as of before the deed, but there had been a legal separation at Tournai. Another case showing not only wife beating but also financial mismanagement is the apparent separation of Pieter Crabbe, identified as the son of Heinric and thus probably a young man, from Lisbette Van Crabbinghen. He pledged to atone his attack on her and not to sell or encumber her lands except for their common profit and with the consent of arbitrators whom she would choose, since they had no children.[46]

Two unsavory characters from the urban aristocracy encounter us in the persons of the tanner Jan Louf and his wife Aechte Blondeels. In 1358 the magistrates declared a truce between Louf and his then wife Mergriet Coelins. Aechte Blondeels in the same year became guardian of her son Annekin, who by 1366 is being called Jan Uten Hove the bastard, whose quarrels with his mother were being patched up by the clan. We do not know when she married Louf, but they were already separated by 1360. Louf died in 1368, and his kindred blocked Aechte's attempt to share his estate on grounds of the property division when they separated.[47] A case in which violence is not mentioned as contributing to marital discord but in which the character of the parties makes it very likely involves Jacob Van der Eeken, one of the most prominent surgeons of Ghent. Between 1357 and 1379 Meester Jacob committed three assaults, one of them while wearing the uniform of the city; was the victim of three assaults; was sent on a pilgrimage for insulting the *scepenen* past and present, alleging "that he could not get justice now any more than in the past," and on this occasion his wife was also sent on a pilgrimage for violence in the presence of the magistrates; and had to make restitution for collusion with another doctor to fix fees unreasonably high. He separated from Lisbette Willays on October 31, 1373. The settlement seems to favor him, for he was given all real estate acquired during the marriage, but he also agreed to pay their joint debt, and this may have been enough to justify it. An interesting twist is that she took his surgical instruments and medicines when she left him, and he agreed to pay her 12 lb. gr. if she would return them.[48]

Other cases of recourse to violence involved attempts to enforce a promise to marry or to clarify what in modern terms would be a common law arrangement. In 1350 Jacob Van Maelte demanded that Truve Parijs leave his house, for it had been awarded him in a contract of separation. She admitted the contract but claimed that they had lived together since then and that she had dower rights on land that he had since sold. She innocently offered to do all that a wife should for her husband. Jacob admitted cohabitation but claimed that he had been forced to take her back by threats against his life. The *scepenen* awarded him possession of the house and ordered her to leave it until a valid marriage between them could be performed, a neat way of skirting the issue.[49]

We have noted a pattern of childless marriages of ten to twenty years duration as specially prone to separation. Most of the recorded separations seem to have involved either first marriages or subsequent unions of longer duration that followed a brief first marriage. But there are some cases of couples, usually young, who decide almost from the beginning that they cannot live together. The separation of Jan Cariman from Zoetin Van den Zomple in 1358 contained most standard provisions, but it also provided a fee to help defray the costs of the wife's childbed, while Jan was to receive the tools of his trade. Zoetin was also to receive an annual payment from Jan's rents, an unusual but not unheard of early form of alimony. Violence had evidently been threatened, for Cariman was threatened with ten years banishment if he attacked his wife or the arbitrators physically or verbally. Zoetin acted with her husband's consent the next year in acquitting the widow of a kinsman. She had died by March 18, 1369, and this apparently restored friendship between her estranged husband and her kindred, for another Jacob Van den Zomple was surety for Jan Cariman in 1370.[50]

Since most separations recorded in fourteenth-century Ghent did not involve children, we get little insight into that very human dimension. Children normally received one-third of the common property and each parent one-third. As we shall see more clearly when we discuss childrearing, there was no notion whatsoever at this time that mothers were intrinsically better suited to raise children than were fathers. When the dyer Heinric Gheleins and his wife separated in 1353, the husband continued to live in the family business, one-third of which went to their child; it is thus likely that the child remained with him. Parents might make arrangements for the child's property at the time of separation.[51] When Fransois Van den Boengaerde and his wife separated in 1374, their son Meuskin was given a separate guardian, an arrangement changed in 1381 on grounds that the parents were separated and the boy had been given one-third of their property.[52] Child custody and support money might be provided as an adjunct to a separation. In 1379 Jan Van Zinghem and his wife Mergriet Graumans established a trust for their son from their common property, with the income of which his mother was to support him. If the father sold any land, the child's right to half the proceeds and the mother's rights of dower were guaranteed.[53]

Children could put a strain on any marriage, particularly when a step-parent was involved. Kateline de Clerc, mother of four children by Arnoud de Jonghe, who had died by September 3, 1371, was remarried by November 16, 1372, to Willem Bachout, whose previous wife had died about the same time as her husband. Bachout's intentions toward the children were evidently honorable at the time, for he settled 4 lb. gr. on them, but in 1376 his wife and the paternal guardian of her children sued Bachout for taking money belonging to them. The *scepenen* sustained this claim and allowed the children to recover their damages on their stepfather's residence. We are never told that the mother and Bachout had separated, although it is likely; she was acquitted as his widow by his maternal heirs in 1381, suggesting that they had no children of their own. She was not deterred by one bad experience, for she had married a third husband by February 3, 1382.[54]

The prospect of children discouraged some persons from marrying, then as now. Most marriage litigation is dry and formal, but complex human dilemmas can be revealed when it can be combined with additional information on the background and situations of the parties. Kerstine, bastard daughter of Jan Van der Houven, had inherited considerable property from her mother in 1377. By May 3, 1389, she was married to the baker Jan de Bitere, but her husband is expressly mentioned as being absent when his wife's guardians rendered their final account. We are told next that Jan de Bitere tried to leave Ghent without his wife in 1390, but her kindred and the *scepenen* forced him to "take his good wife and live and keep house with her in the city of Ghent as a good man is bound to do with his legal wife, and he is not to leave Ghent to live unless some future misfortune makes it unavoidable."

The husband was much older than the wife. Son of Pieter de Bitere, he had been given a guardian in 1365, and one surety for his mother had been

Jan Van Zinghem, who later appears as uncle and guardian of Kerstine Van der Houven. Jan de Bitere was emancipated in 1371, suggesting that he was some fifteen to twenty years older than his future bride, with whom he had a friendship if not a family connection through Jan Van Zinghem. Before his marriage to Kerstine he had made an unsuccessful marriage to Kateline de Puttere, mother of one Pieter de Pape. He had been separated from her when she died in 1380. Since her son is not given a "kin" suffix, as was normal although not invariable with minors, Jan de Bitere evidently married first a woman older than himself and then some years later married a teenager. A document of May 1390, about the time when he was trying to flee Ghent, has him acknowledging a gift from another party, which would be invalid if his wife died without heirs. The chronology suggests a pregnant or just delivered young wife with a husband, conceivably in his fifties, who simply did not want children. The reconstructed marriage seems to have lasted, for Jan de Bitere collected a debt in the name of this wife in 1397.[55]

Our discussion of marital violence and separation has shown that sexual activity was not confined to conjugal relations. While it is not surprising that people trapped in unhappy marriages or unable to remarry after separation would find paramours, this problem must be seen against a background of the casual sexual mores of the time. To this subject we now turn.

Chapter Three

What Man Joins, Let Not
God Put Asunder:
Standards of Sexual Conduct

ll families were concerned that their children, both daughters and sons, enter marriages approved by the clan. We have seen that marriages among the propertied were generally arranged by the clan, but the evidence on this point is less clear for those with less wealth. A woman committed a civil offense if she married contrary to the wishes of her clan. Yet the evidence reveals a number of cases of elopement and seduction, and rarely if ever was punishment extremely severe.

The constitutions of 1191 and 1297 provide the basic statutes on elopement, abduction, and seduction. The Flemish *ontscaken*, which is most often used in the fourteenth century to describe these affairs, simply means to cause to lose chastity; it can refer to anything involving sexual intercourse outside marriage, from willing elopement to rape, and the motives of the parties are of little account in the legal determination of the offense. Neither of the constitutions is very enlightening on the question of motive. According to the statute of 1191 if a woman or her kin complained of violent abduction, the victim was to be sequestered by the *scepenen* away from both her abductor and his clan and from her own kin. The culprit was to present himself for trial within three days of this or face outlawry. At the trial the woman would be placed midway between him and her own kindred. If she went with him, she recognized him as her husband and there would be no fine; but if she chose her own kin, he was to be executed.[1] The constitution of 1297 is more exact, perhaps a reflection of too many damsels choosing to go with the abductor. If a woman who is an orphan or has either parent alive is abducted without the approval of her closest kin—one could hardly expect them to applaud it—the man was to be banished for three years, while the woman's property was to descend by rules of inheritance as though she were dead. This rule applied even if she was taken with her own consent, for the town fathers did not want heiresses abducted for their money. If the deed had been done against her will, but thereafter she chose to remain with the man against the wishes of her parents or her closest kin, she still forfeited her property, and the man would be punished. Only if the clan authorized the marriage or some other arrangement, presumably including the girl's refusal to marry the abductor, might she keep her property. This statute refers only to women not married previously. A man who lured a girl to allow herself to be seduced would forfeit his nose and suffer banishment for as long as the magistrates thought appropriate. The punishment for abduction or rape of a woman who called for help was beheading.[2]

The cry for help was crucial. Ghiselbrecht Van Leeuwerghem was accused in 1374 of having "seduced and raped" Griele Van den Kerchove. The girl had not called for help and refused to press charges. In 1376 Pieter Van Duerle was accused of raping Callekin Van der Wostinen. The bailiff allowed composition in this case because the girl, who this time did press charges, admitted that she had not cried for help and because an unnamed person had told the bailiff that Callekin had gone with Pieter willingly because of bad counsel. Although the kinsmen were involved in bringing the abductor to justice, only the victim was legally competent to bring charges, and in most extant cases she refused. In 1376 Jan Van den Berghe and his party were accused of raping Adelise Van Crabbingen. This time there had been a cry for help, and the girl's friends had rescued her. But she refused to press charges despite the bailiff's express urging.[3]

One would expect few men to risk the penalties, but one would thereby fail to take account of either the warmth of lovers' passions or the softness of parental hearts. Not a single man is known to have been mutilated or executed for seduction in Ghent during the fourteenth century. Most of the girls involved clearly had had enough contact with the seducer beforehand to want to go with him, and this in itself shows that girls did not spend all their time cloistered or chaperoned by male relatives. Clandestine marriages with the consent of both parties were valid. The parents' approval was desirable but not required. While at Ghent as elsewhere wealthy parents arranged or tried to arrange their children's marriages, the church required only the consent of the couple. Those with less property were less subject to the constraints of the kindred than were the elite.[4] While the couple who went to a renegade priest knew that they might have to deal with outraged fathers or brothers, they acted in the expectation of being caught and in the firm knowledge that family affection would keep the punishment milder than the letter of the law prescribed.

Seduction and attempted seduction are our best documented instances of public morality and outrage, but whether angry fathers whose daughters followed the vagaries of nature are typical is best left to the reader. Amicable relations, at least on the surface, were generally restored fairly quickly between the lady and her husband with their clans, notably hers; there are far fewer cases of the man's family being angry about an elopement, suggesting that the male fortune hunter was more common than the female.

The language of the texts usually leaves it unclear whether the lady went willingly or was forced. In 1383 Hugh de Bake and his kin took Jan Blideleven, the widower of Hugh's daughter, to court concerning the *ontscaken* of the lady. The girl had evidently wheedled some property, perhaps her dowry, from her father, then had eloped with Blideleven and died shortly afterward.[5]

The right of the kindred to confiscate the property of a fallen woman was not generally enforced. More commonly the pair or the man would be placed under a loose receivership, sent on a pilgrimage, told to consider themselves in disgrace, or be given some similarly lenient penalty. The clan could insist on its rights, of course, and might try to prevent trouble by informing a girl that it would do so if she misbehaved. The two daughters of Jan Van den Nieuwenhove were warned that "if they married without the consent of their entire clan, the kin reserved the right to sue for their property." A dowry might be made conditional upon the daughter marrying according to the advice of her father and the clan.[6] But since such stipulations were even thought necessary, they show that girls could normally choose their own husbands. The only real barrier to a valid marriage by a girl who had reached her majority was the financial leverage exercised by the kindred.

The escapades of some Lowland Lotharios make picturesque reading. In the winter of 1362 Avezoete, daughter of the Ghent noble Boudin Van Steeland, was en route with her mother to Ghent from northern Flanders to visit her sick grandfather when Wouter, brother of another noble, Mer

Roem de Scouteete, abducted her. He was in the entourage of Avezoete's mother. The girl's connivance is not certain, for while they agreed separately to accept arbitration, he did so three months before she did. It seems probable that in the interim the ceremony provided by the constitution of 1191 was used and that she chose to go with him, for she surrendered all her property "just as if she were lying dead on the floor." But her kindred agreed to give her the revenues of her lands for her lifetime. She might not alienate the properties to her husband—but no wife could during a marriage—and he was to have no dower rights if he survived her. The agreement does not take account of any children who might be born during the marriage. The financial rights of the man are clearly being circumscribed, but his wife, and he through her, would have a decent income as long as she lived.[7]

Other cases suggest that the girl was being manipulated, even if willingly. Betkin, daughter of the prominent tanner Jan Heinmans, was apparently a teenager when she was taken at night from her grandfather's house in late 1375 by Jan, son of Pieter Van der Wostinen. His father quickly agreed to have him atone the "disgraceful attack and misdeed" against the girl's father, his three sons, and other kindred. But Betkin had obviously been willing. The judgment gave her the maternal inheritance, and "from grace" some additional property for furnishings and chattels, together with some land and rents that could not be alienated by the girl or her husband. All property would revert to its side of origin if she died without children having reached their majority. The uncles evidently suspected Van der Wostinen's motives, for they specified that he had no right to her property if they did not remain together. They evidently decided that it was best to safeguard the future while not depriving the daughter of all support.[8] Another case in which the punishment was quite lenient, amounting to depriving the parties of the right to alienate property for a time, is the seduction of Kateline Rijnvisch by Jacob Van Ghend. While most outbursts of passion in these records seem to be between persons of comparable age, usually young, Kateline may have been some years older than her paramour, with whom she eloped in 1363. Her kindred prohibited them from alienating or encumbering any property that she held when the deed occurred, but she was given the revenues. She was also forbidden to encumber anything acquired subsequently, but she could have her property divided from that of her siblings; when relations were amiable, most estates were simply kept together to provide a larger fund for investment. Jacob was sent on a distant pilgrimage.[9]

Childhood sweethearts sometimes married against the wishes of their elders. In early 1361 Kateline, daughter of the cloth wholesaler (*lakensnider*) Lennoot Uten Dale, eloped with the bastard son of the late *lakensnider* Willem Van den Pitte. Her sister Mergriet was married to yet another *lakensnider*, Juffroit Caroen. Family and professional association fed the affections of the young people. Although Van den Pitte agreed to accept the penalty set by Uten Dale and his wife—seduction was an offense against the mother as well as the father—there is no record of punishment being handed down, for Uten Dale's wife died soon afterward. This would have been a logical match for Kateline had it not been for her husband's illegitimacy. Friendly relations were apparently restored quickly. Willem Van den Pitte died in late 1366, leaving one child. Kateline had died by July 13, 1368, but she had meanwhile remarried, to the nobleman Gerard Van Neufvile.[10]

Some runaway couples may not have had marriage in mind, but nuptials were forced upon them by the kindred, since the woman had been compromised. Often the restrictions placed upon the husband's discretion over his and his wife's property would be lifted when they had a child, whose presence would mean greater likelihood of a permanent household and would end the possibility of reversion of the marital assets to the parents' respective clans. Certainly the records show the impetuosity of youth. In the summer of 1362 Simon Trijl married Volcwijf Rabau while he was still under guardianship. His guardian could not annul the marriage, suggesting that Simon was of legal age although unemancipated. He and the "overseer" agreed to support the couple, but Simon pledged not to seek emancipation until he was ready to support himself; he was emancipated on February 20, 1363. Although the marriage did endure, Simon Trijl and his wife were apparently not the most responsible of persons. By the 1370s they were in serious financial embarrassment and were selling real estate and annuities.[11]

Even among the municipal aristocracy, which was small enough that one would expect some personal knowledge and acquaintance with one another's reputations, there are some astonishing acts of carelessness. Ypocras Van Nevele, a scion of the noble family who were lords of that village and a kinsman of a leading physician of Ghent, had led Kateline Uten Hove, who was also prominent, to believe that he was single. She accordingly went to live with him on his promise of marriage, a fact indicative in itself of sexual mores, and he then appropriated property that she had inherited from her parents. She then discovered that he was married.

A separation was arranged involving some division of the property which they had held in common, although unmarried. Ypocras then had had the gall to sue her and the man she subsequently married, Gillis Van der Meere, for a substantial sum of money, but the *scepenen* quashed his claim. It is at least conceivable that Ypocras was acting in good faith, however, for some cases show people who honestly believed that they were married to each other but were not. We are not told the impediment in these cases. Records were kept at the archbishoprics at Tournai and Utrecht, and doubtful cases were referred there. Lisbette Van Audenaerde in 1381 was acquitted of the estate of Jan de Cleyne, "whom she considered her legal husband, but this was found not to be the case" from a document which Lisbette herself brought from Utrecht.[12]

Another aristocratic elopement occurred in 1388 with the younger Willem Uten Hove and Jehane, youngest daughter of Ogeer Tsuul, from whom she had inherited an enormous estate in 1384. The words used are *ontscaken ende wechleeden,* and the latter term definitely places the initiative with Willem, although there is no implication that Jehane was dragged off against her will. Both parties were evidently young and acted with accomplices. They agreed to accept punishment, of which no record has survived, but soon afterward she was allowed to receive her inheritance. An Uten Hove would not have been a disastrous match from the financial standpoint, and one suspects that a pair of teenagers simply did on their own what their elders would have preferred to arrange among themselves a few years later.[13] Potentially more serious was the elopement of Alexandre, daughter and namesake of the Ghent noble Sanders Van Vaernewijc, with the Frenchman Guy de Bloc in 1384. As was true of Jehane Tsuul, both of Alexandre's parents were dead, and supervision may have been lax. Alexandre was an older woman, for she was selling real estate in her own name as early as 1375. Two days after she and Guy agreed to accept punishment, they divided the estates of both her parents with her brother Jan. In 1386 they were prosperous enough to renounce the estate of Alexandre's paternal grandmother on grounds that her dowry from her father, of which she evidently had not been deprived, had been worth more. Guy de Bloc is recorded with and without Alexandre in various property matters during the late 1380s.[14]

The seduction of the daughter of Willem Eemeric by Jan, son of the shipper Roger Everwijn, ran a similar course. As was standard practice, the couple agreed to accept the punishment set by her parents, but the girl also accepted a penalty for leaving their home without their permission; even in this agreement she was represented by her husband. But by May 1387 Everwijn was collecting debts for his widowed mother-in-law, and with other children and in-laws he had consented to the father-in-law's testament.[15]

A more severe penalty where resentment was felt long after the deed is seen with the seduction of Mergriet, daughter of Jan Smeeds, who was placed under wardship in October 1383 and had eloped with Olivier Van der Meere by February 1385. She was evidently younger than most girls who were abducted, for the fact that she was an orphan under guardianship is expressly mentioned, but she was still thought to bear some responsibility. Certainly her property was sufficient to be tempting. Her clan allowed the couple the income of her property, and no limitation was placed on Olivier's discretion with whatever came from his side, but he was sent on a pilgrimage to Rome. The couple also pledged never again to give food or drink to Bette Van der Meere, who had transmitted messages from Olivier to Mergriet before the seduction. The four judges only acquitted Olivier of the terms of this penalty in 1399, fourteen years after the deed.[16] We are not told Bette's relationship to Olivier, but the identity of the family name suggests that they were probably siblings or cousins. It was obviously easier for a girl to confide in a female chum than to speak directly to a man. Yet Olivier and Mergriet must have known each other well enough in other contexts to make them want to pursue the relationship.

Elopement and seduction thus were far less severely punished in practice than the law prescribed. When Lisbette, daughter of Wouter Coepman, eloped with Jan Van der Erdbrugghen in 1339, her guardian, who was a woman herself, went to court to declare that Kateline had forfeited all her property according to law and that it should go to her heir, who happened to be the guardian. But having made her point, she then returned the estate to the girl and presumably her husband on condition that they not encumber or alienate it without the guardian's consent.[17] It is thus difficult to determine generally accepted standards of sexual behavior and morality, since most of our documentation is a litany of the exceptional. Yet the unblushing acceptance of behavior totally at variance with the norms inculcated by Christian moralists, together with the widespread concubinage and high incidence of bastardy, make it clear that at the very least standards were higher than actual practice. Hence we must examine the surviving documents and attempt to reach a balanced assessment of the norm.

We know little of prostitution at this time. The art was more developed in Bruges, where the bailiff took a fee from the ladies of the night. There was a Prostitutes' Street (Huurdochterstraat) in Ghent, which may have deserved its name, but a number of eminently respectable citizens also lived there. In 1378 a house was sold in Onderbergen, not far from the Huurdochterstraat, and the buyers agreed not to allow anyone to live in it "who keeps pigs or cannot live there with the toleration of holy church."[18] A municipal ordinance of 1350 forbade single women "to sit in the compartments of the city walls," presumably to discourage prostitution.[19] In 1375 Pieter Coene found Bernard Van Belle, a nobleman who lived at Ghent, "lying with a woman," evidently on the street in front of Pieter's house. Pieter went inside, got weapons, and returned to the spot where Bernard lay "with his pants down." He would have run him through had not the "little lady" stopped him by telling him who Bernard was. Since he did not know his antagonist, it is likely that the scene outraged him. There was a home for reformed prostitutes, the Filgedieusen, on the northern edge of the city. Women of questionable character are sometimes found keeping company with groups of men. In 1370 a fight erupted over bad words that Lievin Van den Nieuwenweghe "uttered publicly about the wenches who were in the group where he was sitting."[20] Some women had bastards by more than one father, but one should probably conclude promiscuity rather than profession in such cases.

Social norms were set by men, who had rather different standards for their wives and daughters than for other women with whom they consorted. A respectable woman had to avoid all appearance of unchastity, and if a woman was accused of behaving improperly, the burden of proof was on her rather than on her accuser. In 1366 Lievin Van der Loeven was sent on a pilgrimage for striking the daughter of Jan Van den Brouke and for making unfounded accusations against her with foul language, allegations that could have led to discords and marital separation had they been true. Interestingly, she is identified by her father's name rather than her husband's. Standards of public decency could provide legal grounds for altering living arrangements. In 1354 Mergriet Van Crayloe was awarded annual house rent from her mother. But while the arbitrators did not dispute Mergriet's ownership of the property, she was ordered to vacate the premises herself because she had been living there with a man to whom she was not married.[21] There was a clear double standard, for no limitation was ever placed on the right of a man living with a concubine to occupy his own property with her or even to give it to her.

The males of Ghent exercised constant vigilance to make certain that females did not engage in unladylike behavior or utter words unbecoming of the fair sex. Since most direct quotations involve allegations of misbehavior or theft, it is difficult to say just what kind of swearing unsexed a lady. Some moralistic denunciations become rhetorical; nice women had far less freedom of expression than did men. Goessin Van Peelkem did a pilgrimage on behalf of his sister for her impure and disgraceful words "unbecoming for a respectable woman to speak." When men injured one another in tavern brawls, each party normally paid for the injuries of the other. But when Lisbette Uten Berken committed "vile and loathsome behavior" with her companions in a tavern "where good fellows were sitting, she thoroughly deserved" what happened to her and got no compensation for her injuries—another case that shows there was no restriction against women of a certain type frequenting the public houses. In 1377 Wouter Van Pudenbrouc was accused of trying to rape Bette sKevers, "who was sitting with him drinking." She filed a complaint but then dropped it, and the bailiff "thought that he could prove no other force than that he may have hit her with his fists, and they were a pair of noisy drunks anyway." Kateline Van der Ellen did a pilgrimage for uttering words "which were dishonorable for a good woman to say," but she was a victim herself when a man publicly displayed an unflattering poster about her. Some idea of what constituted unladylike deeds, if not words, is shown us by Mergriet Van den Hende, who in 1365 paid damages to Jacob de Cousmakere for a "homicidal" attack on him in her house, "unwomanly and totally without justification, and he is a nice, sick old man."[22]

Attempts to come between husband and wife were severely punished, whether they were committed by men or women. They frequently led to violence. In 1367 Gerem Van Lovendeghem had to go in processional for his lies about Jacob Drinhout's wife, "saying that she is a good woman of body and conscience, as is well known throughout her neighborhood," and did a second pilgrimage for words for which her husband was incarcerated and suffered damages, presumably alleging misbehavior against him.[23] The words of Jane Ebberechts against Heinric Roetaerd's wife, which the authorities thought might have sparked a riot, were "unnatural, unfeminine, and foul." A woman's good name was a jewel to be guarded zealously by her men. In 1374 Jan Bierman, a married man, was ordered to come before the neighbors and kinsmen of Jan Liefghetal's wife and "there to utter all that he had said or done toward Jan Liefghetal's wife, in love or in friendship, and to say that he would not have done it if her husband had been present" and that he considered her a woman of good name. Thus she established that she had not encouraged his attentions and got public recognition of her innocence. Gillis Weyns was accused in 1378 of "stealing the wife and even the property" of Jan de Hond, but the case was dropped since "the hussy went with him willingly."[24]

In principle women were not supposed to be alone with men, but in fact there was a great deal of casual contact between the sexes. A girl complained in 1376 of "force" used against her by Staesin de Hamer, but she dropped the charge after the *scepenen* told the bailiff that she had been "keeping company with Staessin." A father who assaulted a suitor who had been bothering his daughter in 1353 left it to the girl's discretion whether she wanted to speak to the man again.[25] In what was apparently a piece of youthful fun, Kateline, daughter of Wasselin Kindekin, declared of her own free will that "concerning the fact that she was taken to Jacob Willebaert's house on Friday, March 9, 1357, she considers herself well paid by Daneel Willebaert and those who took her there, and from anyone toward whom there might conceivably be hostility, for she declares that there was no cause for complaint, since she was received so courteously and pleasantly there among Daneel's friends." Evidently her relatives had been upset that she had spent time unchaperoned with the Willebaert boys, and she voluntarily came to clear them of any imputation of wrongdoing. These were aristocratic people who would guard their daughters' persons very carefully, and the episode thus shows that men and women had much more freedom to associate with one another at this time than was the case later.[26] In 1376 Jooskin Van Deftingen and Pieterkin de Pape were accused of coming by night to the door of one Callekin, who let them in as friends. The bailiff incarcerated them for trying to lure her away but, as usual, lost the case because no force was exercised, no cry for help was made, and Callekin did not press charges. If little money was involved, courtship was apparently conducted primarily between the principals, with the parents only becoming involved if marriage were actually being planned. A contemporary ring of two brothers fighting over the same girl is given in the promise of Benedictus de Clerc to cease "all annoyances or hindrances toward his brother Jan, particularly concerning Lisbette Ardiels." There is no suggestion of the involvement of either set of parents in what was evidently a courtship.[27]

Yet other cases suggest that maidens of the middle class were kept under some surveillance. Boudin, with the collusion of his father, Willem Van den Pitte, tried to seduce Kateline, daughter of Gillis Van der Beke. The man who had carried messages between the pair and knew all their secrets testified that she had never been with Boudin anywhere where "disgrace" might have occurred. But father and son had tried to entice her into having commerce with Boudin, which "such a young lady, a friend of respectable people, should always avoid, and from which great shame might come." To this point the evidence suggests that she was mildly interested in him. But as the courtship faltered, the Van den Pittes decided to take matters into their own hands and abduct her forcibly. She had resisted the assault, in the course of which her would-be husband had tried to cut off her nose but managed merely to leave a scar. Several pilgrimages were ordered as a result of the affair, certainly a mild enough punishment. It may have caused permanent psychological trauma for both victim and assailant, who seem to have remained single for life; the sentence was acquitted by the girl's unmarried sister as her heir many years later. The arbitrators concluded on a note of horror that such a loathsome deed could be visited on a respectable girl of good family "in such a splendid city as Ghent, which God preserve!"[28] And yet for such a level of interest to be sparked the girl must have had at least some personal contact with Boudin, even if only in the presence of others.

Respectable ladies were not to be seen in questionable places without their husbands, let alone with other men. When Jacob de Scoteleere took walks with the wife of Clais de Drayere, the men fought. When peace was reestablished, de Scoteleere was to initiate no further contact with the lady, but he was given assurances that he would not be fined if the resumption came from her. Jan de Parmentier did a pilgrimage for having pursued Clare de Scoufeleere "contrary to her wishes, attempting to diminish her honor undeservedly," but he was also assaulted by Jan de Scoufeleere for his pains.[29] While a woman could refuse to marry a man who had raped her, one suspects that many agreed to marriage because they did not want to condemn the man to death and in so doing involve their own kindred in a retaliatory feud. A hint of this is given in a case of late 1360, when Lievin Banghelin the younger was sent into exile for attempting a nocturnal rape in the Béguinage of a lady "to get her property." He must have expected her to marry him and bring him some property if the assault had succeeded.[30] We have seen that the count's bailiffs had a great deal of trouble getting victims to press charges against their abductors.

Most references to sexual offenses in the Ghent records are maddeningly vague. In 1352 Pieter and Gillis Ramont did pilgrimages for housebreak against Lisbette Ramont and another for the "scandal and blame done her, through which her honor and standing have been diminished." Contrary impulses seem at work when a brawl erupted between Jacob de Scot and an unnamed companion against Jacob Van Loe and Lievin Vulnose as the latter pair were trying to protect a woman whom the de Scot party mistreated. The men paid for one another's injuries, but there was evidently no punishment for the treatment of the woman, who may not have sustained physical injury.[31] In 1377 two men evidently struck a woman in her genitals when she tried to come between them as they were fighting. Although they had to compensate her for the injuries, it is significant that the *scepenen* apparently thought that she had given them cause.[32] In 1379 Willem Clappaert did a pilgrimage and paid damages for having put glowing tongs between the legs of Beele Baert, trying to get at her sexual organs, then opening the tongs and making two wounds. Although the record calls the penalty an example against such behavior, the fine is actually far less than what would be expected from comparison with other injury cases.[33]

Women might also be punished for unseemly behavior, such as dishonoring a man by grabbing him by the rump. Some women evidently carried small weapons for protection when they were on the street. Laureins Rabau was assaulting Callekin Van Laerne "immorally above and below" when she pulled a knife on him; he then righteously complained to the magistrates that she should compensate him for his injuries. The *scepenen* disallowed compensation on grounds that he got what he deserved, but significantly did nothing to him for what was apparently a sexual assault on a teenager.[34]

Many cases show that women of the upper classes could be as skillful in combat and in sexual misbehavior as their less privileged counterparts. A prominent example is Clemencie de Scouteete, probably of the aristocratic family of that name, who was the mother of a bastard by the prominent hosteller Tonis Melaus in 1365. She was the object of foul language the following year by Kateline Rebbe, probably a kinswoman of the moneychanger Celie Amelakens, and in return attacked her physically. By 1373 Clemencie was married to Jan Strichout and evidently was involved with him in the wine trade. She passed on her talents to a daughter; "young Clemencie de Scouteete" had mothered a bastard of her own by 1380.[35]

Sexual standards are shown in some spectacular cases that by their very atypicality show the vulnerability of women and a certain ecclesiastically inbred callousness on the part of the authorities. Jacob Van den Hende was guardian, evidently as maternal uncle, of Kateline, daughter of Wouter

Van den Berghe. He allegedly mocked the girl, caused her to lose respect, then "took from her her purity and also the marriage which she would have made through her father and friends," suggesting that loss of chastity was assumed to prevent marriage. The girl's father had violent arguments with the "funny uncle" while this was going on, but to no avail. The uncle impregnated Kateline. The child died soon after birth, and Jacob took it from the mother, allegedly to bury it in consecrated ground, but in fact he simply disposed of the body. The uncle paid minimal damages, including the cost of reburying his child in a proper cemetery. He and the girl's father did pilgrimages for fighting each other, but there is no fine or compensation to the girl for her emotional stress. Nowhere is she stated to have consented, although her father would probably have been more successful in warding off the uncle if the girl had objected to her uncle's attentions. The church court only became involved because of the clandestine burial.[36]

The language of the Van den Hende case suggests that rape rendered a girl unsuited for marriage, but other texts indicate that sexual assault did not necessarily deter suitors. The daughter of Jan Beatrisen was the victim of *fortse ende crachte* in 1368. This formula is normally reserved for sexual assaults, although it does not necessarily imply penetration. The young lady was married by 1370.[37]

Girls belonged in principle to the kindred. A case demonstrating this but also proving that parents did not sequester their daughters totally even after seduction involves Jan de Keyser, who paid a minimal fine to Michiel Augustine and his wife for having seduced their daughter, then having hidden her from the *scepenen* while all parties were under summons from the magistrates, who wished to examine her, presumably to determine whether she was of mature years or had lost her virginity. He did one pilgrimage in honor of the girl's parents and a second for the *scepenen,* but there was no pilgrimage for the victim herself.[38]

Even married women were not immune from pursuit by men, who had various legal options not available to women. Gillis de Scacht accused Agnes, the wife of Heinric de Scumere by the time the case was recorded, of pledging to marry him. She was acquitted by the local church court, but Gillis appealed to the archiepiscopal court of Reims, which outlawed her from the Christian community and forbade anyone to give her shelter. Seeing that she was destitute, her friends convinced her to give all her property to Gillis in return for an annual living allowance, in hope of being restored eventually to her property when the court judgment was reversed.

But Gillis continued to hold her property for nine years. Meanwhile, her husband had gone to the comital court, which sustained Agnes. Gillis continued to use procedural delays and prohibitions from the church court. Eventually Heinric's property was also gone, and he appealed to the *scepenen* of Ghent. We do not know their verdict.[39]

We have considered seduction and elopement separately, but we must also consider rape and its legal consequences for the woman. These are cases in which there can be no question of the woman consenting to sexual intercourse. A vicious gang rape occurred in 1375, which may be tied to the murder of Andries Van der Straten, a burgher of Ghent who lived outside the city, whose children inherited from him considerable rural property in parishes near Dendermonde, east of Ghent. Nine men were accused of raping his widow, Lisbette de Cousmakere, but as burghers of Ghent they could choose trial at Dendermonde, where the deed occurred.[40] We next read of the case more than two years later. The men had lured her from her house, overpowered her, taken her by horseback into the woods, and held her there in a pit threatening her. Although rape may have made some single women unclean and thus unworthy of marriage, the issue seems to have been virginity, for Lisbette had remarried by 1386 and with her new husband was contesting the estate of Andries Van der Straten with his blood heirs.[41]

Yet a rather curious case that suggests that widows, too, lost legal rights as a consequence of rape involves the property of the daughters of Jan Van Peelkem. The parents were separated, and the mother had dower on lands whose title was vested in the children. On her own volition she pledged that she would surrender these incomes if she ever remarried or "if she ever lost her chastity, whether with her consent or not."[42] The reference probably indicates that a seducer would be a husband presumptive and that a marriage would follow; but according to the constitution of 1191 she could also lose her family property even if she did consent.

The high incidence of bastardy, which we shall examine in chapter 8, suggests a fairly loose sexual standard. Even more indicative of moral standards are the relationships of men with their mistresses. However indifferent men might be to the chastity of their mistresses during their lives together, they had grave concerns for the ladies' moral character when the strong hand of the male was removed. The case of the priest Lennoot Veys is typical. Evidently expecting death, in November 1371 he willed property to his mistress and their two bastards. But when his estate was settled on the children the following July, the lady's share was declared void if she ever situated herself with another man without marrying him.[43] Concubinage with priests was a generally accepted practice, although comparatively few priests were leaving property to their bastards. But there could be sad consequences with such liaisons. In 1349 the priest Lievin Van den Berghe and Mergriet Van der Haghe willed to each other life possession of their joint residence. The two families were political allies; her brother Lievin stood surety in 1353 for the party of Jacob Van den Berghe in a homicide action. But at some point Mergriet and Lievin parted, and she entered Doornzele abbey. This may have been an aspect of a more far-reaching estrangement between the clans, for in 1372 her onetime paramour is stated to have died outside Flanders in penance for killing Jan, son of Ser Lievin Van der Haghe, who would have been Mergriet's nephew.[44]

The Van den Berghe case suggests that under some circumstances life outside wedlock was tacitly accepted by the families of the parties. Mergriet Van den Speye was given half the estate of Andries Van Wambeke, with whom she had lived "outside legal marriage," not by him but by his heirs. Perhaps this attitude was inevitable in view of the impediments to marriage and remarriage contained in the legal systems of the time. Naturally, there are cases that lead to the opposite conclusion, for example, when legitimate children try to defraud bastards of the bequests from their fathers and cases of heirs who balk at paying bequests to mistresses. Men might have common property with their mistresses, and the rules of transmission when one party died were the same as for married couples, but in such cases the man normally acknowledged that some of their joint holdings belonged to the woman. Hence, in 1377 Heinric de Meyere declared that half his property in Ghent belonged to the lady who lived with him, and he willed her another 4 lb. gr. for "services." If they parted through her fault before his death, the bequest was annulled, but she would still get half the chattels, which were her half of their common property. A woman who had lived with a man outside wedlock might be the holder of his estate when he died and accordingly bound to furnish a list of his property to the *scepenen*. Yet at least once the magistrates accepted a mistress's argument that she was not so obligated.[45]

Two types of women seem to have been especially vulnerable to the amorous artifices of men: farm girls and maids. Whether the former were employed on the rural estates of their paramours is usually unstated but seems likely. The small number of these cases in which the man left property to the girl or her children suggests either that the practice was not widespread, which seems improbable, or that most men were more callous in their dealings with these girls than with their mistresses in Ghent, who obviously could be much more vocal about ill-treatment. With farm girls and especially with maids the bequests are often stated to be in compensation for "services," the nature of which is best left unstated here as it is in the sources, and for loans, some of which were quite substantial.[46] Many bequests to mistresses suggest affection, and most presume that the liaison will continue but also show that the woman was in a form of bondage to the man that made it impossible for her to refuse his demands either for sexual favors or for money. Hence Jan Van der Mersch willed 6 lb. gr. to Marie Van Buxelaer to repay a loan, but the debt was annulled if she predeceased him without having a child by him. Zeger Scoenenzoon willed all his furnishings and chattels and half his moor properties to his mistress, a lady of Wachtebeke, in northeastern Flanders where there were rich peat bogs. He did this because he had used the enormous sum of 50 lb. gr. that she had inherited from her parents for his own profit. In 1378 Heinric Van Belzele and his current maid agreed that the survivor would keep the entire joint right on their residence in Ghent. Such an arrangement would have required the heirs' consent if they had been married to each other. Between the date of this contract and the time the *scepenen* recorded it in 1385 Heinric acknowledged a debt of 15 lb. gr. to the same lady. The theme of financial entrapment of a woman by a man who was siring children by her is illustrated by the case of Jacob Lancacker, who gave 3 lb. gr., effective immediately, to his two bastards by Kateline Van den Steene. The housekeeping arrangement was permanent, for any other children by her would share the bequest. If the two children died without issue of their own, half would go to the estate of each parent, which suggests that half the money was Kateline's. Jacob also repaid her for damages that she had incurred by loaning him money, and the word used, *scoufieringhe*, suggests moral blame or derision. But surely some sort of record must have been set by Jan Waelkin the younger, whose assassination in 1351 left two mistresses pregnant.[47]

We close this chapter with a case probably more typical of standards of sexual morality than the more spectacular examples noted earlier. On July 13, 1354, Lisbette, daughter of Jan Van den Dale, admitted having been deliberately unchaste with Jan de Bastard van Massemine and having left her parents' house with him because of their great affection for each other. She did not say that she had married him. Her parents then acknowledged that Lisbette had been alone with Jan de Bastard with their consent, suggesting that such was probably a normal courtship practice, but implying that they blamed themselves to some extent for what had happened. They were receiving her back into their home and accordingly make no complaint.[48] The parents clearly disapproved of what their daughter had done, but they had trusted both her and the man and were not willing to take further action against either. The number of such cases that were simply handled between parties without making it into the written record cannot be estimated.

Chapter Four

Freedom in Bondage:
Unemancipated Women
in the Business World

We have seen that women could inherit and acquire property on the same basis as men, but that most were legally incompetent to transact business without the express or implied consent of a male guardian; the only exceptions were women who had been emancipated from tutelage by their clans but did not marry and "free merchant women." Most women did marry, and in these cases the husband became the legal guardian of the wife and the manager of her property unless he renounced his right to act for her. We thus must investigate the role of women in the economic life of the family and of the city at large. We shall demonstrate the quantifiable evidence showing women transacting business and disposing of lands or incomes. We shall then examine the role that wives played in their husbands' businesses and the extent to which they understood their husbands' affairs. Finally, we shall consider business-women, who acted on their own recognition or with only the implied consent of a man.[1]

Women did not hold a great deal of real estate on their own. The rent books kept by the churches and abbeys of Ghent and by the city government, though extremely important for other aspects of urban life, tell us little of the role of women. Women are statistically insigificant as payers of *landcijns* (tax) or rents. Most who do appear are listed jointly with their husbands or are widows who hold with their children. Most foundations did not compile new rent books annually; when names are crossed out to denote change of payer, women are usually replaced by men, probably signifying remarriage in most cases. That inheritance at Ghent was so strictly partible also meant that it was a rare tenement that had only one owner. In such cases one person, usually the one with the largest share, would pay the tax or rent.

But we get a very different impression when we examine other sources: the number of transactions contained in the *Jaarboeken van de Keure* in which women appear as principals; the records of the *exuwe* tax; and the loans paid to the city during the wartime emergency of 1336–49.

The *scepenen* of the *Keure* were the chief magistrates of the city. Their judgment in doubtful cases took precedence over that of the *scepenen* of *Gedele,* or *paysierders.* Their records have not survived in continuous series, nor can they be considered complete in any way. Most business dealings were recorded in guild archives, at the cloth hall, in private ledgers, or by *vinders* (arbitrators) stationed on the marketplaces, and virtually all of this material has perished. The *scepenen* handled only the weightier cases. But there is no reason to think that the surviving registers give disproportionate attention to cases involving women; given the political impotence and legal disabilities of women, they are probably underrepresented in the records. These considerations make all the more striking the data that are assembled in Table 4.

Table 4 excludes four categories of cases involving women: rape and seduction; marital separation and related matters, such as child support; donations to mistresses and/or bastard daughters; and those concerning female minors. It includes cases in which the woman is the principal transactor of business, even if her husband is named and his consent is specified, and those in which she appears in the same party with a man not her husband, so that she has only a partial interest in the transaction.

Table 4 shows that in most "ordinary" years women were involved as principals against men in between 20 and 28 percent of the recorded cases. The percentage rises sharply in the war years, as many more men than women lost their lives and their estates were being settled. The composite average for the years surveyed is 27.69 percent. There are far fewer cases in which women figure as principals on both sides; only in 1382–83, the year of the disastrous defeat of the city militia at Westrozebeke, does this figure rise above 10 percent of the total. But the pattern of greater involvement of women during the war years, and particularly from 1382, is present in this column as well. The average percentage for the combined totals of col-

Table 4. Female Involvement in Transactions
before *Scepenen* of the *Keure*

Fiscal Year	1	2	3	4	5	6	7	8	9	10	11
1345 (–6)	56	5	8.92	–	–	8.92	2	3.57	12.49	2	40.00
1349	409	76	18.58	6	1.47	20.05	35	8.56	28.61	21	25.61
1353	327	65	19.88	11	3.36	23.24	27	8.26	31.50	23	30.26
1357	298	75	25.17	5	1.68	26.85	42	14.09	40.94	18	22.50
1360	440	104	26.64	22	5.00	31.64	49	11.14	42.78	37	29.37
1362	283	41	14.49	9	3.18	17.67	47	16.61	34.28	12	24.00
1365	358	77	21.51	18	5.03	26.54	48	13.41	39.95	25	26.32
1368	531	152	28.63	23	4.33	32.96	54	10.17	43.13	55	31.43
1371	424	103	24.29	8	1.89	26.18	54	12.74	38.92	29	26.13
1372	348	94	27.01	8	2.30	29.31	45	12.93	42.24	24	23.53
1373	427	99	23.19	9	2.11	25.30	53	12.41	37.71	32	29.63
1374	392	81	20.66	11	2.81	23.47	59	15.05	38.52	21	22.83
1375	462	103	22.29	12	2.60	24.89	70	15.15	40.04	25	21.74
1376	540	114	21.11	14	2.59	23.70	65	12.04	35.74	37	28.91
1377	511	120	23.48	20	3.91	27.39	59	11.55	38.94	48	34.29
1378	539	128	23.75	10	1.86	25.71	62	11.50	37.21	39	28.26
1379	270	77	28.52	10	3.70	32.22	19	7.04	39.26	24	27.59
1380	316	89	28.16	15	4.75	32.91	41	12.97	45.88	35	33.65
1381	406	130	32.02	21	5.17	37.19	26	6.40	43.59	45	29.80
1382	331	141	42.60	35	10.57	53.17	27	8.16	61.33	70	39.77
1383	464	162	34.91	33	7.11	42.02	41	8.84	50.86	77	39.49
1384	439	154	35.08	13	2.96	38.04	59	13.44	51.48	54	32.34
1386	1181	413	34.97	68	5.76	40.73	123	10.41	51.14	255	53.01
1387	1083	353	32.59	55	5.08	37.67	85	7.85	45.52	184	45.10
1388	884	273	30.88	49	5.54	36.42	80	9.05	45.47	144	44.72
1389	873	258	29.55	39	4.47	34.02	54	6.19	40.21	133	44.78

Key to Column Headings
1. Total number of cases in *Keure Jaarboek* between individuals or between individuals and an institution.
2. Cases between woman and man or male institution, or between female institution and a man.
3. Column 2 as percentage of column 1.
4. Cases involving women as principals on both sides.
5. Column 4 as percentage of column 1.
6. Total percentage of columns 3 and 5.
7. Women acting with living husbands in property transactions, i.e., the husband is principal, but the wife has a common property interest.
8. Column 7 as percentage of column 1.
9. Columns 3, 5, and 7 as percentage of column 1.
10. Number of cases involving widows, including those who have remarried.
11. Column 10 as percentage of columns 2 and 4.

Source: SAG, Registers of *scepenen* of the *Keure*.

umns 2 and 4 is 31.85. Women thus appear on at least one side as principal in nearly one-third of the total cases adjudicated between individuals by the *scepenen* of the *Keure* during these years. After 1357 the fraction drops below one-quarter only four times in the twenty-three years for which registers survive. The figures become even more striking when one includes the number of women who, although not principals, are included in transactions with their husbands because of a common property interest. This figure rarely drops below 10 percent of the total cases, except during and after the war, when the change can be explained by the extreme loss of life among males during the war. When these figures are combined with those involving women acting on their own, we find that 42.38 percent of the cases between individuals in the years surveyed involved women in some capacity as property owners.

Table 5 shows the involvement of women and their heirs in payment of the *exuwe* tax, these records of which are not very detailed before 1351. They deal with cases in which property left the tax competence of the city government. The most important of these instances occur when someone left Ghent to reside elsewhere, statistically insignificant before 1386; when some or all heirs of a burgher of Ghent were not citizens of Ghent; when someone entered holy orders; or when someone made a charitable donation to an individual or foundation outside the city.

The figures are not entirely consistent, for in column 3, cases involving women or their heirs, we include persons designated as "widow of." There is usually no way to determine whether the persons named are being taxed on common property left by their husbands or paid on their own, and this figure thus may be somewhat inflated. But the *exuwe* figures do corroborate to a striking degree the suggestions furnished by Table 4: the involvement of women hovers around 25 to 30 percent except in the plague years of 1360–61 and 1367–68, when it is higher, and the period of civil strife in 1380–81, when it is lower. This suggests the obvious conclusion that fewer women perished during the civil war than men, but also leads one to surmise that the plagues took a somewhat more severe toll among women than among men. Women at all events were paying this tax on considerable property.

Detailed records of forced loans have survived only for the period 1336–49, although scattered records less usable statistically do exist for some other years. Data from seven levies have been collected in Table 6. For four loans the records are grouped by parish, while the others give totals for the entire city. The parish returns fluctuate too widely to permit firm conclu-

Table 5. Female Involvement in Payment of *Exuwe* Tax

Fiscal Year	Total Cases	Cases Involving Women or Their Heirs	Percentage of Female Involvement
1352 (−3)	71	34	47.89
1353	67	17	25.37
1354	64	16	25.00
1355	78	38	48.72
1356	199	36	18.09
1357	155	35	22.58
1358	115	41	26.45
1360	468	172	36.75
1361	219	61	27.85
1362	139	39	28.06
1364	99	31	31.31
1365	156	46	29.49
1366	170	47	27.65
1367	194	83	42.78
1368	401	170	42.39
1369	111	32	28.83
1372	123	37	30.08
1376	102	29	28.43
1377	119	36	30.25
1380	107	11	10.28
1381	255	42	16.47
1382	167	64	38.32
1386	225	73	32.44
1389	214	54	25.23

Sources: SAG, Ser. 400, 9–10; *Rek. Gent 1351–1364*; *Rek. Gent 1376–1389*.
City accounts do not survive from years not in this table.

sions about the proportion of female to male taxpayers in any of them. On a citywide basis women accounted for roughly one-fifth to one-quarter of the total number of taxpayers except in the second loan of 1336 and that of 1349, the first such record after the installation of a revolutionary régime by the Flemish count. The same is true of calculations of the amount paid by the women. St. Pieters, the poorest of the parishes, did not have many wealthy women, while the totals for St. Niklaas, the central city parish that contained the great markets and accordingly the wealthiest, contained many affluent ladies, particularly widows and noblewomen.[2] Comparison

Table 6. Women as Payers of Loans to City, 1336–1349 (Flemish pounds groat)

Year	Parish, if given	1	2	3	4	5	6	7	8
1336	Jan	48	82 lb.10s.	10	20.8%	21 lb.	25.5%	6	60%
	Pieter	20	28 lb.10s.	1	5	20s.	1.8	–	–
	Michiel	13	16 lb.	4	30.8	3 lb.10s.	21.8	–	–
	Niklaas	21	28 lb.15s.	5	23.8	6 lb.	20.9	2	40
	Jacob	2	5 lb.15s.	–	–	–	–	–	–
	CITY	104	133 lb.	20	19.2	31 lb.	23.3	8	40
1336	Jan	24	40 lb.14s.	6	25	8 lb.	19.7	2	33.3
	Pieter	5	29 lb.	1	20	1 lb.	3.5	–	–
	Michiel	44	123 lb.13s.8d.	4	9.1	8 lb.10s.	6.9	–	–
	Niklaas	21	41 lb.10s.	–	–	–	–	–	–
	Jacob and Hg. Kerst	26	74 lb.10s.	4	15.4	9 lb.10s.	12.8	1	25
	CITY	120	309 lb.7s.8d.	15	12.5	27 lb.	8.7	3	20
1339	CITY	25	3080 lb.	13	52	1480 lb.	48.1	8	61.5
1342	Jan and Pieter	56	91 lb.19s.2d. 1 ingl.	5	8.9	3 lb.8s.5d.	3.7	1	20
	Niklaas	42	19 lb.3s.3d	13	31	6 lb.1s.8d. 2 ingl.	31.8	8	61.5
	Michiel	25	8 lb.11s.8d.	5	20	1 lb.17s.6d.	21.8	1	20
	Jacob and Bavo	21	9 lb.13s.8d. 1 ingl.	6	28.6	2 lb.15s.	28.4	2	33.3
	CITY	144	129 lb.7s.1d. 2 ingl.	29	20.2	14 lb.2s.7d. 2 ingl.	10.9	12	41.4
1347	CITY	169	120 lb.18s.3½d.	40	23.7	29 lb.19s.8d.	24.8	17	42.5
1348	Niklaas	6	5 lb.12s.6d.	3	50	2 lb.17s.	36.8	2	66.7
	Michiel	19	49 lb.3s.7d.	2	10.5	17s.6d.	1.8	–	–
	Jan	16	10 lb.13s.6d.	6	37.5	3 lb.13s.2d.	34.3	1	16.7
	[Jacob	8, with sums given for only three]							
	CITY less Jacob	41	65 lb.9s.7d.	11	26.8	7 lb. 7s.8d.	11.3	3	27.3
1349	CITY	278	344 lb.13s.1d.	19	6.8	119 lb.14s.8d.	34.7	15	79

Key to Column Headings
1. Total persons paying loan.
2. Total amount collected.
3. Number of women who paid.
4. Column 3 as percentage of column 1.
5. Total amount paid by women.
6. Column 5 as percentage of column 2.
7. Number of women identified as wife, sister, daughter, or widow of someone, i.e., man was primary source of identity.
8. Column 7 as percentage of column 3.

Source: *Rek. Gent 1336–1349*, 1: 119–127, 378–379; 2: 165–170; 3: 285–288, 336–344, 165–171.

of columns 4 and 6 shows that there is a rough correspondence between the percentage of women as taxpayers and the percentage of the total tax that they paid in the earlier loans, but there is a marked disparity from 1342 except in the levy of 1347. A small number of wealthy women paid a very large tax in 1349.

Perhaps the most consistently valid conclusion to be drawn from Table 6 concerns the numbers and percentages of female taxpayers who are identified with reference to a male relative. On a citywide basis it drops below 40 percent only twice, in 1348 and the second loan of 1336, and reaches a high of 78.95 percent of the total number of female taxpayers in 1349. Clearly, the wealth of most women was still identified by the magistrates as accumulated through their husbands and blood kinsmen.

Flemish inheritance law safeguarded women's rights, as we have seen. When a marriage ended, normally by the death of one party, the survivor received what he or she had taken into the marriage, together with life use of half of the movable property of the decedent, whether or not this had been acquired during the marriage. A surviving spouse received half the property acquired during the marriage, even if it was acquired with the deceased party's property, and dower on half of the other half, the same share as on the property which the decedent had held before the marriage. Remarriage did not affect dower rights on the estate of a previous spouse. There was no distinction between sons and daughters in the inheritance divisions, or in principle between children of first and later marriages, although the fluctuating economic fortunes of the parent could mean that there would be a difference in the estate left to children of different unions.[3] The common property notion was well developed at Ghent; even when transfers of property did not take the form of "X and his wife Y," her half was nonetheless safeguarded.[4]

Parties of both sexes, but particularly women, had to beware of the fortune hunter. Dower rights made previously married persons of both sexes attractive, but the husband could generally control his wife's property, including her rights on the estate of a prior husband. Cases survive in which a man acknowledges a debt and arranges payment in installments; but if he inherits any property or marries, the debt is to be repaid immediately, for the assumption was that he would be able to spend his wife's property. No debt owed by a woman was ever handled in this way, although a subsequent husband might legally be responsible for them.[5] And how many prospective spouses even now, and even more in the fourteenth century, ask to see the intended's business records before contracting to marry?

This arrangement worked both ways. Cases survive of women who had no idea whatsoever of the extent of their late husbands' indebtedness and thus did not renounce the estate, then remarried and thus made the second husband legally responsible for the wife's share of the debts of the first.[6] There are cases of shocking ignorance on the part of women, even among the aristocracy, where one would presume more knowledge or interest. Some men clearly did not trust their wives' business sense. In 1357 Jacob Tac left 2 lb. gr. to his wife and an as yet unnamed good man whom she would choose to satisfy any complaints against his estate.[7] We shall see that many wives also distrusted their husbands' financial judgment, and with reason.

The ignorance displayed by some aristocratic women is not limited to their husbands' finances. In 1375 Ser Willem Stuul became guardian of the four children of the shipper Jan Mayhuus. The father had remarried by April 1377 at the latest and held property belonging to his stepson, Pieterkin Van den Kerchove. In 1379 Mayhuus became guardian of his own children. By 1389 Pieter had married his stepsister Lisbette Mayhuus, an unusual but not unheard of proceeding in Ghent, and was suing the heirs of Stuul, her first guardian. The *scepenen* sustained the heirs' claim that the girl's father had been her guardian, for their own records contained the change, and Van den Kerchove was left unprejudiced to sue his father-in-law. But it is clear that Lisbette either was not consulted or did not know that her father had been her guardian, which he could easily have told her if she had known about the suit, since he was still alive.[8]

The husband did not have total discretion over his wife's property. Certainly most wives were willing to cooperate with their husbands, and there are cases in which women consent to the sale or actually manage the sale themselves of their own property to pay their husbands' debts. We cannot know whether this was more often done from marital affection or because of compulsion behind the scenes.[9] Evidently realizing the possibility of constraint, the magistrates preferred and sometimes required that children or women whose property was being affected appear in person before them to acknowledge that they understood the nature of the transaction and consented to it. A husband could not always represent his wife in an inheritance question in court when property was being contested in her name, and women were frequently asked to be present when their property was being sold or mortgaged. Men could take the income of land that their wives brought to them and even lose that income, but they could not surrender the land unless the wives participated personally. This provision was obviously intended to protect women, but it could be an embarrassment, for example, in rendering it impossible for a man with a mentally incompetent wife to transact business concerning her family property, although this restriction did not extend to the common property that she held with her husband.[10]

A wife could withhold consent if her husband tried to will property to his bastards from common property, although we know this only from cases in which, whether under pressure or not, she did agree. This restriction extended to her husband's bequests in general. The blood heirs rather than the widow were responsible for fulfilling the terms of the testament. The widow divided common property with the heirs and each party paid half the debts incumbent on the estate, but each party might make bequests only from his or her half. Although a husband might refuse to ratify gifts made by his wife effective during her lifetime and could annul any business deals that she made without having his consent or proxy, he had no control over her testament. The wife of Jan Ghiselins gave 10 lb. gr. to her grandson, Moenkin Van der Elst, effective at his majority, but provided that the money would be taken from her estate at her death if her husband refused consent. A similar principle is involved in the suit of Fransois Van Hansbeke against the wife of Gillis Van Goecs concerning money which she had pledged to assist in a criminal atonement. Since her husband evidently had refused to allow her to make this alienation from her own funds, the *scepenen* awarded Van Hansbeke the money at the lady's death or that of her husband, whichever came first.[11] How serious a gap this created in the husband's power to manage the family property can only be conjectured; but since half the common property was the wife's, the possibility was present even if infrequently realized.

Husbands who wished to disassociate themselves from debts incurred by their wives could have a public proclamation to this effect read at the five parish churches; a tradesman who skipped the service could find himself saddled with an unenforceable debt. But wives and children had the same recourse. Numerous cases survive in which the husband's rights over his wife's property are circumscribed. In 1364 the husband of Zoetin Amelakens, daughter of the moneychanger Celie Amelakens, was prohibited from alienating their share of the family's house on the Vismarkt without his wife's consent. A wife might be asked to give express consent to a transaction by her husband which did not concern her property directly but which would bind her if he failed to meet his obligation. The husband could dispose of the wife's dowry only with the consent of her kindred, both paternal and maternal. Alice Coels, mother of the wife of Pieter de Maerscalc, had intervened in a quarrel between the couple, and Pieter complained about it to the *scepenen*. Friends heard of it and obtained a postponement to try to settle matters peacefully; but Pieter came during the delay to Alice's stand on the Friday Market, smiled and greeted her as he passed, then whirled around and knocked her to the ground, continuing to pummel her until he had given her two black eyes and she was bleeding profusely. Pilgrimages were ordered, and he was forbidden to sell or alienate the marital settlement that Alice had given her daughter without the consent of her kin and friends. Significantly, the text does not say that he had to get his wife's consent; her mother evidently had more leverage over him in this case than she did. In 1351 Jan de Scuttere, who was heavily in debt, asked the *scepenen* to confiscate all property that he and his wife held jointly. She contested this, claiming than an exemption had been made previously. The magistrates accepted this argument, but the property which de Scuttere had brought to her in marriage was given as common to his creditors.[12]

When the husband agreed to accept limitations concerning his wife's property, he might place his assets into a receivership administered by his father-in-law or simply allow his wife to manage her own property. Husbands who wished to avoid subsequent entanglements with their spouses could make renunciations applicable to particular cases. A wife could free herself from the obligation to pay a husband's debt if she disassociated herself from it at the time it was incurred, but this act would presumably require the husband's consent. We have seen that financial irresponsibility was frequently a cause of marital separations. Grandparents might take action to make certain that a father did not deplete the estate intended for his children. In 1352 Marie Temmerman complained that Lievin Van der Couteren, her son-in-law, had mismanaged her daughter's property. While there was little that she could do about her daughter, she wanted to see that her grandson got her property when she died without it falling into his father's hands. The *scepenen* agreed to appoint three managers of her property—significantly, in the context of the politics of the day, a baker, a weaver, and a fuller—while warning the father not to disturb the boy, who was living with his grandmother. It was common for men to borrow from their in-laws, and conditions might be attached if the indebtedness became heavy.[13]

Some men, fearful because most women had no binding power to make contracts without the consent of a male guardian, simply refused to do business with them. A case illustrating the impact of this attitude, together with a woman's inability to maintain her rights over the property of a previous husband after she had remarried, is the suit of Mergriet Libbe, widow of Pieter Musch and wife of Jan Van Westhoven, against the saddler Jan Miten. As guardian of her children, she had rented him the house adjacent to her own residence but had to sue him for arrears. He refused to pay because he had rented it from Van Westhoven, who was in exile at the time of the suit, and not from the wife. The woman argued that only she and her children by her first marriage had rights on the house and that she had agreed to support the children on the proceeds of the rent. The magistrates ruled that the tenant had to pay the arrears of the rent on the share of the house owned by her children, but not on her own, on which her new husband had rights. She could collect the rest either with her husband later or after she had received a proxy from him. Women evidently sometimes used the fact of being under legal wardship as an excuse for delaying or cheating on debts. Widowhood changed this, and a woman who wished to prove her good faith could "on her own initiative make herself a widow, her own woman, outside all guardianship."[14] The rural court of Sinaai refused to allow a woman to secure a rent on lands belonging to her and her husband unless she could find a surety until he returned to Flanders. Even an emancipated single woman had to find a man to act on her behalf before the rural court at Canegem. There are cases where the husband's consent is questioned, but the wife's action is sustained if testimony, presumably oral, showed that he had agreed to it. Caution was obviously needed, for some husbands did nullify transactions done by their wives without their knowledge.[15]

Against the evidence that many wives were ignorant of their husbands' affairs, there are cases in which the couple were business partners of a sort, and the wife knew rather well what was going on. Several women testified in connection with the settlement of the estate of Wouter Van Vinderhoute how much Wouter had owed to themselves and their husbands. They knew the amounts owed and evidently the nature of the business, and one woman, the mother of Gillis Mond, acted on her own as a wool merchant. Since most men lived in the same building with their businesses, their wives, save perhaps of bankers and foreign traders, probably were rather well informed. And since businessmen whose dealings were not tied to an exclusively local market had to be away from home for much of the time, considerable latitude was often given to trusted wives. Jan de Roele did a pilgrimage in 1351 for foul language against Jan Straetkin, but Straetkin's wife was empowered to prosecute housebreak on her own, since this had occurred when her husband was outside the city and de Roele had known it. The language of the document makes clear, however, that it would have been an offense against the husband if de Roele had not known.[16]

That most wives, save of men with extraordinarily complex businesses, knew what constituted marital property, assets, and liabilities is demonstrated by the fact that when either spouse died, the survivor was normally the "holder" of the estate and bound to summarize the property for the *scepenen* and therewith offer division to the heirs. No widow could do this who was in ignorance of her husband's activities.[17]

That women could embarrass their husbands by financial irresponsibility shows in itself that they were being left to manage household finances. If a wife mismanaged the family accounts, the damage could be deducted from her or her heirs' share of the common estate, even though the husband would be bound to the debts during his lifetime.[18] In 1372 Clais Van Wettere publicly disclaimed further responsibility in the standard form for his wife's debts. His action against her credit rating was warranted, for he had to acknowledge an enormous amount in petty debts, payable in annual installments of 2 lb. 10s. gr., about one-third the amount needed at this time to support a household of four for a year.[19] Most tradesmen evidently assumed that wives had their husbands' permission to contract small debts, which only became serious when the amounts accumulated and the husband was kept ignorant of them.

The magistrates were obviously sensitive to the de facto independence of many women, and there is no direct indication in the records of a woman being pressured against her will into an arrangement, however much coercion may have been applied before the parties reached the city hall. Women at times consented personally to arrangements that their men had made for them, although what their options would have been had they not agreed is not made clear.[20]

Particularly during the war years women assumed duties for absent husbands which they would not ordinarily have performed. Clare Van der Ponten, for instance, handled wool sales for her evidently absent husband in early 1384 and later in the year bought with him half interest in a large suburban estate.[21] Some of these cases mention the husband's name but do not expressly state that he has consented. Other cases mention a formal proxy, normally from the husband. A wife who held her husband's seal was assumed to have his proxy. In cases of emergency the kindred or even the *scepenen* might authorize a woman to act for her absent husband. The wife of Jan de Scot obtained the magistrates' consent to sell real estate in 1385, since her husband was away. Wives were sometimes given proxies by the magistrates to act for physically or mentally incompetent husbands. At the request of the clan of Jan Van der Clusen, a delegation of *scepenen* and their clerk went to his neighborhood and took testimony from the parish priest and others, who agreed that he had needed a guardian for more than three years. As a result his wife was made his guardian and Ser Hugh Van Lembeke, a prominent man who served several times in the city government, became the overseer. Neither might act without the other.[22]

Whether counterparties were willing to deal with a woman seems to have depended on circumstances; one must remember that for a case to find its way into the surviving records it would deal either with a specific set of legal circumstances or considerable property. For example, in 1390 Joos Van Landegem acknowledged a debt of twenty-six English nobles to Nijs Van den Vivere, who was evidently absent. But Nijs's wife was claiming another seven nobles, and Joos successfully postponed action on this claim until her husband had returned. He apparently was willing to deal with her for the uncontroversial part of the debt, while he suspected that her husband might make trouble about the rest. Casual and uncontested transactions of a domestic sort, which clearly involved numerous women, have left little trace. Strong-minded women might make demands to which their kinsmen and the magistrates would accede. One case suggests that a woman was entitled to be present if she so demanded when transactions involving her property were completed. The corollary of this, of course, is that since most women simply left business to their husbands' discretion, most preferred to confine themselves to domesticity. But even a minor girl might be allowed to take decisions involving her property if she so requested. Orphans were entitled to an interest payment on their investments. Bette de Mindere, who was so entitled, was permitted by the *scepenen* to decline it in 1360, simply "because she does not want it." No reasons were given.[23]

The case of Kateline, daughter of Jan Van Lede and wife of Jan Van den Hamme, illustrates the constraints that bound a strong-minded woman, but within which she might also become the dominating force in her family. The couple had married by May 1366, but we hear little of substance about them until they together settled her father's estate in 1384. In October 1384 Kateline bought a rent on her own authority, a deed which may have aroused objection, for on April 4, 1386, she acknowledged a debt "by necessity without her ecclesiastical guardian, as is known, since she is in charge of handling common property." In May 1385 her husband had settled his own mother's estate, but with his wife's consent stated. The couple bought and sold rents and real estate in 1387–88, but on April 2, 1389, Jan Van den Hamme, "acting in accordance with a prior agreement with his clan," gave her complete procuratorial power to manage his affairs. She acted under this proxy several times during the next two years, and the earliest of these acts specify not only her husband's consent, but also that of his clan. We are not told why Jan Van den Hamme did not manage his own business.[24]

Many women, most of them married, were active in trade and industry. Some were clearly partners of their husbands in forms implying no subordination. An atypical case in our records, but one whose thrust may have been more common than can be proven, is the marriage agreement of 1390 between Nijs de Pijl and Odine Philips, which is coupled with an apprenticeship arrangement for the man. They were to live with the priest Jan Van den Hecke, who would become their partner in candlemaking. The couple and the priest would contribute equal capital and share profit and loss. In return for this the priest would teach Nijs the trade. The wife was clearly to be a partner in the operation and may have been professionally competent when she married.[25]

Whatever influence unemancipated women may have exerted behind the scenes on their husbands and sons, their position in the economic life of Ghent was less conspicuous, though perhaps no less significant, than that of their liberated sisters. A few emancipated women became prominent professionally. Some managed to penetrate trades dominated by males, although often only as a substitute for a deceased male relative. Still others were employed in menial occupations. That women as well as men were expected to support themselves meant that even unemancipated women had at least to help their husbands in their businesses, or failing that to find work outside the home or provide an income from inherited property.

Chapter Five

Bondage in Freedom:
The Independent
Businesswoman

Though the quantitative evidence that women were actively involved in their husbands' businesses is not large, the very offhandedness of the references that do survive shows that there was nothing extraordinary about women in the business world. To be sure, most cases either involve women managing property that they have inherited or, in the case of businesswomen, small amounts of money or activity in the "traditional female occupations." But when one considers the extent to which manufacturing and merchandising in Ghent, as in all preindustrial cities, was concerned with the preparation of food and drink and the various stages of making cloth and clothing, all areas in which the strengths of women supposedly lie, it was inevitable that whether on their own or as "helpers" of their husbands, they would play a major role in the economic life of the city. One can only surmise the number of men who were the public masters while their wives did the work. Most marital separations seem to have presumed that the woman either could live from the investments of her property or had a profession which she might practice during the separation; a case of 1355 says that "they have long lived apart, practicing different trades and paying their own expenses."[1]

Table 7 gives information on the activity of women as moneychangers, moneylenders, hostellers, and *lakensniders* or cloth wholesalers who bought at the halls. Those who practiced the former two professions paid

84

Table 7. Women as Moneychangers, Moneylenders, Hostellers, and *Lakensniders*

Year	1	2	3	4	5	6	7	8	9	10	11	12
1314 (−15)	12	–	–	8	–	–						
1315	14	–	–	19	2	10.5						
1317							27	3(3)	11.1			
1321	7	–		11	–							
1322	6	–										
1323	5	–										
1325	5	–										
1326	4	–										
1327	4	–										
1328	4	–		17	2(1)	11.7						
1329	5	–										
1330	5	–		18	1(1)	5.6						
1334	3	–										
1336	4	–										
1338				15	1(1)	6.7						
1339				17	1	5.9						
1340				26	3(1)	11.5	23	1(1)	4.4			
1341							21	2(2)	9.5			
1342							16	1(1)	6.3			
1343				25	6	24	18	1(1)	5.6			
1344				13	3	23.1	19	–				
1345				29	6	20.7	21	2(2)	9.5			
1346				15	3	20	23	–				
1347	6	–					23	2(1)	8.7			
1348	7	–		10	2(1)	20	8	–				
1349	11	1	9.1	14	2	14.3[a]						
	8	–					13	1(1)	7.7			
1352	10	1	10									
1353	8	1	12.5									
1354	11	1	9.1									
1355	13	1	7.7	28	3(1)	10.7						
1356	11	1	9.1	16	1	6.3						
1357	13	1	7.7	13	–							
1358	13	1	7.7	9	1	11.1						
1360	13	1	7.7	19	2(1)	10.5	21	1	4.8			

(*continued*)

Table 7, continued

Year	1	2	3	4	5	6	7	8	9	10	11	12
1361	8	1(1)	12.5	26	2(1)	10.5						
1362	12	1	8.3	40	8	20						
1364	9	1	11.1	33	5	15.5						
1365	12	1	8.3	28	5(1)	17.9	23	2(1)	8.7	19	–	
1366	12	1	8.3	27	8	29.6						
	11	3(1)	27.3				20	2(1)	10	32	9(2)	28.1[b]
1367	12	1	8.3	25	7	28						
1368	11	1	9.1	17	3	17.6	17	–		17	4(1)	23.5
1369	11	1	9.1	10	1	10						
1371							5	–		45	8	17.8
1372	8	1	12.5	30	7	23.3	13	2(1)	15.4	17	–	
1373							9	1	11.1	32	7(1)	21.9
1374							7	–		20	3	15
1375							5	–		23	3(3)	13.1
1376	7	2(1)	28.6	27	7	25.9	7	–		27	4(1)	14.8
1377	7	2(1)	28.6	30	6	20	6	–		26	3	11.5
1379							2	–		14	–	
1380	6	2	33.3	13	3	23.1						
1381	5	1	20	17	4							
1382				10	4	40						
1386	7	–		12	2	16.7						
1389	8	–		23	2(1)	8.7						

Key to Column Headings
  1. Number of moneychangers.
  2. Number of women as moneychangers.
  3. Column 2 as percentage of column 1.
  4. Number of moneylenders.
  5. Number of women as moneylenders.
  6. Column 5 as percentage of column 4.
  7. Number of hostellers.
  8. Number of women as hostellers.
  9. Column 8 as percentage of column 7.
 10. Number of *lakensniders*.
 11. Number of women as *lakensniders*.
 12. Column 11 as percentage of column 10.
 ( ): Number of women in preceding figure who are identified in the same source as widow, wife, or sister of a man.

[a]Figures in this line are from a rough draft of the city account; the second line contains data from the final copy.

[b]Figures in this line are from the book of receivers and sureties; the top line is drawn from the city account.

Sources: *Rek. Gent 1280–1336; Rek Gent 1336–1349; Rek. Gent 1351–1364; Rek. Gent 1376–1389;* SAG, Ser. 400, 9–10; SAG, Ser. 301, books of receivers of city assizes and of hostellers and *lakensniders* and their sureties, bound behind *Keure Jaarregisters;* Ser. 93 bis, no. 7, 14r.

a fee each year to the city, and most surviving city accounts list them by name. The hostellers and *lakensniders* had to post bond, and some ledgers of their sureties have survived. All were professions practiced mainly by the wealthy except to a certain degree the moneylenders. Anyone who extended even casual credit at interest had to pay the fee, even if it was not being done professionally. Thus it is perhaps not surprising that women appear most prominently as lenders, generally without reference to their husbands. But only after the advent of the régime dominated by the weavers and small guilds in 1360 do they constitute a substantial percentage of the moneylenders. They also appear frequently as *lakensniders,* and the same chronology seems to hold true for this profession as for the moneychangers. Although many women assisted their husbands as hostellers, they rarely practiced the profession on their own, and most who do appear in the lists are linked to a man. Very few women were moneychangers, although one, Celie Amelakens, was one of the most prominent practitioners of that trade.

The statistical information can be supplemented with commentary in the lists and occasional references in other sources. Given the nature of the innkeeping business, involving both lodging and brokerage at the halls, it was only to be expected that women would assist their husbands. A statute of 1369 allowed oaths to be taken concerning madder purchases from hostellers, brokers, or their wives, suggesting that men in these professions were frequently represented by their spouses in making purchases.[2] The wife seems to have handled the food and drink side of the innkeeping business.[3] The female hostellers of the 1340s show interesting and characteristic features. Between 1340 and 1343 Marie Rijm, daughter of a prominent Ghent family and widow of the Italian financier Conte Gualterotti, was a hosteller.[4] Perhaps more characteristic is Quintine, daughter of Ghiselbrecht Van den Zande, who appears only in 1341. Her father had been a hosteller in 1317, the only year before 1340 from which a comprehensive list survives. She was married at some point to a Ser Volkers, by whom she had a son Jan. She died between March 4, 1358, when she founded a chantry in St. Michiel's church, and July 1359 and is identified as the late wife of Simon Van Vaernewijc, who himself was a hosteller from 1346. She evidently took over her father's business briefly, then passed it on to her second husband.[5] Gillis Naes is mentioned as a hosteller throughout the 1340s, but in 1345 his wife was allowed to take over his business under strict surety until he or Willem Van Vaernewijc, evidently his partner, returned from England. She could only handle transactions paid in cash or with payment due within two weeks. She was again a hosteller in 1349 under the same conditions.[6] Celie Amelakens, whose principal occupation was moneychanger, also took lodgers and four times posted bond as a hosteller. In 1372 Aechte, the widow of Gillis Talboem, did so; Jan Talboem, but not Gillis, had been a hosteller previously, and in 1373 Aechte, although not a hosteller herself, did surety for Michiel Talboem, who practiced what was apparently the family profession.[7]

The case of Aechte Spitaels or Uten Pollepel is curious, for she seems to have been a hosteller, succeeding her husband, for some years without posting bond. She had married the hosteller Jan Van der Crayen by February 1354. He posted bond in 1360, but neither he nor his wife appears thereafter in the lists. He was still alive in early 1369 and was known as Jan Van der Crayen in den Groten Pollepel, after the inn on the Friday Market which he and his wife maintained. Even by 1365, when she was sent on a pilgrimage for assault, the woman was known as verAechte Uten Pollepel. She died in 1383 without remarrying, and for the next several years the heirs disputed her testament.[8]

The inn Ten Drien Coninghen did a thriving business, evidently catering primarily to German merchants. The proprietor in the 1380s was Thomas Van den Weerde, who with his wife Aechte Van der Eeken was involved in a lengthy suit against Jacob Van Heyle as widower of Alice Van den Plassche, also called Ten Drien Coninghen. When Alice had married Van Heyle in 1373, her four children by two previous marriages were guaranteed half interest in Ten Drien Coninghen. Jacob Van Heyle was evidently a hosteller involved in the Sluis trade. In 1375 his wife, acting without his express consent, bought several rents in and outside Ghent from her daughter Aechte and the latter's husband. In 1382 Gillis Walkier and his wife Kateline Van der Eeken bought the rights of Van Heyle and Alice on Ten Drien Coninghen. The city confiscated Walkier's rights for political reasons, and Thomas Van den Weerde and his wife, evidently the eldest daughter of Alice Van den Plassche, bought it in turn from the buyer on December 14, 1383. In 1386 Van den Weerde and his wife, apparently fearing challenges to their purchase because of the restitution decree of 1385, sued Alice's husband for a division of her estate. Conflicts continued for several years and eventually involved not only Ten Drien Coninghen but also properties at Sluis and Middelburg bought by Van Heyle or his wife. Although most of the action concerns the activities of Alice Van den Plassche, her daughter was appointed without reference to her husband by a Duisberger in 1388 to collect debts owed him in Ghent. With her husband and a man of Oudenaarde she was made proxy in 1390 by a Dordrecht man to collect debts owed him. Each of these ladies was involved closely in dealings concerning her own property and with the business of innkeeping and brokerage. Alice Van den Plassche was described by her heirs as "her own woman, free businesswoman, keeping an inn."[9]

The wife of the prominent hosteller Gillis Van der Pale received money on behalf of herself and her husband while he was absent, and she contracted at least one sizable debt on her own. In 1350 her husband went to Rome on city business and received there a loan from the Bardi of Florence on behalf of the government of Ghent. In what was evidently a bill of exchange, Alice turned the money over to the city receivers, who acknowledged a debt to her on this account. Her payment to the city took account of the rate of inflation or interest, depending on how one interprets the transaction, and shows conclusively that she understood the mechanics of international exchange completely.[10] There are other isolated instances of women acting in an official or semiofficial capacity. During the war of Flanders with Brabant between 1356 and 1358 the count's mother evidently sent money to pay sergeants to the wife of the Ghent knight Wasselin Rijm.[11] Alice, the widow of Jan de Meester, was evidently a notary doing business before the city hall. An unnamed female appraiser valued the chattels and furnishings in an estate in 1383, and the context suggests that women were frequently used for this purpose.[12]

Just as the wives of small innkeepers cooked the meals while the spouses of big operators became involved in foreign trade, so the wives of another type of innkeeper assumed responsibilities. The jails of Ghent were used chiefly to intern persons of both sexes awaiting trial and particularly for debtors; the incarcerees had to pay for their own upkeep, sometimes directly to the jailer's wife.[13] As one might expect from such examples, some women had accounts at the inns or the exchanges, but the only surviving cases involve very wealthy women.[14]

Little can be said of most of the female moneylenders beyond their names. The single exception is Aechte de Pottere, who as we have seen took over her husband's business when they separated. In 1355 both Lievin Van der Weeden and his maid paid the tax as moneylenders, but neither is in the lists thereafter.[15] While many of the others practiced the trade only for a single year, perhaps liquidating their husbands' businesses, there are several exceptions. Calle Van der Waerde paid the fee between 1339 and 1346, Kateline Toete in 1340 and 1345, Alise Van Ghent between 1372 and 1377, Mergriete Zoete between 1376 and 1382, and Gierne de Mey between

1363 and 1378, and these are only the most conspicuous cases. To judge from the amount of tax paid, they were among the least active of the moneylenders except for Aechte de Pottere. This was clearly not a full-time profession for most of its practitioners.

With inadequate records we can say very little of the role of women as *lakensniders*. It seems to have been a trade not practiced continuously either by many men or women. The widow of Philips Van Turtelboeme did surety in 1373, but since her husband is not in the earlier lists, she was not following him in his profession. The wife of Jan Scelpe appears as a hosteller in 1365 and 1366, but not afterward. Jan Scelpe appears for the first time as a *lakensnider* in 1368. Neither he nor his wife is in the book of receivers for 1371, but Scelpe himself did surety thereafter as a *lakensnider* until 1375, when his wife did so. She continues in the lists until 1377–78. The couple thus seem to have been partners, with the husband succeeding the wife as the active partner in the mid-1360s and being succeeded by her at his death. The widow of Pieter de Coninc was a *lakensnider* for several years during the mid-1370s. Probably the most characteristic is the widow of Willem de Cupere, who posted bond only to settle her husband's estate. Her sureties guaranteed her only for the "purchases which she and her husband had made jointly." She does not appear in the later lists, but the implication is clear that she had been active enough in the business to be able to deal knowledgeably.[16]

Only one woman was prominent as a moneychanger, but she was one of the most interesting personalities in the business world of fourteenth-century Ghent. The first woman named is the Joncvrouwe Valkeneere, who appears in the rough draft of the account of 1349–50 but is replaced by Oste de Valkeneere in the final copy. This is probably another of the cases so common in the 1340s of a woman taking briefly the profession of an absent spouse or male kinsman. In 1361–62 the widow of Jan Van Laerne is listed as a moneychanger. Her husband had practiced the trade the year before, but her name does not reappear in the later accounts.[17] A similar situation is found in 1366–67, when the Book of Receivers lists three female moneychangers, including Kateline de Kempe, whose surety was her father Jan, and Wijvin Zeghers. The account of 1367–68 lists Lievin Zeghers and no de Kempes, while the main city account of 1366–67 lists neither of the women. A Marie Zeghers was a moneychanger in 1380–81, while in 1376–77 the sister of Simon Van Houtem is listed. Simon himself appears in the record of 1380–81; his sister could have been a substitute during his absence or conceivably an older sibling taking on the profession until he was old enough.[18]

With these exceptions the only female moneychanger during this period was Celie Rebbe, generally known after her marriage as Celie Amelakens. Her establishment was on the Vismarkt, the financial center of Ghent. She was a business partner of Joos Van Landegem and Joos de Zadeleere in leasing the assize of the Fish Market and Meat Hall in 1345 and of Gillis Van der Canebeke in 1356. In 1356 she also leased the tables of the Fish Market without a partner.[19] She thus became one of only two women to engage in tax farming in Ghent during the fourteenth century. She came from a family of fishmongers, and she was the first Rebbe to become a moneychanger.

Celie Rebbe paid a 10 lb. fee as a moneychanger in 1352; as Celie Amelakens she paid 20 lb. in 1353, suggesting an increase in business.[20] The age of her children by the 1360s shows that she was already married before this time to Godeverd Amelaken; the change in name may have been purely formal to make way for her kinsman, Clais Rebbe, who became a moneychanger in 1355, although Celie Amelakens and her son were later practicing the trade simultaneously under the same name. Her husband was evidently considerably older than she. A Godin Amelaken, whether he or his father is unclear, was already a hosteller in 1317, and Godeverd is found in the lists throughout the 1340s.[21] In 1353, as an innocent man on behalf of his absconded son Jan, he atoned the death of Pieter de Taeffelmakere, and Celie joined him as surety for the blood price. He is called "Der Godeverd," a title indicating the senior male of a clan and generally someone of advanced years. He died between June 1363 and September 1364,[22] when his four lay children, three boys and a girl, acquitted their mother Celie of his estate. They allowed her to hold their share of her residence on the Vismarkt while reserving their own rights to it, and Jan Van der Haghe, her son-in-law, agreed not to sell or encumber his share of the house except with his wife's consent, suggesting that the daughter was already closely involved in the family business.[23] Since all the children were adults by 1364 and at least one was grown by 1353, Celie must have been at least in her late forties when she was widowed.

Even before Godeverd Amelaken's death Celie was the dominant force in the family. During 1356–57, while she was leasing two assizes as she continued her moneychanging business, the *scepenen* held several conclaves at her establishment, as they commonly did in the homes of clerks and other municipal officials.[24] In this same year there was a scrap between cousins, when Goskin Rebbe and Coppin (Jacob at his maturity) Amelaken were sent on pilgrimages for assaulting each other, suggesting that both were teenagers. The mothers of both boys were warned that words or deeds beyond what had already happened would be rewarded by a pilgrimage to Avignon. Celie's surety was her son Jan Amelaken, evidently returned from his own exercise in homicidal self-expression of three years before. Celie was apparently supporting Gilkin de Tolnere during this year and accounted for his property.[25]

Jacob Amelaken, evidently the second eldest son and the one who joined his mother in the moneychanging business, had apparently reached his majority by 1360.[26] Jan and Jacob were sureties for a murderer in 1363; Jacob and Gillis Amelaken did pilgrimages for assault in 1363 and 1366, respectively. Jacob's propensities assumed more serious forms in 1370, when he assaulted a mason who had been ordered by the city government to build a wall to separate the Amelaken property from another.[27] He first appears as a moneychanger in 1362, and he and his mother regularly appear together in the lists from that time.[28] Jan Amelaken, the eldest son, became a wine merchant. He too zealously upheld the family honor, doing pilgrimages for assault in 1365 and 1367, and in 1373 he retaliated for bad language about him by hitting a woman in the eye.[29] No Amelaken after 1353 assumed primary responsibility for homicide, but serving as sureties for those who did normally means complicity in these records.

We know little of Celie Amelakens during these years. She continued to pay the fee as a moneychanger. For two periods of two years each, 1365–67 and 1372–74, she is also identified as a hosteller.[30] The first of these could have been to settle her husband's business, but we do not know what caused the expansion of her activity in the 1370s. In 1376 she willed 20 lb. gr. apiece, a substantial sum, to Godin and Zoetin Amelaken, who are identified as her sister's children.[31] She secured the bequests on her one-fifth share of the house "de Rebbe" on the Vismarkt. Since she had four children alive in 1364, apart from a sister in the leper hospital, they evidently owned the other four-fifths, but of equal significance is that to have this name the family residence must have come from her family and not the Amelakens.

Matters blew up between Celie and her son and partner Jacob in 1377. She claimed that he had earned 8 lb. with her share of the business, and the *scepenen* awarded her 4 lb. with some additional compensation for having supported him. They were living together in the Vismarkt property, and Jacob claimed that she owed him rent; if Jacob's claim that the house was worth 10–11 lb. gr. yearly in rent had been correct, it would have been one of the most valuable properties of which we have record. Jacob was awarded no arrears, but Celie was to pay him rent in the future. He also claimed smaller debts, and the magistrates allowed those that she swore that she owed him as being earned in common profit. Either the Amelakens had no written records or the *scepenen* did not examine them. Although Celie and Jacob had always paid the tax separately, the suit suggests that only in 1377 were they actually dividing the business.[32]

Celie apparently felt the end approaching. In January 1378 she divided her property, effective at her death. Each child was to get 20 lb. gr., as had her niece and nephew in 1376, further evidence that Celie was not overly fond of her offspring. Since Jacob and Zoetin Amelaken had received marriage settlements, their totals included these amounts. She had lived rent-free in the share of the house belonging to Jan since his father's death, and she pledged him an additional 20 lb. in compensation. What makes this settlement peculiar is her bequest of 20 lb. gr. to Mergriet Mabels. In 1375, identified for the first time in twenty-three years by her maiden name, Celie had willed 5 lb. to Mergriet "for services rendered." Mergriet had served in the Amelaken household for sixteen or more years, and evidently between the dates of the two bequests she married Jan Amelaken, Celie's eldest son, who must have been at least forty in 1378, with his wife not much younger.[33]

Jacob Amelaken continued to be the male moneychanger of the family, but the registers of the *scepenen* have more references to Jan. Celie evidently died in late 1382, for she disappears from the list of moneychangers with the fiscal year ending August 14, 1382, and by January 17, 1383, Jan and Jacob were suing each other over the estate. Jan Amelaken was ordered to vacate his mother's house and to have no more right over it than Jacob. A settlement was only reached on August 28, 1383, and by that time Jan Amelaken had died. His widow Mergriet Mabels handled the case.

The conflict centered over Celie's claim in 1378 that she had made Jacob a marriage gift of 20 lb. gr., which was demonstrably false. Her relations with her son were clearly poor at that time, but why he would not have caught a transparent lie is a mystery, unless perhaps she made the settlement during his absence. For Jacob had received a gift of only 15 lb. at his father's death in 1364. The arbitrators rejected Jacob's claim of the annual rental value of the house in favor of a much lower figure. Jan Amelaken had married Mergriet Mabels eleven years after Godeverd Amelaken had died, or in 1375 or early 1376, about the time of the first bequest to her. The arbitrators also found that Jan and his wife had lived in a house with Celie and taken its profits and that Celie during that time had had a maid in addition to paying the daily expenses of Mergriet Mabels. Celie's claim that she owed rent to Jan was thus intended only to defraud Jacob and was disallowed. We are never told why Celie and Jacob disliked each other. After his youthful escapade in 1353 Jan seems to have been the more amiable figure, but one gets the feeling from the language of the settlement that he may have hoped to get his mother's money.

Quarrels over Celie Amelakens's inheritance sputtered on until August. Much of the controversy involved the division of chattels. There was obviously some question of her mental competence at the end, although she had still been professionally active in the year of her death. Jan and his widow had incurred expenses in handling the estate, for they obviously were in control of the house, her person, and certainly her emotions. The career of probably the most remarkable woman attested in the fourteenth-century records of Ghent thus ended with a continuation of her business by a despised son and squabbles among all her children arising from her evident favoritism of an eldest son and his wife, who had been personally close to Celie Amelakens for many years.[34]

The case of Celie Amelakens was obviously exceptional, but there are many references to wealthy women active in the business world. Lisbette Van den Calchovene, wife of Heinric Scolle, traded at Bruges, and her husband had to pay large sums to satisfy her debts there.[35] Another lady who was very active in commerce was Lisbette de Wilde, wife of the fishmonger Godeverd Scakelinc. Her husband died in 1381, and by 1383 she was acting independently as a moneylender, although she did not pay the fee to the city. Of particular interest is an acknowledgment by Michiel Boene of a debt for money that she loaned him "at win, at gain," which seems to have been the Ghent version of the *commenda*.[36]

Women were also active in the wine trade. Gerem Strichout and his wife filed suit in 1378 against Romboud Scoreel and Fransois de Bruwere "concerning expenditures and receipts from their partnership in the wine trade." The plaintiffs were awarded damages, and Scoreel, his daughter, and de Bruwere were ordered to swear that they did not use money that Strichout had paid into the exchange (*wissel*) for their own profit. Scoreel's daughter was clearly a business partner, and Strichout's wife probably was. In 1377 Juete Monds was fined for selling wine behind closed doors.[37]

Many references to women in trade suggest that their presence was not at all remarkable. In 1376 Kateline, widow of Jan Ser Ghelioets, joined Jan Van den Scotte in a grain sale. In 1390 the smith Jan Capelleman and his wife Kateline declared that they had done much merchandising (*coepmanscepen*) together and therefore were giving each other 15 lb. Since there is no mention of consent by the heirs, the labor of each evidently caused this to be considered legal compensation for services rendered. When Mergriet Cortoys, wife of the prominent businessman Sanders Van Leden, was released from wardship in 1357, it was justified because "she is mature both in terms of discretion and of years and has already managed her property for many years."[38] Since it is inconceivable that everyone who did business with her was constantly running to her guardians to find out if it was all right, wardship in her case was more a threat to use until her discretion was completely established than a serious hindrance to normal activity.

The city accounts show many women acting professionally. To cite only a few examples, Lisbette Talboem in 1323 sold cloth to the city for uniforms of the captains and their deputies. Women normally brought food for the participants on the annual religious procession to Tournai. After the death of Jan Van Artevelde, a cloth merchant prominent in the 1320s, his widow continued in business on her own for many years. The wife of Jacob Van Artevelde even conducted diplomacy on behalf of the city. Mergriet Godewals was either a silversmith or the wife of one, selling her wares to the city. The daughter of Philips de Schachtmaker was reimbursed in 1380 for cooking utensils and table linens lost on campaign, while women regularly followed the militia with provisions.[39] A woman was the resident caretaker of the hall of the *scepenen* of *gedele*.[40] Meere, the wife of Jan Van Bruesele, and three men were fined in 1376 for having sold a type of knife illegal in Ghent. Clare and Marie Van Verdebrouc were alleged to have incurred so many petty fines levied by the *vinders*, civil justices stationed on the marketplaces, that the total reached 72 lb. par.[41]

We have seen that women were frequently business partners of men not their husbands. Mergriet, daughter of Jan de Costere and wife of Willem Cleyne, in 1372 sued Pieter Boudins for arrears on their transactions together, but he countered successfully that he had settled with her.[42] Lisbette Van den Coukele, described as a "female mercer" (*merseniericghe*), collected a debt from Jan Bollaert incurred by his wife, and Volcwijf de Backere practiced this trade on the Kouter in 1385. Mergriet Van Maelmolen rented a house from Heinric Scolle and with it his right to sell fat products.[43] The condition of "merchant woman" was a legal status that permitted married women to act independently of guardians and relieved the husband of liability for his wife's business dealings.[44]

Women were expected to earn their own keep if single, to contribute materially to the family enterprise if married. A suit of 1386 mentions support pledged to a girl "until she could earn her own bread," while Jan Van der Bellen in 1370 was to teach an unspecified trade to the daughter of Jan Van Boven. Kateline Racorts was so severely mutilated in an accident that "she may never again be able to earn her living," a clear implication that she had been doing so. When the list of property of the two daughters of Jan Van Zottegem was renewed in 1377, the girls were now stated to be earning their own living, and all profits would be added to their estate.[45] We are not told what they were doing; it may have been nothing more than work around the house which was being compensated, although the words used suggest work outside the home. But it is evident that they were making money while still under the supervision of guardians, who had final disposition over their earnings. It is equally evident that there was nothing unusual about this arrangement. Girls were not expected to sit around the house being decorative. When the widow of Willem Maes remarried in 1378, she held the property of her two children. The boy was to get his maintenance, "shoes, schooling including reading and writing, and thereafter be taught his trade, while [the girl] would be taught sewing and tailoring linen," and these are professions which had guilds.[46] In 1385 both the son and daughter of Willem Van der Stekenen were to be provided with a trade (*ambocht*).[47]

The prospect of girls working is seen in the case of Marie Scrents, who in 1379 felt that her guardian was not giving her enough spending money and tried to live apart from him. The magistrates ordered her to live with him rent free but at her own cost, and she was to live on 13 scilde from her own property. If she needed more money, she was to get a job and "earn her bread," for all other income from her properties was to be used for her profit until she was otherwise situated on the advice of her friends. She was told, in short, to shut up and live on her allowance or get a job.[48] Jobs befitting a girl of property were thus clearly available, and women who took them were laborers, rather than management in the modern sense.

Women of "good name" could have quite menial occupations, such as Mergriet Van Belle, who was evidently delivering pastries for Jan Wieric when she was assaulted in 1372. Men and women had some conflicts within the same guild. Jacob de Lakenbleekere did a pilgrimage for attacking Kateline Van den Cnocke during a truce made while they had turned to their guild for judgment. A serving girl who was attacked while defending her master's interests would act independently in arranging punishment for her assailant.[49]

The wives of bakers and brewers were clearly crucial to the success of their husbands' businesses and sometimes acted independently. These were enterprises normally conducted in the family home, although not invariably so in the case of the brewers. The women did not generally have guild rights except through their husbands. The widow of Jan de Paeu in 1384 rented the half of their bakery that had descended to his heirs; it is unlikely that she would have done so had she not intended to continue the business.[50] Kateline Inghels, widow of Ghiselbrecht Stroepers, even took a boy as an apprentice baker. The case of Ermegart Scatteman, widow of Philips de Smet, suggests that the bakers were comparatively open to the notion of women in the trade, although evidently not as masters. When her husband died in 1374, Ermegart divided the estate, including a bakery, with her son Pieter, who was evidently an adult since he was not called Pieterkin. She rented Pieter's share of the bakery for 1 lb. gr. yearly, suggesting a large operation. Whenever Pieter wished to matriculate in the guild, he was to rent her half at the same rate. The option was Pieter's, rather than his mother's, but she evidently intended to work for a while. She could have had professional training from a blood relative, for a baker Jan Scatteman is mentioned in a source of 1376.[51] We have no list of bakers from which to be more specific about women's roles.

This is not true of the brewers, however, for lists of masters survive in the *Neringboek,* and there is other evidence. In 1372 three brewers pledged for themselves and their wives not to tap illicit hop beer in the city.[52] A case in which a brewer's wife may have had more influence than the father upon the son's profession involves Lisbette de Hond, wife of Jacob Van den Zomple, and her son, also named Jacob. The parents had married by June 1355, and a list of property has survived from 1359 for young Jacob, including a quarter interest in three-quarters of a house, but the entire property had been rented for another three years beyond 1359. In October 1362, as the rental term expired, Lisbette bought another quarter of the house, here called a brewery, and half the brewing implements. The son later bought another brewery. Under the circumstances it is unlikely that his mother had bought the shares of the brewery as a rental property. She came from a brewer family herself and evidently had the necessary professional competence to train her son or the connections to have him trained.[53] In 1377 Jan Van den Velde inherited half the brewery of Jan

Walijn and rented the other half from the widow. He then sold all his rights, including the rental contract, to Joos Rijnivisch, who was bound to restore the house as it had been before Van den Velde acquired it, "because the widow does not want to keep a brewery."[54] She clearly had the option of continuing her late husband's profession, even though she did not choose to exercise it; and although the house, from which she had evidently removed the brewing implements, had been reconverted to use as a brewery by Van den Velde and Rijnvisch, this could not be permanent without her consent. The guild book of the brewers contains the names of several women who succeeded their late husbands, but each is crossed out for unstated reasons.[55]

Many daughters were also given some professional training. A woman without profession needed either a husband or inherited wealth. Simple prudence thus dictated that even when women could not become masters in the family trade, they were given training that could be used for their support. When the wife of Jan Van den Driessche died in early 1377, she left two adult sons and one daughter, who agreed among themselves that the daughter would "continue to live with her father and practice the brewing trade with him, as they have done heretofore." They were to be partners, sharing profits and losses equally. Other property is mentioned that apparently went to the sons. When the father died, the daughter was to get half their common property and divide the rest with the other heirs according to law. Jan Van den Driessche is listed in the guild book for 1363 but had apparently died before the next list was compiled, and his daughter is never listed as a master brewer.[56]

Most guilds of Ghent were much less restrictive in the fourteenth century than they became in the fifteenth, but the push to hereditary mastership was so strong by then that for the guilds to maintain their numbers there had to be some sort of transmission through the female line. Peter Laslett, based on later evidence for England, has called attention to sons-in-law carrying on the family business, since there frequently was no continuity between generations in the male line. Men who did not have their own shops could rise above their station by marrying the daughter of a master artisan.[57] The evidence from Ghent is inconclusive on this point, although rarely if ever did a man gain automatic admission to a guild or preferential treatment by marrying a master's daughter. When Roger Van der Wostinen agreed in 1383 to teach painting to a boy, he stipulated that if he defaulted, presumably by dying, his mother would "complete his training with whomever she shall be working, but Gheenkin will pay the guild's fees himself."[58] She thus was not able to teach him the trade herself, but she promised to have it done with the master for whom she herself worked after her son's death; one assumes that she was working for him in 1383.

Women could be members of the barbers' guild in good standing. The fourteenth-century constitution mentions both sexes. Fathers could pass on the trade directly to their daughters, but the daughters could not emancipate their husbands. In 1402 the guild sued Pieter Tavernier, who claimed that because his wife was the daughter of a free barber, he as her guardian obtained the right. The guild was upheld, but Tavernier's wife was expressly given the right to be a barber. The situation was apparently similar with the spice merchants. In 1360 the guild sued Clais de Ruddere for practicing the trade without authorization. His wife, who is not named, was to pay the entry fee and thus be free in the guild as a master's daughter. Clais himself was to undergo a four-year apprenticeship with her, after which he would be recognized as a free journeyman.[59] This is quite unusual and suggests that in this trade, which is rather close to the "traditional female occupations," the lady had learned the trade from her father but had married a man who had no knowledge of the business and had to learn it from her.

While women were not master trousermakers, wives of masters were subject to the jurisdiction of the guild court when they did something affecting guild sovereignty, and the context suggests that the wives generally were involved in the business.[60] There is one case of a girl apprenticed to learn the furmaking trade. Women could be free in the wagoners' guild, and the guild constitution of 1324 took account of women doing transporting without guild membership in return for a fee.[61]

Women apparently could be in the fruitmongers' guild, but only through inheritance; certainly a husband could not use his wife in the shop to handle his business.[62] Women were not members of the fishmongers' guild, which was one of two trades to obtain heredity of mastership in the male line during the fourteenth century. But men seem to have used their wives frequently to sell their fish for them. Suggestions elsewhere of a reaction with the régime of 1349 against women in business are confirmed by a prohibition of 1350 against women selling fish, with its corollary that the practice had been tolerated before. According to the statutes of the fishmongers of 1366, women were forbidden to buy fish for resale or have it done, and fishermen could not use their wives as sales agents. Women were, however, permitted to buy eels and alewives from fishmongers and sell them in neighborhoods around the city.[63]

Women are also found as candlemakers,[64] and at least one woman was a tanner. They are also found in the health care field, although in the traditional roles, notably as midwives and nurses. We have few specifics. A midwife was once accused of causing a miscarriage. The *scepenen* quashed the malpractice suit, adding that "people ought to handle such things privately." Some nurses were permanently employed doctors' assistants, not independent operators. Mergriet Van Lichtervelde was awarded 12s. gr. for a cure in 1387, an amount suggesting that she could handle difficult cases. Some nurses were married.[65] Women also owned and operated bathhouses. For perhaps obvious reasons the baths were considered unsavory. Most had accommodations for both sexes, but some were reserved for women.[66]

The occupations of many women are shown in a declaration of debts owed by Justaas Van Abbinsvoorde and his wife. Money was owed to sixty-two persons or foundations, together with a long list of bills at taverns. Sixteen of the debts were owed to women. Several mention only name and amount, but others give the purpose for which the debt was contracted: for linen, silver, woolen cloth, an annuity, embroidery, wine, and a debt to a brewer's maid, presumably for beer. All but one of the debts were small, and most seem to be rents or connected with comestibles or cloth.[67]

As one would expect, many cases show women in the work force in the various branches of the textile industry. Women could be in the guild of doublet-makers, although apparently only with special permission of the *scepenen*. Lisbette, daughter of the embroiderer Jan Van Tienen, took over his trade after he died. An unusual case of a woman entering a trade late in life involves Lisbette Van Pollaer, who was to be taught embroidery for two years, with the costs to be paid to the master by her nephew. In 1360 Mergriet de Ploughere, widow of Heinric Van Hoedonc, declared that during her husband's lifetime they had bought two sacks of wool on condition of paying for it by turning it into cloth. The phraseology leaves no doubt of her participation.[68]

Women evidently could not be master weavers, but they did own looms.[69] These could have been used by women in a family operation for which a husband or son was legally responsible or leased to another weaver. There is little evidence in our records of spinners of either sex, but there is no reason to assume that women did not practice the trade at Ghent as elsewhere. There is more record of them in the various branches of the dyeing profession. A case of 1367 denied a woman the right to inherit mastership in the dyers' guild from her father, evidently on the basis of a statute of 1334–35.[70] Yet Lisbette Ghiselins had a family or business connection with the prominent blue dyer Jan Van Libertsa. She was living in a dyeing establishment in 1361 and is expressly called a dyer in a text of 1363. The widow of the dyer Jacob de Meester acknowledged a debt contracted with her husband for madder, while in 1387 Alice Hueghe was owed a large sum "for dyeing cloth."[71]

The blue dyers constituted a separate guild at Ghent, although they had considerable contact with the dyers. Women definitely practiced this trade. The younger Jan Van Libertsa acquitted his mother of the paternal estate in 1365; and since they were to continue to practice the trade jointly, they did not divide the business assets, including an enormous amount of woad and ash. In 1383 Anees de Quinkere, widow of Jan Moens, was willed life use of three-quarter interest in a *blauwerie* (blue dyeing establishment) by her daughter, whose heirs agreed to surrender their rights on the other quarter if the daughter's husband died childless. The donation included the blueing equipment, and it is thus likely that the mother and daughter had practiced the trade together, perhaps with some help from the son-in-law. In 1387 she is called the "widow Moens," dyer. In 1390 Anees willed the business, here called a *verwerie* (dyeing establishment) rather than a *blauwerie,* to her sister, but it was then to descend to the sister's son if he survived them.[72] Jan Moens is never called a dyer, although he probably was. This case provides clear evidence of continuity of a family trade through the females but eventually descending to a male.

There were so many women in the blue dyers' guild that the "free journeymen" considered them a threat, for "certain women who are emancipated in the guild are diminishing and destroying the [position of] the free journeymen in that they want to stand at the vats and work in their place"—in short, they were taking work away from men. They claimed that this was unjust, for the journeymen and apprentices had to pay their share of guild costs, and by implication therefore the women were not paying, although the document does not state this directly. The guild officers responded that there would be unrest if their wives and free widows could not work at the vats, and they had never seen or heard of the contrary. But the journeymen were sustained by the overdean of the small guilds on grounds of the cost issue and because "it is man's work." But this ruling was made with the reservation that "any woman may help to do her own work and may inspect it as often as she wishes." The issue thus seems to be that female blue dyers were using one another to oversee and inspect one another's work.[73]

Some cases of women in the textile and sewing trades involve an option for the widow to continue the business of her deceased husband, but this assumes that the master artisan would teach his wife the full skill of a master. In 1377 Annekin de Moenc was apprenticed to the tapestry weaver Arend Van Uutkerke with the stipulation that if Arend died during the three-year term "and his wife keeps the same trade," she will complete Annekin's apprenticeship.[74] This is admittedly unusual; it was more common for the heirs of a deceased master to be bound by the contract to find another master, and it is likely that the tapestry weavers would have had more room than other guilds for women. Still, few apprenticeship contracts of any sort have survived, and the practice may thus not have been uncommon.

An informative case regarding women in the textile trades is Aechte Van den Scake, who was already a grandmother when we encounter her in the 1350s. Her daughter Kateline, who was dead by 1349, had been the wife of the shearer Sanders Mont. Aechte was sued in 1353 by another daughter, the wife of Pieter Van den Houte, over the inheritance of her unnamed father. Aechte had evidently threatened to disinherit the daughter from her own estate if she pursued claims on her paternal inheritance. Sanders Mont had remarried and died by 1354, leaving two sons by the second marriage; Aechte Van den Scake was "overseer" of her grandson by his first marriage. In December 1357 she was a principal buyer of four bales of alum; she was supporting her grandson for three years before he reached his majority in 1363. She evidently died in the plague of 1368. She had held, as many women did, a stall in the cloth hall for the sale of white and blue cloth; she had transferred her rights on this business to her son-in-law, Pieter Van den Houte, with whom she had evidently been reconciled, although the magistrates only found this out when they tried to give the stall to another woman.[75] Her case shows not only the involvement of women in the textile business, but also the impossibility of maintaining rigid occupational divisions, for the same family was involved in shearing, dyeing, and the merchandising of finished cloth.

Although the number of stalls in the cloth hall was limited and was a grant by the *scepenen,* most were held by women, even if there might be a male claimant,[76] although the rights could be transferred by one holder to a successor with the consent of the *scepenen.* In 1349 Simon Van Aalst, representing his wife, told the *scepenen* that she had surrendered her stall in the cloth hall to another lady with the approval of their predecessors.[77] In 1338 the brokers agreed that the women operating these stalls might sell white and blue cloth and buy up to fifteen stones in weight of wool without going through a broker. Mergriet Veys joined three men in 1354 in leasing the assize owed by the stalls in the cloth hall. The holders of these stalls were petty retailers, but some women became major textile entrepreneurs, either on their own or with their husbands. Kateline de Brune, wife of the cloth merchant Jan Wittebroet, was entrusted with substantial linen purchases by her husband. The wife of Boudin Goethals was obviously an active partner of her husband. She was sent on pilgrimages in 1368 for violence and in 1372 for foul language about a municipal official. Although burgesses of Ghent were forbidden to buy cloth outside the city, she made an enormous purchase at Brussels in 1383 from two men who were also from Ghent. She acted in partnership with Jan de Keyser, who with her husband was still making payments on this transaction in 1390.[78]

Although women were obviously important in the economic life of the city, they had no political rights. No woman ever served as a guild official or was on the town councils. Only two, Celie Amelakens and Mergriet Veys, leased assizes or rents from the city. They seem to have taken very little part in the political agitation that so divided Ghent during the fourteenth century. A document of July 12, 1330, lists 608 persons exiled from Ghent and the environs for conspiracy against the city and the count. All were males.[79] In 1359 the count repatriated 540 persons who had been exiled from Ghent. Thirty-three were women, but fourteen of these were identified as someone's wife, while another three were identified by a male relative other than the husband. Of the sixteen others, twelve bear diminutive first names, suggesting either youth or, if an adult, someone of loose moral character.[80] Over half the women listed thus seem to have accompanied their men into exile, and the numbers are small enough in themselves.

Yet there is one isolated case suggesting a woman whose influence on civic life was greater than a literal reading of the sources would allow. Aleit Van den Potijser had been banished for rebellion by the magistrates of Ghent in 1359, presumably for siding with the weavers, but the count remitted the sentence on August 3, 1359, at the request of the dean of the small guilds. The weavers had returned to power between the time of the banishment and its withdrawal. For the dean to intervene in her behalf she must have been an important lady. By 1362 she was the wife of the brewer

Heinric Spene, and she may have practiced the trade after his death, for in 1375 she secured a rent on her residence and its brewing implements.[81]

Much of our information about women in the work force concerns domestic servants, the most exploited group. For a woman of little or no property and no professional training, domestic service in a wealthy household was a way of making ends meet. Unfortunately, many maids were subjected to financial exploitation and often extortion and sexual harassment. We cannot say how widespread the use of household servants was, but Ghent would be exceptional for this time if they were not numerous. Most of our information about them comes from bequests by good masters to maids who have served faithfully, while bad masters with guilty consciences left property to their children by the servant girls and sometimes arranged for the repayment from their estates of money "loaned" them by the maids.

Men often left small amounts in their testaments for "alms," "services," or both to women stated to be living with them or called maids or servants.[82] There were many variants on these basic themes. Many men made donations to their mistresses and bastards on the eve of the campaigns of 1379 and years following, evidently fearing that they might not return from military duty.[83] Girls, particularly those who had lost both parents, were expected to do housework for those supporting them, such as a stepmother. Other kinswomen, for example a sister-in-law, could be used as domestic servants, but most cases suggest younger women, such as nieces. Maintenance was often their only compensation during the master's life. Accumulated wages would be taken from the estate, but often the servant's heirs would have no recourse if she died unpaid. Of course, the delay in payment was a way of binding the servant. A case unusual in providing eventual payment, albeit accompanied by unfavorable terms, meets us in 1374, when Jan Compeer willed 10 lb. gr. to his niece, Kateline Volkaerts, but this was annulled if she predeceased him or if she married or left Compeer's house for any other reason. If they could not get along, he agreed to pay her a small sum for each year that she had lived with him. The lady evidently did not marry, for she was collecting a debt in 1387 without mention of a husband.[84]

Maids thus might be expected to do lifelong service in return for a bequest, and the gift could be nullified if the servant left. As was true of accumulated wages, bequests did not generally descend to the maid's heirs, although there are exceptions, particularly in cases where the maid had loaned money to the master.[85] Some bequests were rather generous; a few masters provided decent retirements, such as an annuity or a small cottage, for old servants. In the case of a maid who had stayed with the master for many years and died in his service, he was recognized as the holder of her estate and settled with her heirs.[86]

Maids obviously had a great deal to do with household management and accordingly had some control over valuables. There is at least one case of peculation, while in another a master expressly releases his maid from any claims which might be raised against her by his heirs.[87] But since many maids loaned money to their masters, one wonders in vain where the girls got the capital; if they had property, why would they enter domestic service? These questions cannot be answered adequately, and there is a case of a maid and her husband becoming severely indebted to her master.[88]

Married women who did not live in the house where they served thus might be maids. In 1383 a Gentenaar willed 6 lb. gr. to the child of his maid without indicating that he was the father. She was evidently a "working woman" with a child to support.[89] Relations with the lady of the house were not always amiable, perhaps understandably in view of the various opportunities for illicit behavior. Lane de Temmerman evidently became very close to Jacob de Puur, whose wife she had served, after the wife died. Although they are never stated directly to have cohabited physically, they lived in the same house, and Jacob made substantial bequests to her, some of which were nullified by the *scepenen*.[90]

Maids of priests seem to have been particularly vulnerable. In 1371 the priest Lievin Goethals willed 20 lb. gr. to his maid but admitted that 12 lb. of this was for twenty-four years of unpaid service. She was obviously getting her maintenance in addition, but he also owed her 8 lb. for a loan. She agreed that he keep the money for his lifetime, and it was to go for masses rather than to her heirs if he predeceased her.[91] Such arrangements could afford a maid some security. In 1373 the priest Thomas Uten Berghe willed his house to a maid who had served him without pay for thirty years and had loaned him money. Some priests were obviously living openly with women for long periods, treating them as wives, and the arrangement was viewed as normal. Men of the cloth who got their maids pregnant and then remembered the girls' "services" in their wills include Ydier Mond and Jan Zelle. Zelle seems to have been more conscientious than most. He willed 3 lb. to his maid in return for services and for her care of him during illness, and another 7 lb. to his natural daughter by her. If the child died, half was to go to the mother.[92] Most such bequests were to revert to the donor's legitimate heirs if the child died childless. In 1378 the priest Jan

Priem willed substantial properties to his mistress and to his two bastards by her. Children born subsequently to the couple would share the gift. The priest hoped that his son would continue his holy vocation, if not his avocation, for he stipulated that the boy would get all his books and his vestments for mass if he became a priest, but they would go to other beneficiaries if he did not.[93] How pervasive such situations were cannot be said. That they are generally found without apology and presented as a perfectly normal state of affairs suggests that maids generally and those of priests in particular lived in a state of precarious virtue.

A document of 1367 suggests that it was common for servants to be drawn from a migrant population, when the *scepenen* denied a woman a prebend in the leper hospital "because she has lived nowhere in the city except in service." If she left again in service, the city would have no right to collect the tax incumbent on citizens in such cases.[94] We have seen that farm girls were as prey to the amorous artifices of their well-to-do employers as were house maids in the city. Everard Van Zwijnaarde willed 4 lb. gr. to each of his six bastards by a girl who was evidently a domestic on one of his farms. The mother got lifetime access to the estate, a residence there, and one cow. Jan Van der Vicht, whose wife was childless, had one illegitimate daughter by Amelberghe Scuerbroet and four by Beatrise Daus, evidently a later mistress. He willed them 40 lb. gr. in common and another 5 lb. to Beatrise in 1378, with the proviso that if he fathered any more bastards they would be included in the bequest. Since it is not specified that they be by Beatrise, he may have been leaving her.[95] The dangers to girls in domestic service is pathetically illustrated by the case of Merkin, daughter of Willem Andries. She was a minor who sustained "disgrace through force and violence by which her honor is greatly diminished" from her employer, Willem Plucroese. The offense was probably rape, but that word is not used, probably because it was being settled by private composition. The fine was allegedly set high to serve as an example. Yet while it is higher than most fines involving injuries to children, it was a mild penalty of 100 lb. lichter or 2 lb. 10s. gr.[96] An "exemplary" fine obviously took account not only of the character of the offense but also of the social level of the victim.

Part Two

Honor Thy Fathers:
The Children of Ghent

Chapter Six

The Nest and
Its Occupants

he example of Ghent in the fourteenth century fur-
nishes a clear corrective to Philippe Ariès's belief that childhood did not
exist in the medieval mind. Children worked, but adults played. While
most of our sources deal with children's property, they leave no doubt that
children were considered beings to be nurtured and protected, and that
while standards of parental discipline were undeniably more severe than
now, what occurred between most parents and their children in a fourteenth-century Ghent home would not have seemed grossly out of place in
1850.

The registers of the *scepenen* of *gedele* are our best source for the history
of childhood in Ghent. They deal in principle with orphans' property.
When a child lost either parent, the surviving parent, or failing him or her
the kindred, provided a *staet* or list of the child's property within forty days
of the death. Property of all orphans who had at least one parent a citizen
of Ghent is included in principle; a wardship was established in 1356 but
then crossed out with the explanation "this is null because neither the
father nor the mother was a burgher." Delay might be permitted if a widow thought she might be pregnant.[1] A guardian was appointed, normally
from the side of the deceased parent. There was usually also an "overseer,"
most often the surviving parent or someone from his or her clan. The

surviving spouse would account to the guardian for the estate, and that reckoning would then be recorded with the *scepenen*.

Children's names regularly bore the suffix "kin," such as Annekin for a child named Jan or Betkin for Lisbette. While persons under age are occasionally given the adult form, and an adult less frequently bears the diminutive, it is usually safe to assume that a person called "kin" is a minor under guardianship. That special language was used for children seriously weakens Ariès's thesis.

Yet problems of terminology persist. The Flemish *kind,* usually translated "child," does not always mean that.[2] Just as a group of adult friends today may colloquially refer to one another as "the boys" or "the girls," we find *kind* used at Ghent to refer to any young person, including some who had obviously been emancipated. The accounts of Ghent refer frequently to the "King of the Ribalds and His Children," a paramilitary thug brigade used especially to terrorize the rural areas by the government of Ghent and not children by the stretch of anyone's imagination.[3] Some persons with "kin" names were sent on pilgrimages to places outside Flanders; such "children" were sometimes gone for years at a time and presumed dead. They must have been teenagers at least to be sent abroad, presumably with the means to support themselves. A case of 1364 has two parties, apparently a separated married couple, fighting over who should be responsible for a child "who is wandering about unsupervised." The "kin" suffix is applied to a man who had to be at least twenty in 1381.[4]

Children, however defined, were beings to be protected. A person left in charge of a child was liable for negligence that led to injury. Children were considered innocents. Lisbette and Mergriet Martins had to do pilgrimages and pay Aghate de Pape 25 lb. par. for a head wound; but Aghate did a pilgrimage for slandering the girls, "who are innocent children," although clearly large enough to wreak considerable havoc in defense of their honor. Payments for damages, whether intentionally committed or not, tend to be low when done to or by children, which may indicate disrespect for children but certainly does not mean that they were considered small adults. That a deed was "child's work" was a mitigating circumstance. In 1390 the late lord of Eksaarde, who had also been a citizen of Ghent, was declared to have been incompetent to manage his property in the years before his death because "he was so aged that he was a child and had no control over his five senses." This formulation clearly equates senility with childishness, which shows that children were considered mentally and emotionally incompetent to manage their own affairs and thus in need of guardians. "Childish" behavior was also frowned upon when committed by older "children." Coppin Tac, who was evidently young since his name is a diminutive, was prohibited from contracting debts because of his "bad behavior and childish attitude."[5] We shall examine more carefully the custom at Ghent of paying interest on money invested for children without regard for the usury prohibitions of the church. The justification evidently was that children were incapable of increasing the value of their property themselves and that as "innocents" they were not responsible to God for the sins committed on their behalf. The same principle allowed interest to be paid on the property of elderly people who were under the care of others.[6]

That special records were kept of orphans' property in itself shows that the notion that children were not cared for is without foundation. Adults could and did handle such matters for themselves; and since a child was entitled to an immediate division of the estate when one parent died—there was no idea of parents entailing their common property until the second death unless the heirs consented—a record had to be kept until the child reached an age at which he or she could act independently.

Most *Staten van Goed* take the form of "Property of . . . ," then list the children by name, normally from eldest to youngest male, then eldest to youngest female.[7] The father is normally named, but some *staten* also list the mother if she is the parent from whom the children are inheriting. Dispositions for guardianship or support are then given, and the guardian acquits the surviving parent of the estate of the decedent. The *staten* are notoriously incomplete, even for the areas which they purport to cover, and they do not deal with the property of persons whose parents did not die before they reached their majority.

Children were given guardians, nominated by the clan of the deceased parent and normally approved by the *scepenen* pro forma. The surviving parent is normally not the legal guardian (*vocht*) unless there is an unusual degree of trust or the *staet* is being changed after an interval. The clan was expected to nominate its most suitable male, such as an older brother who had reached his majority or more often an uncle; after the estate was settled, guardianship might be turned over to the surviving parent, even if it was the mother. If there was no obvious male candidate for the position or there was a dispute, the *scepenen* would appoint a guardian.[8] As we shall see when we deal with the extended family, there frequently is no distinction made or felt between members of the blood line and the in-laws, a common feature of social systems having bilateral inheritance and clan membership.[9] An older daughter's husband was a brother to the family and hence was a suitable male to be guardian of her siblings, even replacing her uncle.[10] Children were supposed to be present before the *scepenen* when they were being assigned a guardian. One assumes that they were asked their opinion if they were old enough to talk, although this is not stated expressly.[11]

The legal standing of children thus has similarities to that of unemancipated women. The guardian managed the property and generally had the right to handle custody of the child, even to the point of situating the orphan away from the mother, although most did not exercise that right unless there were special circumstances, such as an ineffectual mother or an unwilling stepfather.[12] That remarried widows could not manage their own children's property without their husbands' consent meant that the guardian sometimes had to make other arrangements, but this could also be true when a surviving father felt himself incapable of caring for his children, was simply unwilling to do so, or had married a woman who did not want them. We are generally not told the circumstances under which custody arrangements were set. That death rates were high and that most persons who survived into their thirties or forties had married more than once doubtless give some credence to the "wicked stepmother" stereotype of literature, but there are also many cases suggesting not merely tolerance, but strong affection between children and their stepparents.

Guardians might be nominated by the clan as soon as the parent had died.[13] Any claim on any estate, whether by orphans or not, had to be raised within a year and a day of the death, and these regulations seem to have been enforced.[14] There are many cases in which a wardship is established without a *staet* following it, but most of these seem to have been appointments of new guardians for children previously orphaned. There are cases in which *staten* were evidently furnished but kept in a separate register that has been lost[15] or were never summarized in the registers from the rougher forms in which they were brought to the magistrates.

The guardians seem to have been quite busy during the forty-day period to ascertain and summarize assets and liabilities. Most do not give a detailed account of petty debts owed to and by the orphans, but merely totals. Whenever possible, they paid off the debts on the estate before bringing the *staet* to the *scepenen,* confining the actual list primarily to assets, and this sometimes caused delays in reporting. In most *staten* the surviving parent is stated to have taken the chattels while holding an amount of money representing the children's half of their value. This was to be held for the children until their majority or until the magistrates gave permission to spend it on them, and hence there was a sort of enforced saving.[16] It was the only dowry that some orphan girls had.

Although orphans' property was administered through the *scepenen* in principle, there was actually considerable latitude for the guardian and the kindred as long as the principal of the estate was not diminished. Guardians sometimes spent their own funds on the maintenance of the children or their property, then received permission from the magistrates to recover their expenses from the wards' estates.[17] Upon request the *scepenen* might assume a very active role, such as approving investments of orphans' money in advance of the fact. When Pieter Van St. Jacobshuus willed money to his grandchildren, their father wanted to buy rents with the bequest. The magistrates approved in principle but reserved the right to approve the rents before purchase, apparently to make certain that they were secured adequately.[18] When an orphan had an encumbered estate, the *scepenen* had to approve any alienation of the principal to pay the debts. They might also be asked to regulate the amount of money to be used to support the child, although such matters were normally left to the guardian.[19]

The magistrates took a more direct interest in the care of the children of mentally incompetent parents with small estates. There was no effort whatever to prevent retardates from marrying or having children. The magistrates took an active role when no suitable kinsman was available to act as guardian. After the children of Lievin Hoybant were assigned to their grandmother for custody, since both parents had died, the *scepenen* agreed to provide for their support if she predeceased them. When no kinsman was available, a guild brother of the father might become guardian. At times the magistrates appointed "chamber guardians," who were not blood relations, evidently in cases where the parents died in Ghent but were not citizens and the clan could not be located. The practice was especially common during the war of 1379–85, and the action was often taken "from grace."[20] But it shows that the town government felt a social obligation toward orphan children not limited to those for whom it had legal responsibility.

The constant involvement of the magistrates in the financial affairs of orphans meant that a complex fiscal apparatus was in place. One of the clerks of the *scepenen* of *gedele* handled orphans' money. The same clerk usually handled the business for several years at a time and did not, as far as we know, render annual accounts to the *scepenen* but simply kept his own ledgers. No originals of these records have survived. A transcript exists of the accounts of orphans' property and blood price payments as transferred to the clerk who took office in 1360 by his predecessor.[21] It is a standard accounting of receipts and disbursements by name, in some cases indicating the purpose of the expenditures. The clerks were keeping track of property involving several hundred families, and the business was complicated.

Guardians were supposed to render annual accounts to the *scepenen*,[22] but we do not know how strictly this requirement was enforced. Some accounts are preserved in the registers, but they are from longer periods, most often three years, and usually amount to a simple acquittal of the guardian.[23] Most come from the more complex estates; the simple ones are given once, or sometimes again when the surviving spouse remarried or died. One case does suggest that most guardians kept annual accounts but that the *scepenen* did not usually ask to see them unless they suspected problems.[24] The guardians clearly had to keep accurate records for their own protection in the event that the *scepenen* became suspicious or there was conflict with the orphan at the latter's majority. The less money was involved, the more ad hoc the arrangements for child support were likely to be, without parties being overly concerned about responsibility. Since most estates remained undivided during the children's minority, there was usually no conflict of interest in having children under the tutelage of persons who shared the same inheritance. Whenever there was a potential conflict, the guardian would be replaced by another person for the particular transaction but then would return to his duties.[25]

The magistrates stopped physical abuse of children when the matter was brought to their attention, but that permits considerable latitude. In 1377 Jacob Zoetamijs was sent on a pilgrimage for threatening words and *vreeze*, a term normally denoting intimidation but in this case apparently a beating, against his ward. The case probably would not have come to the magistrates' attention had the surgeon not gone to them to enforce payment of his fee for her care. The girl was evidently living in Zoetamijs's house and being maintained by him, and the magistrates declare that for the sake of "promoting love, peace, and quiet between him and the child, who stands to be an heiress of Jacob's property," they are assessing a lenient penalty.[26] What kind of peace and love the girl would expect after being received back into the home of a guardian whose brutality had sent her to a doctor is not described.

There may have been some problem with persons in whose custody girls were placed taking long-range decisions for them without consulting the guardian and the clan. In 1358 Willem Van den Scoete and his wife, who are not stated to be kin but probably were, pledged on pain of an enormous forfeit to support the daughter of Jan Van Meyleghem "without bringing or directing her to any engagement or condition of matrimony, cloistering, debts, or any other sort of obligation." She would be situated on the advice of her clan at her majority.[27]

Most orphans seem to have been cared for by their families, a testimony in itself of the strength of the extended families. Only two orphanages are mentioned in Ghent during the fourteenth century, in the St. Michielsstraat and the Burgstraat, and the sources suggest that their population was quite small. In view of the small number of recorded cases of malfeasance by guardians, together with the evident care and vigilance of the city government, the system evidently worked rather well. Most guardians performed conscientiously, if in a few cases reluctantly. Some guardians who managed especially difficult estates received a small payment for their services, but most acted without compensation. A rare instance of abuse involves the guardian of Callekin Van Steeland, who arranged to have his son rape the girl while the boy's mother sang loudly to drown out her cries. The magistrates, noting piously that every guardian was bound to bring orphan wards to their majority "without marrying them off unless the entire clan consented," assessed pilgrimages on all three and forced the guardian to surrender the guardianship and control over the girl's property. A similar case but without the aspect of rape involves Marikin, daughter of Hugh Janssone. The guardian's own brothers claimed that he had tried to marry her off without the consent of her clan on both sides, although she was not yet ten. Testimony was heard and the child was "seen," presumably meaning examined for sexual maturity, but evidently no testimony was taken from her. The *scepenen* ordered the guardian to undo all pledges that might bind the girl, including at Tournai, surrender physical custody, and "situate her to buy her maintenance in good, moral places and with a decent lady in the Bijloke abbey or the Béguinage of St. Lisbette with whom she may learn virtue and honor." He was forbidden ever again to situate a "child" of either minor or major years—child here clearly includes those who have reached their majority but are unemancipated—without the knowledge of the clan and the *scepenen*.[28] No one, including the guardian or the surviving parent, might undertake fundamental changes for the child without the consent of the entire clan and the city government.

When both parents were dead, there would be a guardian from each parental clan. While they usually acted jointly, they sometimes rendered separate accounts for the two branches of the estate. Half-siblings normally had different guardians.[29] And in view of the power that husbands had over their wives, it is not surprising that while in the daily running of a household a stepmother's attitude might have a great impact on the emotional development of children and thus give rise to the literary stereotype, our records, which in principle deal with the family's relations with outsiders, say more of stepfathers.

The picture is mixed. Many stepfathers behaved correctly and conscientiously and even showed affection. The stepfather had to consent to his wife being legal guardian or even having physical custody of her own children. Many *staten* were redone when the mother remarried, and some have survived in first recensions only from that time.[30] The mother could not hold their property without his consent; if she was doing so when she remarried, he could force her to surrender it, although this was unusual.[31] Occasionally a stepfather became guardian of his wife's children after an interval had elapsed and the deceased parent's clan had had an opportunity to observe him.[32] The *scepenen* had the right to alter the custody arrangement for a child if the mother's situation changed, presumably by marrying an unsuitable man or taking holy orders. Stepfathers were clearly more likely to have a conflict of property interest with the children than were the blood kin, and thus for a stepfather to intervene directly in the childrearing process apart from providing shelter required the consent of the magistrates. Even for the stepfather to take his wife's child as an apprentice required official approval.[33]

Stepfathers had the option not to support their wives' children permanently, although most seem to have supported their stepchildren on the income of the children's property, just as a natural parent would do. They were entitled to compensation for support provided.[34] A widowed stepparent of either sex evidently had the duty to support a child until the spouse's estate was settled, for when money had been invested for the child, it might require some time to recover.[35]

The frequency of deaths and remarriage undeniably put a strain on children. The five children of Pascharis de Borchgrave were orphaned before July 1379. Their mother had remarried, to Jan Rijquaert, by the autumn of 1381, and he "pledged to be a good friend to his stepchildren." The mother had died by February 1383, and an evidently amicable settlement was reached with Rijquaert, who continued to hold part of the children's money, even though they no longer resided with him.[36]

There is surprisingly little evidence of squabbling among half-siblings, considering the extent of remarriage and intermarriage, perhaps because inheritance rules were rigid and the magistrates took such care to resettle the estate at the death of each parent. The Parisian system of customary law required division of an estate into equal shares per marriage bed, rather than equal shares per child. Ghent shared this, but with the difference that the property of each bed was separated when it was terminated by one spouse's death. The inheritance of the child of a second marriage would be the property held by the remarried parent with his or her second spouse, and this would not be the same amount that had been held with the first.[37] A stepfather, of course, could come to grief through his involvement with the property of his wife's children. By 1374 Jan de Keyser had married the widow of Jan de Moenc and was holding 70 lb. gr. belonging to her six children. The lady had died by early 1378, leaving two more children by de Keyser. On April 1, 1378 he was ordered to refund half the money that he had secured and that he had evidently invested at interest with other persons, but the children were ordered to repay him for funds of his own that he had spent on their properties. Although both the de Keyser and the de Moenc children had large estates, Jan de Keyser evidently lost heavily on these investments, for in 1384 his house was confiscated for a debt still owed to his stepchildren.[38] But this case is clearly exceptional, and the general impression of equilibrium which the sources convey is perhaps due to the likelihood that a second marriage would be childless. Although we have too few sources to establish a statistical sample, we encounter stepparents most often as childless widows or widowers being acquitted by the spouse's children.

When stepfathers had agreed to support a child or to provide financially for it, the arrangement would be enforced by the *scepenen*. Occasionally they had to force a reluctant stepfather to pay for a child's maintenance. That we know of so few cases of abuse may testify to nothing except the unwillingness of parties to go to court, but it suggests at the very least that the extended family unit was in reasonably firm control. There are cases in which the mother and stepfather seem to have made party against the lady's child or children, and the clan of the deceased parent was able to stop blatant abuses.[39] A case showing such abuse but also the power of the paternal clan in ordinary cases involves Marikin de Jonghe, who had been situated in the convent at Eeklo. Her stepfather, Gerard Van der Donc, had been empowered to manage her property without alienating the principal by the *scepenen*, but he had sold her land without proper authority.

The girl's mother had then obtained her release from the convent under false pretenses, put secular clothing on her, and had taken her before the magistrates of the village of Destelbergen to handle the sale, which shows that alienation of the property of minors, even if done with the consent of the authorities, normally was done in their presence. She then returned the girl to Eeklo and told the abbess that she had been visiting a sick aunt who was especially fond of her, a fact showing that a person physically in charge of a child would see nothing unusual in special affection for her by a collateral relative. The abbess had complained to the *scepenen* of Ghent and had obtained the girl's return, but she had again been removed from the nunnery in a fashion to cause her death, and this "without the knowledge of the child's friends from the paternal side." The mother was exiled from Ghent.[40]

The comparatively few cases of abuse by guardians may be due to the absence of "institutional safeguards," even though the magistrates tried to be careful. The shipper Heinric Eeckaert and his wife were guardians of her grandchildren, the children of Joos Van den Hoerne, in the late 1360s. They were sued in 1369 for money owed to the children, but Eeckaert continued to be guardian until 1371, when he yielded the position to the man who had sued him in 1369, and then only so that he might lease peat bogs from the Van den Hoerne children. We have seen that whenever a conflict of interest could be demonstrated, an otherwise qualified person could not be guardian of orphans, but there was often a very liberal interpretation of what constituted conflict. Jan Van Huffelghem, legitimate heir of Jan Van den Kerchove, first contested the validity of the latter's bequest of 32 lb. gr. to his bastard son. But after the magistrates had ruled the will legal, he became the boy's guardian and promised to support him as his own child. Persons whose fitness was not above question might serve as guardians. In 1387 Hugh de Spoermakere became guardian of his own children, even though a homicide was imputed to him.[41]

The support of legitimate children devolved in principle upon the father or upon his kindred if he were deceased, although some fathers preferred to situate their children with women for upbringing.[42] This is perhaps inevitable in view of the legal disabilities of women in relations with subsequent husbands. Yet the language of some texts suggest that the father had an option not to support his children. A case of 1356 shows a guardian from the mother's side acquitting the father of her estate, and the father agreed to support the children with the income of her property for as long as he wished. In a case involving two butcher clans, Lievin

Ghevaert, as guardian and maternal grandfather of the daughter of Jan Van Erdbuur, settled his daughter's estate and agreed to pay her father 5s. gr. "to help support her for as long as Jan has her supported outside his house, to end when either Jan or Lievin takes the girl in."[43] This may have been a case of an infant being situated with a nurse. But the grandfather, who as guardian held the money, had to pay the father to help support her.

The right of the father who wished to support his children could not be gainsaid. That most businesses were conducted in the home and that children of both sexes could be used as laborers as they got older meant that fathers had less trouble caring for their motherless children than most do in the modern age, when the occupation is normally practiced outside the home. But the father did have the option of refusing to support his children, at least if no help was forthcoming from the late mother's kindred. Although Volker Van Elverzele was guardian of his children, the maternal grandparents supported them. One girl was evidently old enough to cause her grandmother to promise not to marry her off or otherwise change her situation without the consent of Volker and his clan, but the grandmother was not to be held liable if the girl did it out of desire and "evil will." A crass statement of the father's rights comes in the case of Pieterkin Van der Mersch, who was to live with his father, but the father could escape the obligation to support him by refunding the maternal estate to his late wife's clan. There are cases in which the father is simply placed on his conscience concerning his financial obligations toward his children but is admonished to do "as a good father should."[44]

But the mother, too, could evidently refuse to support her children unless she was compensated from their property, particularly if the estate was poor. Widows, who often had no profession, were victimized by the fact that the estate had to be divided. In a simple inheritance, in which a couple had children only by each other, the surviving parent got half of the common property, while the children divided the other half equally without distinctions of age or sex. The only exception is that the eldest son ordinarily inherited fiefs, but his younger siblings would then be compensated with other property of equal monetary value. The children's half would not usually be divided among them until at least one had reached majority. The surviving parent got dower rights for life on half of the children's half of common property and was normally entitled to the income of their share to help with the support costs. The parent was not bound to let the children's income accumulate. Some did so, but they were generally of the upper classes. When the estate produced more income than was needed to support the children comfortably, the surviving parent sometimes offered to support the children without compensation, or more often a part of their income would be specified as going for their support, with the rest earmarked for investment. Cases of hardship might be recognized and compensation provided by the paternal clan. In 1391 the potential heirs of the daughters of Jan Eeckaert agreed that since the estate was so small, the mother might keep the entire property if the girls died before their majority. If they reached adulthood, the *scepenen* would compensate their mother for her expenses in supporting them.[45]

The father and his kindred clearly had more discretion than the mother. He might pledge support for only a limited time, particularly if the child was nearing majority. He could eject one or more of his children from the "common nest" simply by separating their property from the estate of the children who remained. He need state no reasons, although most cases in which this occurred are probably simple emancipations and not ejections. The father's position vis à vis the guardian was much stronger than the mother's, for he could raise his children if he wished; but if he did not, he could leave them to the guardian, who would be legally responsible for them. These features, together with the practical equation of the notions of "support a child with principal undiminished" and interest, with the children's money invested and the proceeds used for their support, are given with the son and daughter of Jan Houtscilt in 1362. The estate was large, and the father agreed to support them with principal undiminished. But if the boy "behaves and situates himself badly, the father may free himself of him and give him his annual income in order to situate him wherever the guardian and overseer think best." A father's decision about support need not be irrevocable, for he could surrender custody of his children for a time and later recover them.[46]

While rights of legal custody favored fathers and other males, it is likely that most actual childrearing was done by women. We have only a few hints of the practice of wetnursing in Ghent at this time. Some women are called *voestereere* or nurse, but most mothers lacked the income to make a wetnurse a practical option.[47] The norm was that the deceased father's estate should assist the widow in raising the children, although some mothers were unable or unwilling to have the children with themselves. The daughter of Jacob Claus was to be supported with a tiny estate by her mother, but the mother could be freed of the obligation to provide support by returning the money to the guardian, who had the expressly stated power to relieve the mother of custody by giving six months notice.[48]

Some mothers were willing to release their children to their own male kinsmen for upbringing. A case showing this aspect, together with the power of the clans and the tendency to use children as pawns in larger estate considerations, is given by the example of the adult children of Clais Rabau. In 1358 his daughter Celie, who evidently lived outside Ghent, renounced his estate to her brother but agreed to arbitration concerning her parents' debts. They ruled that Clais Rabau the younger would give Celie's son, Joerkin, who was then in Ghent and one assumes being raised by his uncle, 30 lb. gr and would support him for three years on the proceeds of that sum. If the arbitrators, who were kinsmen of the parties, felt after three years that a more profitable arrangement could be made for the boy, they would give the uncle six months' notice; the arbitrators seem to have represented the four branches of the extended family. They had the right to situate Joerkin in the monastic or secular worlds as they thought best, and nothing is said about obtaining the boy's consent. Most incredibly, if Joerkin died before his kin had decided his fate as an adult, his mother was to send another of her children to Ghent under the same terms. It is clear that the future of one and perhaps more of Celie Rabau's children was being determined primarily by the need to make an equitable division of her father's estate.[49]

A mother could become her children's legal guardian, but only with the authorization of her late husband's clan, who could even withdraw her children from her if they chose. The widow of Pieter Uten Wissele became her son's legal guardian and was to support him "as long as the father's clan approve and she is making profit for the child and no longer."[50] In many of the surviving cases the issue may be in large part the kindred's right to determine when the child was to be emancipated or taught his trade, or to set a proper course if the mother remarried, and such restrictions might apply to male guardians as well; but no cases survive of a father being threatened by his late wife's clan with the loss of his children.

The mother's power as guardian was clearly not unlimited. The surviving parent was frequently overseer of the wardship, but when the surviving parent was the guardian, the overseer almost always came from the clan of the deceased spouse, so that some restraint could be exercised over the guardian. Some cases survive of suits brought by the overseer against the guardian on the children's behalf. One of them resulted in the ejection of the mother from her house. Another case, however, was adjudicated in favor of the mother against the overseer, and the *scepenen* invoked the natural role of the mother. A paternal estate was settled on Annekin, son of

Diederic Bonters, in 1375, and the mother became guardian after providing the *staet*. She had remarried by 1377, and the overseer evidently objected to some aspect of the arrangement, for in 1379 the *scepenen,* noting that "no one is better suited to keep the support of the child the mother, of good character as she is," left the boy with her. But they also thanked the overseer, without saying what his complaint had been, "for his worthy affection shown toward the child and which he shall continue to demonstrate for the welfare of the orphan."[51]

Whatever the law may have been, practice meant that the surviving parent would have to spend his or her own funds on the children. When Pieter Minnebode died in 1382 leaving no property, the mother simply renounced her rights to her child, and the clan pledged to raise the child to her majority without expense to the mother.[52] The magistrates might intervene to make certain that a mother did not impoverish herself caring for her children, in giving the mother some relief against the property of the child or the paternal kindred. Pieterkin, son of Gillis de Grande, was placed under wardship in 1371. Fifteen years later he was seriously ill with stones, and his mother, who had not remarried, was caring for him and consulting doctors at her own expense. Since she was not wealthy, the *scepenen* awarded her 8 lb. gr. from his estate if he died childless, but it is clear that she had been caring for him through affection for some time and went to the magistrates only when her funds were nearly depleted.[53] It seems certain that as a matter of practice most orphans simply remained in the custody of the surviving parent without serious questions being raised.

Despite their extensive powers of review, the *scepenen* seem to have been disinclined to intervene with the guardians unless an abuse was glaring. A noncustodial mother who felt that her child was being neglected had little recourse. In 1355 the widow of Jan de Dievel claimed that Clais de Dievel, the guardian of her son Pieterkin, was feeding the boy so inadequately that he had become ill. She asked reimbursement for providing his food. The guardian answered that the mother had taken Pieterkin from him without cause and against his will. The magistrates sustained Clais de Dievel, adding that he was to support Pieterkin properly and thus suggesting that the mother had some cause for complaint, but also warning the mother that if she took the boy away again, it would be at her own cost. Other cases, however, suggest that the magistrates would take a firmer hand, and much probably depended on the composition of the town council in any given year. Jooskin, bastard of Meester Joos Van Munte, had been situated with Clais Van Munte in 1386 but had escaped him and returned to his mother. Clais was holding the boy's money and had been supporting him on its income. But in 1389 the *scepenen* ordered him to pay interest for as long as he had held the money, beginning with the time that Jooskin had returned to his mother, and also to pay the mother's court costs. The magistrates clearly regarded Clais Van Munte as being at fault, presumably on grounds of mistreatment of the boy.[54]

It was unusual for guardians to situate children away from their mothers before they were of an age for apprenticeship. Provisional support was normally provided by the mother for an interval after the father's death. The guardian would then assume legal responsibility, although he might choose to leave the child with its mother. A case showing both the power of the guardians and the extent to which it was mitigated in practice involves the children of Gerard Coppins. In separate actions of July 1374 the guardians acquitted the mother of the father's estate and held a cash sum with which they were to support the children or have them supported. Eight months later the mother agreed to support them with the income of their property, and the guardian was expressly released from the obligation to provide further support, although he was evidently to continue to hold the money and pay the mother the income that it generated.[55]

Even when a child lived away from its mother, she might contribute to its support.[56] Most mothers would clearly do far more for their children than they were required to do by law. Against the occasional case suggesting that the mother wanted to get rid of her children,[57] we have seen numerous examples of genuine care and affection.

Part of the difficulty in determining who had physical custody of minors is terminological. The standard form in the *staten* is that someone, usually the guardian or the surviving parent, will *houden onghemindert*. *Houden* can mean either "hold," in the sense of keeping the child's money without diminishing the principal, or "support." And when *houden onghemindert* refers, as it often does, to a child rather than specifically to the money, the possibility of confusion is compounded.[58] The term did not necessarily mean that the person who held the money had physical custody of the child, but it did mean that that person was legally responsible for the child's support. When this term is used, the income of the principal is to be used to pay the child's costs, while if an orphan's money is invested at *pensioen* or interest, the proceeds were to be saved or reinvested.[59] The rate of return on the two forms of investment was expected to be comparable.[60]

Although the extended family played a major role in decisions regarding children, the conjugal family was recognized as the cell in which they would best be nurtured, even if it could not be the parental family. Annekin, son of Willem Zelle, had lost his mother by April 1360. In 1363 he was situated with Gillis Van Dorenselaer and his wife, who were to support him for five years. But if either Gillis or his wife died, "and it seemed that the child would not be well off with either survivor and they parted," the money would be refunded. The circumstances under which the boy was being reared would clearly be altered for the worse if either the man or the woman died. We have seen that surviving parents were expected to support their children until the estate could be settled and that blood payments went exclusively to males. But when in an exceptional measure of 1360 the *scepenen* agreed to pay for the death of Jan Van der Wostinen during the recent civil disturbances, they gave an additional 50s. gr.—a mere 10 percent of the blood price that went to male clan members—to the widow, "since she has supported the children as a good mother without property" since their father's death. In 1368 Jan Stijl died leaving a pregnant wife. She bought out the heirs' rights and pledged to support the child "as a good mother" if it were born alive.[61]

A case showing the strength of the nuclear family which is probably atypical only in the amount of property involved and not in terms of the living arrangements concerns the family of Ogeer Tsuul, one of the most prominent men of St. Bavo's abbatial village, east of the city. He and his wife had settled 40 lb. gr. on their daughter when she married in 1336, and Ogeer had died the next year. The widow had sole custody, "responsible for the five [other] children sitting and producing in the common nest with the property undivided." Subsequent provision had been made for the other daughters, but the two sons had continued to live at home and did not divide the property with their mother until 1360, and then on her initiative. Noting that they had been faithful and had helped make money for the family, and perhaps expecting her own death, she asked the *scepenen* to make a fair division.[62] The sons thus had let a generation pass without demanding their shares while they conducted the family business, apparently in partnership with their mother.

Comparatively few nuclear families remained intact for an entire generation, and one of the results was a proliferation of divided custody arrangements for children, evidently determined by clan judgments and the temperaments, ages, and interests of the parties. In 1385 Lisbette Van den Velde was to support one of her two daughters with property undiminished, while Jan Van den Steene would support the other with an equal property. The opinions of the extended family were paramount, and even the father had to accede to its collective judgment. In 1388 the younger of the two sons of Jacob Annaert was to be supported by his father, while the older, who was presumably able to work, was to be supported by the clan.[63]

The formula used for the clan in these cases is *maghen ende vrienden,* kindred and friends. The "friends" actually seem to have been the closest relatives among the "kindred." A case of 1350 mentions "the friends who would stand to inherit" a child's estate if she died.[64] The clan thus defined normally decided where or how orphans' money would be invested,[65] and these arrangements were normally ratified by the *scepenen* unless there were compelling considerations to the contrary. In one extraordinary case a boy was to be supported by his mother and the "friends" in alternate years.[66] The extent to which the clan ordinarily overrode the wishes of the parties directly concerned cannot be determined.

There is a tendency, but by no means an invariable rule, for boys to live with men while girls went with women.[67] An older brother who had reached his majority might assume the care of a younger sibling. Quite frequently the legal guardian and the surviving parent would divide custody of the children, particularly in cases where the mother is the surviving parent. Large families seem particularly prone to division, but this is not to say that the mother's role becomes negligible. Gillis Versaren left four children when he died in 1387. The mother was given charge of 32 lb. gr. for the children under the standard "support undiminished" arrangement. She gave out 8 lb. of it to each of three persons, one of them her brother, each of whom was to support one child, including the only daughter. No mention is made of the support of Willekin, the oldest son; but since 8 lb. was left of the 32 lb., he was apparently the only child who stayed with his mother, perhaps to receive training in the family business or to work.[68] This was a large estate, and there was no financial necessity to situate the children away from the "common nest." But the tendency was clearly an accepted and common practice at all levels of urban society.

There is also a tendency, but no more than that, in cases of divided custody to leave the younger children with the mother, while the guardian or other persons took charge of the older children, particularly if they were boys. One suspects unstated apprenticeship arrangements in such cases.[69] Since most guilds gave preference to the sons of enfranchised masters but did not permit boys to be apprenticed to their own fathers, some measure of divided custody of siblings was inevitable. In such cases the boy might be situated with less money than the girl, for he would be expected to compensate the person supporting him with his labor.[70]

An exceptional extent of division of function among custodians is found with the three children of Gillis Van der Wostinen. The mother held 7 lb. 8s. gr., and with the income of that, principal undiminished, she was to furnish their shoes and clothing. The two older children, one boy and one girl, were situated with a man who was to support the boy with 5 lb. and the girl with 4 lb., principal undiminished. The youngest child, a girl, was placed with a second man for four years, and he was "to give her food and drink with sufficient care that the mother and guardian will be adequately paid." Hence there was divided custody with none of the children living either with the mother or the legal guardian, both of whom were to contribute to the support of the children and evidently to oversee it.[71]

There are countless variants on these basic themes. In 1350 Jan Ghiselin agreed to support Annekin, son of Jan Zickelvoet, with 30s. gr. while the mother would support the daughter with 14s. The case is peculiar in that Ghiselin secured the money on his share of a house that he owned jointly with the widow; he must have been her kinsman, for a stepfather would have been identified as such, and a separate support arrangement would have been pointless. There are cases in which a maternal uncle supports a child, even though the father is still alive and on good relations with his in-laws. The father and the legal guardian from the mother's side were to support Annekin Bloume in alternate years. Custody of two girls might be divided between the father and the guardian. Maternal grandparents are frequently in divided custody arrangements with widowed fathers or in some cases simply assumed custody, although the father was still alive. Given the legal preference for the father's rights, one can only assume that they were helping an in-law with onerous domestic responsibilities. In a truly exceptional case of 1363, a woman acted as maternal side legal guardian, although the father was still alive; she took custody of the three girls, while the father raised the only boy. The widow of Heinric Eyfins surrendered custody of her daughter to another woman, evidently the older sister of the mother, and her husband.[72]

Divided custody of children could sometimes be dictated by economic circumstances. The average size of nuclear families in Ghent at this time does not seem to have been large; it was an unusual family which had more than three minor children. In 1356 Jan Van den Scake was left with nine children by his wife. Although the estate was large, consisting of a house, moor property, and 30 lb. gr. in money, it was not enough to support the children. The father and the maternal grandfather, who was also the legal guardian, each took three children to support undiminished of their principal property, while they agreed jointly to support the last three "as best they can." That large families were unusual and were an economic burden even on wealthy families is shown when the widow of Boudin de Groete, one of the most prominent physicians of Ghent, noting that her brother Jan Van den Woelpitte, also a doctor, "has a great burden of small children and by God's grace may have more yet," willed 8 lb. gr. to each of his five children and left open the possibility of additional bequests to children born subsequently.[73] While children were obviously desired by most couples, God's grace could sometimes make too much of a good thing.

Children inevitably come to assume responsibilities in an adult world. Parents realized that children had to be prepared and trained before emancipation. Some *Staten van Goed* mention school as part of the support that would be provided for the orphan. Since it is specifically mentioned in these cases, it evidently was not automatically assumed. Many orphans clearly remained unlettered, but anyone with a substantial property would want his children to have some education. Schools instructing in Flemish evidently were adequate for demand in the city.[74] There was already an assumption that those of good family needed to be bilingual, although the education of most persons was probably confined to the native language. The eldest son of the brewer Jan Baliet was to be taught French at his mother's expense, but only if the "friends" thought it advantageous. Most references to learning French involve the child leaving Flanders for the purpose, although there are some exceptions.[75]

There certainly was nothing unusual about children going to school. That combatants were schoolboys was a mitigating circumstance when the magistrates punished street fighters, and the language of the text suggests that students were a common sight in the city. The schools of Ghent were not for the squeamish. In 1377 Colard Van den Gardine had to pay 150 lb. par. because his son had accidentally blinded Gillekin Van der Meere by sticking an object in his eye while they were "sitting" in school.[76]

Although most poorer boys probably learned only a professional trade, education for those with property was not considered a substitute for becoming professionally competent. In 1394 the brewer Jan Van der Brake, who was evidently guardian of his grandson and namesake, added to a minimal list of the boy's property that he now had a little more money with which he could send him to school.[77] This would be a dual sacrifice for poor parents or guardians, for they would have to pay school fees and be deprived of at least a part of the child's labor.

For those who were educated at all, schooling preceded apprenticeship. Annekin de Houveneere was to be sent to school in 1371 "to learn French, to learn to write in German and French," and only when this schooling had ended "to learn either a trade or merchandising." The principle is also expressed in the case of Lodewijk de Beere, whose father was to have him sent to school until he could read and write, presumably in Flemish, and then would teach him his own trade, although it was very unusual for a boy to learn his trade from his father. In 1353 Jan Abelin was apprenticed to the cobbler Willem Van den Veere. Willem was to hold 3 lb. gr. for him and pledged "to support him until his majority and send him to school until he is old enough to warrant having his trade. Then he will teach him his trade."[78]

There thus seems to have been reasonably widespread lay literacy in Flemish in Ghent in the fourteenth century, but literacy in French and German was exceptional. This culture was also shared by women. The only clear indication of women in the schools during the thirteenth century was indirect: a fable of a teacher who fell in love with his thirteen-year-old pupil.[79] But the fourteenth century brings many indications of literate women, although, just as with the men, all that we can say in most cases is that they went to school and learned Flemish. Lodewijk de Beere, who was to be educated before learning his trade, had inherited several books from his mother, including a bestiary, a concordance, a martyrology, and the gospels in Flemish. We have seen that women were often active in business, and this suggests literacy.

We are told in absolutely unambiguous terminology that some girls were to be "sent to school." We are not told whether they went to the same schools attended by boys, but these references cannot be interpreted as indicating instruction in the home. The four daughters of Pieter Walraven were to be "sent" to school, as were Trijskin de Man, Betkin Aldewerelt, and Betkin Ackerman. Callekin, the daughter of Michiel de Handzuttere, was at least aged eleven in 1380, when she was to be sent to school in Ghent for two years. Mergriet de Buc was to support Line, the daughter of Jan Ackerman, just as if she were her own child for one year, including "food, drink, instruction, and learning."[80] This could be private tutoring rather than formal school instruction, but it does show that supporting the girl as one would one's own daughter would include making certain that she became literate.

As with boys, we may not assume from silence that a girl would be sent to school if the arrangements made for her support did not specify it. The stepfather of Callekin de Pachteneere agreed to support her without diminishing her principal property. The support would not include the costs of her marriage, but would include sending her to school. Some women, probably most, were educated in the home. The evident intention of the magistrates was to provide some minimal education for orphans. Merkin de Moenc was to be taught "sewing, reading, and writing within the home." Merkin Vaneels was to be provided with these talents, but she was to learn them from Kateline Van Gheroudsberghe, and the document suggests that she was to be situated in Kateline's establishment rather than her own home. Callekin Everhems was to be sent to school by her guardian, who would teach her sewing and tailoring at home.[81] As with boys, girls' professional training was apart from the acquisition of basic literacy and usually followed it.

Orphans were expected to contribute toward their own support with the income of their estates or with their labor as they became older, and preferably with both. Education was desirable, but competence in a trade was essential. In the next chapter we shall consider the changing roles of children as they grew older and gradually emancipated themselves from their parents and clans.

Chapter Seven

The Flight of the Nestlings: Children and the Outside World

The ecclesiastical sanctions against usury were evidently followed very strictly at Ghent, although some subterfuges were used. But a payment of *pensioen,* usually around 10 percent, was owed on the investments of minors. This generally went for their support but might be used as an increment of the estate if money were available from other sources. *Pensioen* stopped when the child reached his or her majority, even if legal guardianship continued.[1]

We have seen that children were to be supported with the income of their properties, but that the *Staten van Goed* distinguish between the money given at *pensioen* and that held by the person with custody, for which the term is normally *houden onghemindert.* The notion that *pensioen* could be paid only on orphans' property, but not that of unemancipated adults, was clearly no empty form.[2] But we also find that the distinction between *pensioen* and *houden onghemindert* is often fictive, since the *pensioen* is sometimes stated to be used by the person having physical custody to support the child. In 1379 Clare de Coc reached an age where she could no longer receive *pensioen.* Her guardians were ordered by the *scepenen* to collect her assets and use them "undiminished" to support her until she married. Accordingly, they secured 8 lb. gr. apiece under the *houden onghemindert* formula; a year later we are told that she had 16 lb. at *pensioen* with these very people. In the document where she is forbidden *pensioen,* she is called Clare; in the second and later version, she is Claerkin, suggesting minority. Someone's conscience was apparently being salved, but the end result was still that her money was generating income that was being used to support her.[3]

That orphans' money was distinguished in principle from that of the surviving parent and that such funds were to be invested to make more money meant that considerable sums were available for investment. Often this took the form of short-term loans.[4] When interest could no longer be paid, the money might be invested in real estate, which at least until the civil war of 1379–85 was certainly safe enough but which did not normally realize a 10 percent annual return.[5] The same principle that allowed orphans to receive interest on their money permitted their real estate to be sold at a higher than market value. The city *erfscheeders* would appraise the sale value of property on request; while there was no legal obligation to sell at that price, their verdict was used for purposes of tax assessment and to determine the value of shares of an estate. When Jan Van den Hecke bought a house for 24 lb. gr. in 1388, he had to pay an extra 2 lb., or 25 percent, on one-third of the property, which belonged to an unnamed orphan. The contract calls for payment over eight years, or an extra 3.125 percent per year. Measures were thus being taken to protect the real estate of orphans in long-term sales against inflation.[6]

Money was invested at *pensioen* immediately when a parent died, suggesting a ready market for the funds. Although there were exceptions, most guardians invested larger sums in land or rents, placing at *pensioen* only more modest amounts. When large sums of money went into *pensioen*, the principal was normally divided among several investors to minimize risks. The interest was generally paid to the guardian every six months. Since the guardian was personally responsible for any losses, he had to be certain of the borrowers' reliability. There are a few cases of orphans' money being placed in merchandising or "at gain or loss,"[7] but most took the form of simple personal loans, rather than business partnerships. Money held at interest was secured on other property of the borrower, preferably real estate. There are countless variants on the basic procedure. Some relatives and friends seem to have taken the money simply to be helpful, but in other cases it was given to people who needed loans.[8]

The skill of the Flemings at dodging the usury injunctions makes it very difficult to find out the amount of *pensioen* in most cases or to say much about the workings of the system. The rate could vary, but it was normally determined by the clan when the money was loaned. In a case of 1378 a rate of 5 percent is given for a contract which amounts to the children holding a mortgage rather than loaning their money directly.[9] The rate which occurs most often is 10 percent; but even if the money were held by the borrower for several years and the yield not paid to the guardian to help support the child, the interest remained uncompounded.[10] Higher rates are sometimes found.[11]

Money belonging to orphans had to be repaid in terms of the intrinsic value of the coin, not the face value. Since some tutelages lasted for many years, the children would otherwise lose considerable purchasing power. There is no trace in records of orphans' property and very little in those concerning adults of the Italian idea that it was legitimate to make a profit or sustain a loss on fluctuations in the exchange rate. No attempt was made at Ghent to protect orphans' property from inflation caused by fluctuations in supply and demand, but orphans were entitled to compensation for the frequent debasements of the precious metal content of the coinage. Numerous contracts of *pensioen* specify repayment "in present money value," a determination evidently made by the moneychangers, or the money would be repaid in the same coin as received.[12]

Children were expensive to support. Statistics bearing on this problem have been assembled in Table 8, but they probably raise more questions than they answer. The amount spent to sustain a child would vary with the social standing of the individuals and size of the estate, the age and sex of the child, and whether the child was working to provide part of his or her support. The figures given in the "support undiminished" clauses are unrepresentative, for these range from extreme comfort to "support undiminished" on a pittance that happens to be the total value of the estate. A better indication of levels of support are those texts that provide separate figures for support, including those which separate money held at *pensioen* from that which is to be used directly for child support. In these cases we have figured the support costs as 10 percent of the principal. We have excluded cases in which the labor of the child is suggested.[13]

The averages in Table 8 are determined by the extreme fluctuations in the high figures. The lowest figures are much more constant, only once dropping below 6s. gr. and showing a slight tendency to rise in nominal terms during this period, although this was not enough to keep pace with inflation. Indeed, 6s. gr. seems to have been the minimum necessary to maintain decent support. In 1372 the guardian of the three children of

Table 8. Costs of Supporting One Child for One Year

Year	Highest Figure	Lowest Figure	Average	Number of Cases in Sample
1350	30s. gr.	10.s. gr.	19s. gr.	4
1351	10s.	10s.	10s.	1
1352	20s.	8s.	14s. 8d.	5
1353	No cases			
1354	19s.	19s.	19s.	1
1355	20s.	10s.	15s.	2
1356	25s.	6s.7.2d.	14s.	5
1357	25s.	6s.	14s.2d.	4
1358	50s.	8s.	29s.2d.	3
1359	54s.	8s.	18s.2d.	8
1360	26s.	26s.	26s.	1
1361	32s.	4s.	16s.	4
1362	14s.	14s.	14s.	1
1363	28s.	20s.	24s.	2
1364	12s.	11s.	11s.6d.	2
1365	30s.	12s.	21s.	2
1366	16s.	16s.	16s.	1
1367	29s.	12s.	19s.8d.	4
1368	60s.	20s.	29s.8d.	6
1369	40s.	10s.	19s.10d.	8
1370	40s.	7s.6d.	16s.8d.	13
1371	60s.	6s. 2d.	28s.6d.	6
1372	26s.	6s.	13s.4d.	6
1373	40s.	40s.	40s.	1
1374	60s.	12s.	27s.6d.	9
1375	24s.	14s.	19s.8d.	4
1376	80s.	80s.	80s.	1
1377	13s.	13s.	13s.	1
1378	40s.	8s.	16s.6d.	4
1379	26s.	26s.	26s.	1
1380	28s.	28s.	28s.	1
1381	43s.6d.	40s.12d.	41s.11d.	2
1382	14s.	14s.	14s.	1
1383	20s.	6s.	13s.	2

(*continued*)

Table 8, continued

Year	Highest Figure	Lowest Figure	Average	Number of Cases in Sample
1384	40s.	20s.	30s.	5
1385	48s.	12s.	32s.6d.	6
1386	36s.	16s.8d.	24s.6d.	6
1387	40s.	14s.	26s.	4
1388	36s.	6s.	26s.	3
1389	35s.	32s.	33s.6d.	2
1390	50s.	26s.	37s.6d.	3

Source: SAG, Registers of *scepenen* of *gedele*.

Willem Van den Vivere was to support one on the income of a small amount of real estate, another "undiminished" with 3 lb. gr., which at the 10 percent rate would mean 6s. gr. annually, and the third child he would support as charity. Unfortunately, wage figures are so fragmentary that it is difficult to translate these amounts into purchasing power, but most figures suggest that a comfortable living for a family of four would require roughly 7 lb. gr., or over twenty times the 6s. gr. figure. One text specifies that for 6s. gr. annually a girl was to receive food, drink, one pair of shoes, and one dress—absolutely minimal support.[14] A case of 1361 shows that 3s. 9d. gr. was considered below the poverty line.[15] It was recognized that children cost more to support as they grew older, and some cases provide for adjustments in expenditure. The *staet* of a girl first put under tutelage in 1378 was revised in 1382 because "she can no longer be supported as inexpensively as before, but she will be given decent support from her property through common friends."[16] When children in the same family are supported at different levels, it can reflect one having more property than another or an age difference.[17]

Many if not most children of artisans had begun to earn their own money before being emancipated. It might not be demanded that a child or unemancipated young adult take a job, but the guardian was not bound to deplete the estate of one who refused. When a ward "earned his own bread," the income of his or her property was in principle reinvested, while the wages provided daily maintenance. Children were normally expected to work for those supporting them if requested, but they were to be paid. In 1360 the two sons of Jan de Moelneere were to live with their brother-in-law Ghiselbrecht Van den Zomple, who would support the older boy for one year, giving him food and sleeping quarters and paying him if he worked, but leaving open the possibility that he might not. Labor was to be compensated even if performed for the surviving parent or a stepparent. The widow of Jan Van Crabbinc was to support their children with principal undiminished as long as the guardian and the kindred desired. "And it is understood that if the children work for their mother, she is to pay whatever the guardian and overseer think appropriate for it."[18] This case shows again the extent to which the guardian could intervene actively in the relationship between a widowed parent and the child. In a similar case the widow of Michiel Van den Colcte was to support her son Annekin undiminished with 4 lb. gr., but she was to pay *pensioen* on that amount to the boy's sister Merkin, "since Merkin works for her mother." The widow of Pieter Prester was to support Aechte, her younger stepdaughter, undiminished with 4 lb. gr., suggesting an annual income of 8s. gr., while Kateline, the older, would work for her support. This estate was large, including rural land and another 20 lb. 10s. gr. held at *pensioen* for the girls. Poverty was thus not the reason for having the children work, but rather a desire to acquire money for investment or a dowry.[19]

Child labor was obviously quite common. In the spring of 1382, when Ghent was in danger of being starved out by the count's forces, Marikin Van den Abeele was given 10 s. gr. of her money to use for clothes and 5s. gr. "to leave Flanders to look for work." She asked that the rest of her money be held for her until she returned. The weaver Jan Van der Eeken left substantial properties and looms to his children; one child was to be supported by the estate, but the other three were declared old enough to be earning their own money. That boys would get the family profession was occasionally recognized in *staten* as a reason for compensating the girls. Of an estate of 16 lb. gr. left by the butcher Jacob Haghelsteen in 1368, his daughter got 6 lb. and her brothers 5 lb. apiece, "since they are installed at the meat hall." The estate inherited by the two children of Pieter de Deckere included substantial lands and rents. The boy would be supported with the income of the real estate, but "the other child [the girl] earns its bread," and accordingly the income of her inheritance would be turned to profit and invested.[20] A child who was considered old enough to work but not old enough to live alone might owe his wages to the person supporting him.[21] This situation might last until the individual had been emancipated by marrying. The money of Annekin Streif was to be held until he married, "since he earns his bread with his trade on ship."[22]

That a child worked for his or her upkeep thus does not of itself suggest poverty. Merkin, daughter of Raes Van Wormine, inherited half interest in a house, some land at Aalter, and cash. Two years after the estate was first probated, provision was made for all the income of her property to be applied to her profit, presumably through reinvestment, "for the child is situated in a job paying all her costs, so that leggings, shoes, and dresses will not need to be bought from her estate."[23] It is likely, but unprovable, that many of the cases in which children's money is given to someone not a family member under the "support undiminished" formula involved domestic service, with the money serving as a bond. This is especially probable in cases where the amounts of money are so small that a 10 percent return could not conceivably have supported a child for a year. A more ambiguous case of a child being given part, although not all, of his money occurs in 1351, when Pieterkin de Mulre was given part of his estate "so that he could help himself," presumably by working, conceivably by showing his responsibility to his elders.[24]

The problem of child labor leads naturally to the question of emancipation from tutelage and the circumstances under which a young person might be considered ready for such responsibility. The situation at Ghent parallels findings of scholars for other cities.[25] The age of legal majority was fifteen for boys, twelve for girls.[26] A man normally became his own master when he left his father's house or married—a common formula used is "his own man and married"[27]—although the sources are not entirely consistent on whether a clandestine marriage not approved by the family automatically terminated wardship. Jacob Coevoet evidently achieved emancipation through elopement; but after Simon Trijl eloped, he agreed to remain under wardship until he could support himself and manage his property. Still, his guardians emancipated him five months later.[28]

Formal emancipation could occur only after the clan had determined that the person had the maturity and wisdom to justify it and had its decision ratified by the *scepenen*.[29] Yet the fact that so few formal acts of emancipation survive proves that most persons gained their independence informally. Graph 2 provides by calendar year the number of acquittals by adults of the person who had been a guardian or other holder of property. The figures are strikingly low, reaching a high of sixty-five in 1376. The chronology is interesting, for it shows that the number of emancipations declines during crisis years, such as 1359–60, and in plague years, such as the late 1360s, and rises again thereafter. The drop is particularly striking between 1375 and 1380. The figures then become steady during the first

Graph 2. Acquittals of Guardians by
Emancipated Adults, by Calendar Years

Number of Acquittals

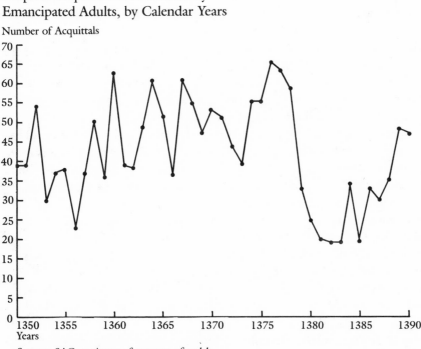

Source: SAG, registers of *scepenen* of *gedele*

years of the civil war and rise again with the peace from 1385. The figures
show that clans were cautious and were reluctant to upset the status quo,
particularly during plague periods. If the adult child's property was controlled by the kindred, there would be no risk of its loss if he or she died.
Emancipation thus does not reflect the time at which one reached the age
of majority, but rather other factors.

Emancipation clearly did not follow automatically the age of legal majority. Annekin, son of Jan de Meyere, was placed under wardship in 1380
and emancipated in 1402, when he would have been twenty-two even if
orphaned as a baby, while Jacob Zoete was at least thirty-six and probably
older when he was emancipated in 1419, for he already had a stepfather by
the time his paternal estate was listed in 1383. Delays in emancipation led to
interesting situations. In a quarrel over the estate of the younger Heinric
Yoens, his father refused to answer on certain points because his son "had
been old enough to be his own man, navigating his own ship and earning
and spending his own money."[30] Although Heinric evidently had not been

emancipated, his father was arguing that his age alone made him partially responsible for his own actions. In 1390 Pieterkin, elder son of the prominent shipper Lauwereins Boele, received the consent of his clan and thereafter of the *scepenen* to sell shares of a house that he had inherited to pay for a boat which he was using to support himself.[31] The clan's action could terminate some of its own responsibility; the father of an emancipated man was no longer legally responsible for his deeds of violence, despite the principle of clan solidarity in such matters.[32]

A case of arrested development that shows the vulnerability of adult members of the family is Annin or Jan, son of Boudin Caye. He was placed under wardship with a substantial estate, which was to be held for him undiminished by his mother. In 1385 she declared to the magistrates that Annin was now twenty-four, an official of his guild, and had used her property, including some that she had lost in standing surety for him. She asked that her losses be deducted from his *staet*. Her son retorted that she had promised him complete support without diminution of his principal and was therefore obligated to pay all his debts. The *scepenen* heard testimony from the clan that the mother had behaved properly toward her son and that the son was conducting his own business. Accordingly, the *scepenen* awarded the mother an indemnity, but much less than she had asked. They also released Annin from wardship and acquitted his mother, while admonishing her to stand by him and help him to manage his property according to her conscience, as a good mother should, implying that his discretion was in doubt and that he needed help, which under the circumstances she might be less than enthusiastic about giving.[33]

A case similar to that of Jan Caye, which also shows indirectly a reason why few mothers were guardians—they were less able than males to compel a recalcitrant youth to behave—is that of Jan Uten Hove the bastard against his mother and guardian, Aechte Blondeels. Their disagreements were settled by a board of kindred. They had been residing together; Jan then left, but whether on his instigation or hers is unclear. Jan now pledged to conduct no business without the consent of his mother and the clan. He also agreed to return to his mother to live; both he and his mother were to treat each other as a good child or mother should, including decent support from her. Curiously, no term is set to this arrangement, but if they later parted, she was to pay him an allowance of 30s. gr. per year, a decent but not lavish amount.[34] The boy had clearly been allowed to manage his own affairs, at least up to a point, had botched matters, and had

had to return home; but his mother was not able to control him without the cooperation of the clan, even though she was his guardian.

There are thus many cases of persons past the age of majority but still under wardship transacting business on their own, and even of persons who still bore the "kin" suffix and thus were probably minors doing so. The making of wills was evidently an area in which the normal incapacity of a person under tutelage to make a binding contract did not invariably apply. In two cases of 1368–69 the issue was whether the person was of age and sane and thus capable of making a binding testament. Both persons were still under tutelage, but that issue is simply ignored. Coppin Tac, who from his diminutive name was probably still a minor, willed money to his bastard in 1355, and the legality of the action was apparently not questioned. The late Jan Boele had given life use of his share of a house to his mother, although he had still been a ward. The *scepenen* approved the deed "because he had been of mature years and had had good judgment." Bequests made by a minor to a parent may have had a special legal standing, for in 1383 the *scepenen* ruled valid such a grant by the son of the butcher Jan Van den Walle, but they nullified other bequests that the boy had made.[35]

Mature persons who still were under tutelage were occasionally asked by the magistrates whether they understood the implications of an action to be undertaken by the guardians and approved of it. The magistrates approved a number of arrangements giving a trial run to youths approaching maturity to see how they would manage their property. In October 1355 Jan Uten Mantele, at the request of his guardian and clan, was given the large sum of 15 lb. gr. with which to engage in commerce (*coemanscepen*) for his profit on their advice. The document emphasizes that he and his other property remained under wardship. He apparently satisfied them of his maturity, for he was emancipated the following May. The word "proof" is sometimes used in these texts. These arrangements were generally confined to disposal over a certain sum or to the use of the revenues of the estate, for rarely could an unemancipated person alienate his principal. Sometimes the amount given was no more than a little spending money for incidentals.[36] Never could one sibling endanger the share of another when the two were still in the "common nest" with undivided assets.[37]

It was thus ordinary practice for young persons of both sexes to manage their own affairs under the loose supervision of the guardians for some time before formal emancipation. When Mergriet Cortoys was emancipated in 1357, her kin declared her to be "mature in wisdom and years, and that she has managed her own property for some years."[38] Her younger brother did less well. In 1358 his kin, including the grand master of the schools of St. Jan, reported to the *scepenen* his serious misconduct and mismanagement of his property during a time when he was controlling his property with the consent of the guardian and the clan. The magistrates revoked his provisional emancipation in terms suggesting that a priest, probably connected with the school, had led him astray.[39] This case is exceptional; most young people, anxious to prove themselves, seem to have convinced their clans that they were responsible adults.

Some "children" naturally became impatient with the long tutelage. Annekin, son of Arnoud Van der Hoyen, lost his father in 1361. In 1376 a new *staet* of his property was made, and his money was held by his step-father, Jan Van Houtem, who was to support him. Annekin was admonished "to behave as a good child should, as he has done until now," until the last of his money was paid. The mother had died by this time, and Annekin was becoming edgy; the estate was to be paid by Christmas 1377. Yet his stepfather was still loaning him substantial amounts of money against the principal held as late as 1382, which shows that Annekin was incurring expenses on his own while his stepfather held his money.[40] The case also shows a stepparent who was willing to assume responsibilities toward a child beyond the letter of his legal obligation.

Yet attitudes about child support could be remarkably casual. Children could be farmed out indiscriminately.[41] The magistrates made no attempt to enforce an arbitrarily conceived plan of how children should be raised. Beyond the platitudes of "treat the parent or child as one should," they intervened not at all in the emotional bonds of the nuclear family. Accordingly, we have trouble fathoming those relationships except to some extent in the case of bastards, who by their peculiar status can hardly have been representative. But the *scepenen* did make absolutely certain that the physical needs of orphans were being satisfied. A curious case of 1386, just after the war, involved the property of Pieter Baaf's daughter. The estate was small, a stepfather was involved, and the land was only now being placed again into cultivation. The guardian was admonished "to be careful in supporting her that he supports her as well when her property produces profit as he is doing now with smaller incomes."[42] Evidently what is meant is that he should support her proportionally better as her income increased, not give her minimal support while taking the added revenue for himself.

While girls were subjected to constraints on their mobility that normally did not apply to boys, there were two areas in which treatment of all children, irrespective of sex, was to be equal: the division of property and affection. Favoritism of one child sometimes led to an attempt to skew a property division in his or her favor. There are numerous references to a parent leaving extra portions of the estate to a particular child in return for services or because that child had been more faithful than the others to the parent in time of trouble.[43] As long as the reasons were genuine and the favoritism not gross, such arrangements were usually uncontested. Yet we have seen the emotional and legal problems caused by the attempt of Celie Amelakens to favor one son over the others. The adult children of Pieter Breebaert demonstrate an exceptional extent of rivalry and infighting among siblings. One son, Hugh, had evidently been entrusted with the support of his mother, and the other children accused him of spending too much on her and of squandering his own property, which was evidently still undivided in the common nest, although none of these people was still under tutelage and a daughter was married. A limit was placed on her support from her own incomes, but the *scepenen* ruled that the siblings could not limit the amount that Hugh spent on her from his own money. The parties agreed that Hugh was best suited for supporting her.[44] The case sounds suspiciously like a son who was trying to treat his aging mother well being troubled by the potential heirs of both.

One area in which males were definitely favored over females is in the division of the blood price. When a person, almost always a man, was killed, compensation was due to the other males of the clan for his loss. The widow, who was not of the blood kin, was excluded; and since it was a blood price rather than an inheritance, girls were also excluded. Thus the *montzoen,* half the payment due, went to the eldest legitimate son if there was one, to the exclusion of the other children, including sons, or failing a son to the eldest brother of the deceased. Nephews took precedence over daughters. The rest of the blood price, the *maagzoen,* went to the kindred of the deceased in fixed proportions, after deductions were made for their expenses in arranging the atonement. Support of the widow and daughters of a murdered man devolved in principle upon her father or brothers, while her husband's brothers or nephews got the blood price. Exceptions could be made if there was danger that the children would not be cared for adequately, but this was solely at the discretion of the kindred. Most of the estate of Jacob Van Maelte, which was settled in September 1389, went to his widow. When the blood price of 18 lb. gr. was divided the following March, half went to the only son. His mother was to hold it for him. The other 9 lb. went to the clan for its rights of *maagzoen,* but, "out of love for the children [the other two were daughters] and because they do not have much property from their father," the clan arranged to have the 9 lb. secured for the girls on condition of reversion to the kindred if they died without issue.[45] Most clans were notably less generous than the Van Maeltes, for other *zoen* payments clearly enunciate the principle that the money is not to be used by the mother for child support. A case of exceptional clarity because the changing circumstances can be traced over several years begins with the death of Pieter de Munteneere, which was atoned in July 1373. He left a single legitimate son, Pieterkin, who received the *montzoen* and rights on the *maagzoen* totaling 15 lb. gr. Another 30s. gr. was awarded by the clan to Annekin, the decedent's bastard, and 10s. gr. to "the girl," whose legitimacy is not stated. The money had been paid by July 1374. By January 1375 the mother was claiming that she did not have enough money to support her children, but the *scepenen* stated categorically that her suit to have part of the boy's *zoen* money for child support was invalid: she was to be given only such extra money as the clan determined.[46] A boy might have the right upon reaching maturity to renounce the atonement of his father's death made by his kin on condition of returning the money already paid. Girls were occasionally made beneficiaries of *zoen* payments, but only with special arrangements and the consent of the kindred. Of the 20 lb. gr. blood price paid for the death of Justaas de Otter, the kin conceded his daughter Callekin 8 lb., but this would revert to the clan for division according to law if "Calle acted against the advice of her two guardians and her friends in any matter, great or small."[47]

Young people frequently perpetrated deeds of violence. They cannot be seen solely as the bereaved if financially advantaged heirs of victims. Table 9 suggests the extent of the involvement of young people in homicides recorded in the *Zoendincboeken.* This is clearly far lower than the total incidence, for our only indications are the use of the "kin" diminutive form of nomenclature and "son of" identifications; particularly in cases such as these, when the "child" is being punished for an adult offense, the adult form of the name was often used. Even with this reservation nearly one-quarter of the homicides involved young persons on at least one side, while a small number had them in both parties. Even when a "kin" form is not used, many decedents left minors as heirs and accordingly were probably young adults themselves, for at least 30.07 percent of the victims left minors as beneficiaries of the blood price.

Much the same picture is obtained from the trial days (*dinghedaghe*), at

Table 9. Involvement of Persons with "Kin" Names in Homicide Atonements

Fiscal Year	Number of Homicides	"Kin" or "Son of" Principals, One Side	"Kin" or "Son of" Principals, Both Sides	Child in Tutelage is Heir
1350 (−1)	23	4	–	5
1351	27	3	–	4
1352	23	3	–	5
1353	19	7	2	4
1354	38	6	1	6
1355	24	4	–	6
1356	29	6	5	6
1357	42	15	–	11
1358	29	9	–	6
1359	43	13	2	12
1360	23	2	–	6
1361	20	4	2	4
1362	16	4	2	3
1363	28	7	–	12
1364	20	5	–	5
1365	17	4	–	6
1366	23	6	–	5
1367	20	2	–	9
1368	12	4	1	3
1369	39	14	1	18
1370	19	5	1	8
1371	21	10	–	8
1372	16	5	–	6
1373	18	6	–	6
1374	21	6	2	5
1375	24	1	4	15
1376	28	8	4	12
1377	21	5	1	10
1378	23	4	2	5
1379	19	5	1	7
TOTAL	725	177 (24.41%)	31 (4.28%)	218 (30.07%)

Source: SAG, *Zoendincboeken*.

which pilgrimages and financial compositions were assessed for non-homicidal acts of violence or the use of foul language. These figures are contained in Table 10, where a remarkable consistency is shown each year in the percentage of offenses attributed to youthful principals. There may be underreporting here, as for Table 9, particularly since a man in his twenties whose father was dead would not be designated as a youth in the source but was hardly middle aged. Yet the fact that the percentages are consistent suggests that they may be reasonably accurate. Since so much of the violence in Ghent was perpetrated by the clans, which were dominated by older men, it is highly likely that older men answered for misdeeds actually committed by their younger relatives.

Our sources are less enlightening for the emotional environment of children than for their economic situation. Persons in whose care children were left were responsible to see that nothing untoward happened to them. Yet the fines imposed tended to be considerably smaller, even if there was malice, than would be true for the same offense committed against an adult. Even when permanent disability resulted, damages assessed were very low.[48] Working mothers used babysitters, who were responsible for keeping the children out of danger.[49] Then as now children liked to play around work areas, and accidents sometimes resulted, but they were compensated only to the extent of the injury without additional penalty for malice.[50]

The magistrates would not tolerate what they considered brutal or negligent behavior toward children, but it is clear that they thought an exemplary thrashing would hurt no one. Hence Gillis Martins and Lisbette de Hollandere were sent on pilgrimages for having beaten Paschkin Warijns; but the violence inflicted upon Pieterkin Van den Moure by Jan de Vos was fined only 20s. par. since it was done in the boy's interest. When Heinkin de Smet injured another boy accidentally, he was to pay the doctor and be punished with a rod.[51]

Children were expected to obey their parents and particularly their fathers. We have seen that they were frequently given or willed money on condition of maintaining proper attitudes toward father and clan. An unusually explicit statement of the children's duty to obey the father is given in 1355, when Gillis Plante was ordered "to give his two children their proper support if they behave as good children should and act according to their father's wishes."[52] We are not told what would happen if the children were recalcitrant.

Children had obligations toward their mothers as well as their fathers.

Table 10. Persons with "Kin" or "Son of" Forms
as Principals in Cases Heard on Trial Days

Fiscal Year	Total Offenses Punished	Youth as Principals
1350 (–1)	80	11 (13.75%)
1351	102	9 (8.82%)
1352	138	11 (7.97%)
1353	117	7 (5.98%)
1354	114	13 (11.40%)
1355	92	10 (10.87%)
1356	132	26 (19.70%)
1357	142	19 (13.38%)
1358	131	27 (20.61%)
1359	155	27 (17.42%)
1360	55	5 (9.09%)
1361	132	21 (15.91%)
1362	118	21 (20.34%)
1363	152	24 (15.79%)
1364	154	30 (19.48%)
1365	194	32 (16.49%)
1366	165	27 (16.36%)
1367	160	22 (13.75%)
1368	98	13 (13.27%)
1369	170	28 (16.47%)
1370	177	25 (14.12%)
1371	145	15 (10.34%)
1372	165	28 (16.97%)
1373	183	30 (16.39%)
1374	225	29 (12.89%)
1375	220	29 (13.18%)
1376	215	29 (13.49%)
1377	250	40 (16.00%)
1378	187	30 (16.04%)

Source: SAG, *Zoendincboeken*.

Note: 1379–80 is a partial year, and the form of the *Zoendincboeken* changes in 1380, making comparisons with the above figures difficult.

We have seen that some mothers made considerable sacrifices to raise their children. Some were willing to reject the wishes of members of the clan if it seemed against the best interests of the child. The *scepenen* were sometimes willing to help a mother who wished to raise her children without harmful interference from the kindred. The small estate of Raes Terlinc was probated in 1350. By 1352 the widow was supporting three surviving sons. In 1357 she complained that two of the boys had been urged by certain of their "friends," which can only mean kindred in this context, to leave the common nest, an "arrangement which would work to the advantage of the friends but not of the children and in positive detriment to the mother, who has raised them on a small estate and taught them their trade." Thus the magistrates allowed her to keep the property of the two who had left home and only to give it to them if they returned and behaved as good children should toward their mother. If they remained away, she was to keep their property until the youngest boy had also left, a clear statement of the principle that the parent had the option of keeping the property of the older children until the youngest was emancipated; for the mother would have had problems supporting the youngest had she separated the property of the older boys from the "common nest."[53]

Most of the criminal practice of fourteenth-century Ghent regarding children diverged very little from the modern. Striking other people's children was actionable even if there was provocation.[54] Children, however, were to take care that they did nothing to provoke.[55] The idea that children worked and did not play is absurdly at variance with conditions in Ghent, but the magistrates' policy was that they should not play with dangerous animals or weapons, particularly after dark. Jan Goetkind was apparently walking peaceably along the street at night when he encountered some children playing with a hunting dog. Since he could not see what was happening, he apparently reacted instinctively and injured one boy. He paid 12 lb. par., which is substantial but covered only the costs of bed, doctor, and court. The *scepenen* added that "it is inappropriate to allow children to play with such dogs at odd times of the night in this manner, for everyone is supposed to keep his children under control."[56] One must remember that children would be unlikely to come to the attention of the city council unless they were misbehaving or had been injured. Hence the admonitions to punish or to be firm, statistically insignificant in themselves, may reflect nothing other than the circumstances of misbehavior. Children sometimes got hold of dangerous weapons or big animals, particularly during the revelry of the town festivals. Annin Arents in 1374 paid

72 lb. par. to Annin Masins for shooting him in the eye with an arrow. In 1360 the *scepenen* declared truce between Juris de Cammere and Jan Ebberechts and their minor sons, and the fathers were admonished "to chastise their children and keep them under control, so that they do not get into such games at the Shrove Tuesday celebrations." Parents evidently took sides in some of these frays and had artificially high expectations of behavior from other people's children, and the magistrates' tone becomes quite testy in handling such cases of hypersensitivity. In 1357 two men and their sons and clans were all included in a truce, "and each one is to keep his kid in his house as long as he is a minor if he does not want to let him play with other children."[57] We have clear instances, at all events, of play rather than work by children who are old enough to do quite a bit of damage.

The natural accidents among children could involve the parents, particularly when responsibility was an issue. The father or parents together were responsible in principle for damages done by the child, except that when the offending party was an orphan, the money came from his or her estate rather than from the property of the surviving parent. The clan was responsible for knowing any propensities of its young toward undesirable behavior and for taking action to prevent it, for example, in the case of a potentially dangerous mental retardate who was allowed to circulate at will. Just as the reputations of adult women were to be protected from malicious gossip, so were those of children, particularly girls, and violations here could be punished as severely as a violent act.[58]

The misbehavior of children then as now was a source of disquiet to their parents and kindred. It was physically impossible to control an unruly adolescent, let alone an even older person who was still under wardship. The father and guardian of Heinric Van Daelpitte complained in 1360 that he had "misbehaved terribly, had stolen and borrowed money and stolen horses" and had been imprisoned in France. The *scepenen* allowed the costs to be deducted from Heinric's property, since the problem was the ward's fault rather than the guardian's. Sending a bad boy away for a while to calm down was one solution. Gerem Portier's clan obtained the consent of the magistrates in 1360 to reimburse themselves a substantial sum that his "mismanagement" had cost them. They also situated him with the wife of Wulfram Van der Pale, who would take him to England and support him there for a year, evidently in connection with a family business. In 1363 the *scepenen* countenanced a further diminution of his property. But he was not the only problem child of this family. Gerem was apparently the third of four sons. In 1357 the paternal estate, which ordinarily would have been held undivided among the siblings until they were older, was divided among the brothers because of the misconduct of Goessin Portier, the eldest, so that the other boys would not be bound to his debts.[59]

The sources thus reveal some spectacular cases of misbehavior by children, but we have no way of judging their typicality. But when an adult prompted unacceptable behavior by a child, the magistrates punished only the adult, whatever chastisement the clan may have administered privately to the child. The child was clearly viewed as only indirectly responsible in such cases. Kateline de Quinkere and her granddaughter sued three persons for a misdeed stated to have been against the child but which in fact involved urging the girl to steal property from her grandmother and give it to the defendants. Family members, including mothers, could threaten or administer severe punishments for misbehavior. Jan Van Lovendeghem was forced in 1368 to pledge that if he ever again played dice, at which he had lost a vast sum of money in a single sitting, he would forfeit to his mother all his rights in a house, the debts owed to his late father, and a cog. Jacob Willebaert had to pledge "to act on the advice of father, mother, and friends, and to do nothing, nor engage in fighting, nor do anything else that might cause him to lose his temper or behave badly." He would lose all inheritance from both parents if he failed to abide by this.[60] A conspicuous case of bad conduct by a child involves Annin or Jan, apparently the eldest of three children of Jan de Bake. The parents were apparently opposed to the revolutionary régime that assumed power in Ghent in 1379, for in 1385 they complained that they had had to support Annin outside Flanders for six years, and he had made trouble for them the entire time. He had married without the consent of his parents and his clan. His mother had even given him the large sum of 10 lb. gr. without her husband's knowledge, a fair comment in itself on the ability of married women to act independently, but he had squandered it. Both parents now declared that they would be justified in having the *scepenen* declare him a "useless" child and hence disinherited. But since he had repented and pledged to make amends, they received him back on condition that he renounce his rights on the estate of either or both of his parents to his two brothers, since he had already taken more than his rightful third through his misconduct. Jan's exclusion was evidently adhered to. The mother settled the paternal estate with her three sons in 1390, but Jan got only his marriage portion, which would have predated the arrangement of 1385.[61]

Children were a source of pride and shame, an expense and a care, but also recipients of boundless if occasionally exasperated affection from their parents. It is the human condition. The extended family and the city government took a more impersonal and proprietary attitude toward the young than did the parents. This is only to be expected, since the clans and the *scepenen* only became concerned with children when the nuclear family was broken or could not cope with its youth. But genuine affection toward children is also shown by relatives other than the parents and also by persons evidently not kinsmen. Such a case involves Pieter Boudins, not a burgher of Ghent, who came to the city to support Wouterkin de Husene, and even agreed to do so without using any of the boy's property. The boy's parents were not burghers, and no guardianship was established because of Boudins's generosity.[62] Grandparents were sometimes lavish in their affection and on occasion took steps to protect their grandchildren against their children. This care could extend to bastards as well as to legitimate grandchildren.[63] In 1389 Heinric de Wevere settled 40 lb. gr. on one daughter and an equal amount on the children of another by her husband, Gerard de Coc, "due to their [the parents'] improper conduct." Childless persons of both sexes sometimes made bequests to the children of others, usually nieces or nephews. In these cases the bequest was sometimes to be nullified if the grantor had children of his or her own. A peculiar case of 1385 has the widow of Jacob Van Doinse giving to Simon de Smet and his wife, evidently her tenants, their residence. At the donor's death, however, the house was to pass to the de Smets' children on condition that they behave according to their parents' wishes. If they did not, the parents got full ownership.[64] The gift was obviously intended for the children, but the parents had a vested interest in declaring them contumacious.

Bastardy seems to have carried more legal than emotional disabilities in Ghent at this time. A case of 1380 hinged on the question of whether Gheenkin de Zwane was legitimate and hence an heir of his aunt Alice Van den Berghe. The boy's mother claimed that he was legitimate and "furthermore that Gheenkin had lived with Alice for a long time and had experienced many joys and sorrows with her and that she had recognized him on her deathbed as her heir." The heirs denied this but were willing to admit that she had willed him 3 lb. gr. from affection. We do not know the outcome, but it is clear that the boy's legitimacy was uncertain, that he had lived apart from his mother with an aunt, and that she had loved him.[65]

The records of Ghent tell us surprisingly little of infant mortality. The guardian was usually appointed before the orphan's property was re-corded, so that the guardian would be involved in the *staet* that he would be responsible to maintain. Only a statistically insignificant number of cases list a child under guardianship but not included when the *staet* is recorded and thus who presumably died in the interim. *Staten* were occa-sionally updated when one sibling died and the others inherited his or her share. There are also cases in which adult heirs of a child acquit the child's guardian of the estate. The total number of cases contained in the registers of the *scepenen* or *gedele* involving the estate of a deceased minor is re-corded by calendar year on Graph 3. This is not an index of total infant mortality, for it is confined to children who had outlived at least one parent or had inherited property from other sources. The youngest children, those dying within the first two years of life, would be included only ex-ceptionally. These figures are, however, important in illustrating years of relatively large numbers of deaths. There is a sudden rise in the early 1350s, a period of famine and high grain prices, but not of such an extent as to

Graph 3. Acquittals of Estates of Deceased Minors, Registers of *Scepenen* of *Gedele,* by Calendar Years

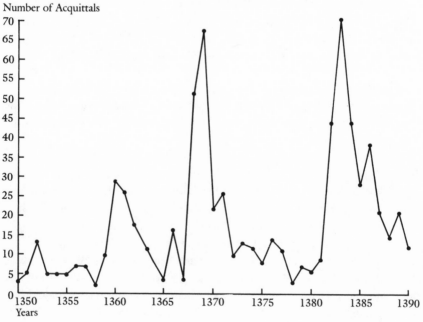

Source: SAG, registers of *scepenen* of *gedele*

suggest a major crisis. Between 1359 and 1362, years of plague and civil turmoil, there is a marked increase in the number of infant deaths. Mortality among minors reaches catastrophic proportions only in the plague years of 1368–71 and the early 1380s, a time of civil warfare, and the figures remain high throughout the 1380s even after the crisis had passed. Yet even when we make allowance for the limitations in our sources, these figures are astonishingly low for a traditional society.

But while infant mortality may have been less severe in Ghent than in comparable cities, the same records suggest that the individual conjugal family was a fleeting phenomenon, for few married couples survived as a unit until their children were adults. When an adult died childless, the law of Ghent provided that his estate would go to his children if he had them, or failing that to the clan by fixed rules unless both parents of the decedent were still alive and married to each other. The number of cases in which parents inherited from adult children in this way averages no more than one a year. Some idea of the duration of marriages can also be gathered from cases in which an adult child acquits one parent of the estate of the other but does not also acquit a guardian, in short in cases in which the parents stayed alive until at least one of their children reached adulthood. These figures are given on Graph 4. The number of such acquittals goes up in plague years, as one would expect. The lower figures during and after the war of 1379–85 reflect unusually heavy adult mortality during the conflicts. Although the records are incomplete, these figures are still very low for a population of some 12,000 nuclear families.

Arguments have been raised against using the *Staten van Goed* as demographic sources because only orphans with considerable property would be included.[66] That they are incomplete is undeniable, but the cause is sloppy bookkeeping by the city government, not any idea that poverty would exclude guardians of orphans from the duty of registering with the *scepenen*. Although most recorded *staten* contain at least enough property to support the children, there are some exceptions due to poverty of the estate or the large number of children, and such children were put on the charity of their collateral relations or prominent persons in the city. The children of Jan Volkers in 1352 inherited 30 gr. from their father, representing about four or five days' wages for a master artisan, perhaps a week and a half for a journeyman. Boykin Thomaes inherited only 2 lb. gr. from his father in 1356. We are not told the size of the estate of the children of Jan Van der Lake. It was evidently heavily encumbered, for when Diederic Van der Lake became their guardian, he did so without surrendering his

Graph 4. Duration of Marriages: Adult Child Acquits a Parent of Deceased's Parent's Estate

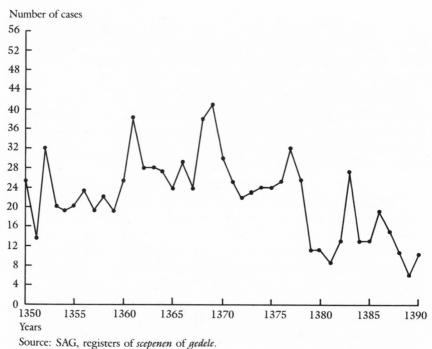

Number of cases

Years

Source: SAG, registers of *scepenen* of *gedele*.

right to financial claims against the children. Perhaps because of this conflict he was replaced as guardian after five months. His successor agreed that if the children inherited or otherwise acquired property, those currently supporting them would be repaid, "for their property is so miniscule that they cannot now be supported with it," a statement not only of the poverty of this estate, but also of the principle that children should be supported on the income of their own property.[67] Poor though they are, such estates included a cash value assigned to furnishings, personal effects, and chattels. It seems clear that if estates of this poverty were recorded, all should have been in principle. Many records simply acquit the surviving parent of the estate of the deceased without mentioning the size of the *staet*. Most of these estates were probably small, since holders of more complex estates would want their properties written down for the record.

There is less evidence than one might expect, however, that widows and orphans were having major financial problems. Most businessmen of Ghent seem to have operated cautiously. There were a few spectacular failures, but the fact that a widow or children could sell property may simply mean that they have no need of it, not distress. Complex estates were hard to administer, and most single women and children seem to have lived on small real estate investments, particularly in the city, and on rents. The sale of rents, a form of long-term borrowing, is a better index of financial need, for no one would sell them unless he or she needed money immediately, but the number of widows and orphans who sold rents is statistically insignificant. They frequently bought them, even converting other assets to cash for the purpose, for what persons in their position most often desired was a steady if modest source of regular income, not property that might bring a greater return but was risky. There can be no doubt that poverty was a serious problem in Ghent during this period, but, despite some very small *staten,* very little of it is reflected in the lists of orphans' property. Most cases where the estate is diminished substantially in money involved extraordinary expenses, such as the purchase of real estate, the payment of a blood price, or an estate heavily encumbered when the parent died. The guardians were naturally cautious with property not their own, and their investments, which had to be approved by the *scepenen,* tended to be conservative. There is very little evidence in the *staten* of heavy losses through merchandising or bad investments by the guardians.

Most married couples thus desired and cherished their children. Yet the loose sexual ethics of the day combined with the ecclesiastically enforced notion of the indissolubility of marriage and ineffective methods of contraception meant that the illegitimate child was a common figure in medieval Ghent. The social, economic, and legal impact of the high incidence of bastardy is the subject of the next chapter.

Chapter Eight

The Legitimacy
of Illegitimacy

Most of our information on attitudes toward children and childrearing comes from cases involving bastards, which are not necessarily applicable to legitimate children. Most surviving cases do not make illegitimacy seem an immense emotional disadvantage; but bastards whose parents were making written provision for them may have been exceptional. Certainly the offhandedness of many of the references to bastards suggest that the condition was widespread. There are isolated cases of bad behavior on the part of illegitimate children, which a psychologist might interpret as a reflection of rejection. Yet the total number of such cases pales beside the misdeeds committed by persons of unquestioned legitimacy.

Bastards definitely suffered legal disadvantages. They could inherit from the mother in fourteenth-century Ghent, evidently on the same basis as her legitimate children, and indeed from the entire maternal kindred.[1] But they could not inherit directly from the father. If he wished to acknowledge his bastards and leave them something, he had to specify an amount as a gift to be paid before his legitimate heirs divided the residue of his estate. We shall see that the total number of recorded bequests to bastards by their fathers is not large; but since they come from the "best" as well as the poorest families, the incidence of bastardy is probably rather high.

Even among aristocratic women there is a surprising amount of concubinage and illegitimacy.

The restrictions on marriage and divorce in medieval Europe meant that many men were in the position of St. Paul's sinful Christian, who was told to marry only if he could not control his passions in any other way. Those who were locked in an unpleasant marriage simply cohabited outside the conjugal bond. Most fathers in making provisions for their bastards say that they are doing it to settle the affairs of their souls; having bastards was clearly considered sinful.

The situation of bastards suggests a great deal about sexual ethics at this time. While families of good name can hardly have welcomed the idea of a daughter turning concubine, there are some cases in which relations with the man seem at least to have been correct, perhaps even amiable. When a lady is identified as the child of her father, it suggests that she is still relatively young and has close ties with her own family. Particularly where ongoing liaison is indicated, there was genuine affection and not simply sexual attraction between the pair. Jan Van Wassenhove acknowledged a debt of 18 lb. gr. to Kateline, daughter of the late Pieter Van St. Jacobshuus, for a loan in 1382, but she returned 6 lb of this to him in the event that he predeceased her and she died then without children. He also willed 8 lb. gr. to his bastard by her. Jan Jaquemins willed a gift to Mergriet Cauweric and their two bastards, but the bequest to Mergriet was unusually large because Jan had received money from her uncle. A suggestion of either the commonness of bastardy or the compassion of in-laws for a once wayward girl who has become respectable is given with Lisbette de Crane, wife of Jan de Sticheleere, who had a bastard daughter by Boudin Scride. She was holding a 5 lb. gift to her child from its father, who was also overseer of his daughter. We are not told whether Lisbette had conceived the child during her marriage to de Sticheleere, but his son was one of her sureties, although his father pledged to acquit him of any damages. We have thus a suggestion of an older man who married a young woman who may have been pregnant already, but this is impossible to prove. Certainly he and his family were "understanding" about it.[2] Little social stigma thus seems to have been attached to illegitimacy.[3]

The peculiar status of bastards led to confusion in nomenclature even more difficult than what we find with women and legitimate children. Bastards seem generally to have taken the father's name if he recognized them as his, even if the mother was guardian or had custody. If the father was not in evidence, but sometimes even if he was, particularly if the parents were no longer living together, the child took the mother's name. In the *staet* of his property, which was substantial and suggests illegitimacy at the highest levels of society, Jan Van der Corben took his mother's name, even though she was still alive and he was receiving a bequest from his late father, Jan Wouters; but in the establishment of wardship preceding the *staet* he was simply called the son of Jan Wouters. His sister Mergriet was called Jan Wouters's daughter.[4]

The incidence of bequests by fathers to their illegitimate children is given in Table 11, which is confined to the *Keure* registers. Fiscal years are

Table 11. Number of Bequests to Bastards by
Fathers, Registers of *Scepenen* of the *Keure*

Year	Sons	Daughters	Total Number of Bastards	Mother Included	Total Cases
1360–61	9	2	11	1	
1362–63	2	4	6	1	
1365–66	8	5	13	0	
1368–69	12	5	17	4	
1371	8	2	10	1	
1372	9	8	17	4	13
1373	9	8	17	3	13
1374	8	0	8	1	7
1375	9	11	20	1	9
1376	11	10	21	8	15
1377	8	9	17	3	13
1378	17	17	34	5	18
1379	10	8	18	0	11
1380	19	25	44	9	24
1381	20	15	35	3	23
1382	24	23	47	12	31
1383	12	4	16	0	10
1384	11	6	17	0	14
1385	1	4	5	2	
1387	3	13	16	1	11
1388	1	7	8	1	7
1389	10	7	17	3	14
1390	6	17	23	6	14

Source: SAG, Registers of *scepenen* of the *Keure*.

used until 1371, calendar years thereafter, except for the eight months of 1385 which were part of the previous fiscal year. When complete calendar years have survived, we have indicated the number of total cases represented by these figures.

The number of donations to bastards is rather steady in the teens until 1378, the year before the civil war began, when it jumps to thirty-four. The number remains high until 1382, thereafter declining to the prewar levels. These fathers clearly realized that they might die and wanted to provide for their illegitimate children. The table shows also a considerable callousness toward the mistresses, very few of whom were remembered along with their children. The distinctions by sex of the beneficiaries are not very revealing, evidently more an accident of the records than a desire in particular years to favor boys over girls or vice versa. The figures for the total number of fathers who were responsible for these bequests show that while most fathers limited themselves to one bastard, a sizable number sired entire families of illegitimate children, generally although not invariably by the same mother.

Table 12 lists the number of establishments of wardship for bastards, together with the number of bequests to them from all parties found in the registers of the *scepenen* of *gedele*. The discrepancies between total number of bastards and the figures from the two other columns comes from some cases mentioning a number of bastards of someone without differentiating sex. These records are clearly a less reliable index of bastardy than are the data from the *Keure*. Only in 1383 is there a substantial jump from a norm of five to ten per year before 1366 and ten to fifteen thereafter. The persons most likely to remember bastards were their natural fathers; but since mothers, from whom the bastards could inherit, would normally not remember them separately in testaments, our figures cannot conceivably be used as a total. Since bastards could be remembered at any time, while legitimate children usually do not enter the records until one parent has died, an index of bastardy cannot be constructed by comparison of the series.[5]

Our sources are quite enlightening about the treatment of bastards. We have seen that the father had sole rights in law over his legitimate children, but this passed to the mother with bastards. Neither the father nor his kindred could control illegitimate children unless the mother wished it or he married her. Most bastards were probably supported informally by their fathers. Most bequests seem to have been made only when the father thought he might die soon, although some fathers lived long enough to

Table 12. Donations to Bastards by All Persons, Including Parents, and Establishments of Wardship for Bastards, Registers of *Scepenen* of *Gedele*

Year	Boys	Girls	Total Number of Bastards	Year	Boys	Girls	Total Number of Bastards
1349	1	0	1	1370	3	6	9
1350	0	0	0	1371	6	6	14
1351	9	4	13	1372	7	3	10
1352	1	1	2	1373	5	8	13
1353	2	2	4	1374	–	1	6
1354	2	–	7	1375	5	4	9
1355	1	0	1	1376	2	0	2
1356	2	0	2	1377	3	5	8
1357	1	0	1	1378	6	4	10
1358	3	1	4	1379	4	2	6
1359	1	3	4	1380	7	5	12
1360	2	1	3	1381	3	7	10
1361	1	0	1	1382	8	6	14
1362	9	6	15	1383	25	13	41
1363	2	3	5	1384	11	8	20
1364	5	1	7	1385	13	6	26
1365	1	1	2	1386	8	11	19
1366	1	0	1	1387	8	6	14
1367	6	4	10	1388	3	7	10
1368	9	6	15	1389	8	8	16
1369	8	9	17	1390	13	10	23

Source: SAG, Registers of *scepenen* of *gedele*.

revoke their donations later. The father could impose conditions of any sort on the bequests. A case of 1358 directed that the money never fall into the hands of the mother or her clan and made the awards conditional upon the guardian coming from the father's side. Although this was unusual, the fact that the mother's clan did not contest it and the *scepenen* ruled it valid clearly establishes its legality, although the language suggests that the magistrates might have ruled differently had there been objections.[6]

The rights of bastards to inherit could become quite complicated. Most bequests, whether made by the father or some other person, were to revert to the legitimate heirs if the bastard died childless. Although the property of deceased bastards was not automatically confiscated by the officials of

Ghent, as it was by the count's men in the rural areas, only bastards' children could inherit from them. All others had to surrender the property when a bastard died, and this was a significant part of the city's income from the *exuwe* fine.

The principle is clearly stated in the suit of Jan Van den Zande on behalf of his wife against her cousin's estate. Both women were legitimate themselves, but their mothers had been the bastard daughters of two legitimate Borluut brothers. The *scepenen* ruled that in such a case a collateral relative could not inherit, and they warned Jan Van den Zande against any more threats against the city tax collector, who was only doing his duty. In 1354 Jan Loetins and his sisters were excluded from the estate of the late wife of Ser Jacob Van den Rijsekin, "since they were descended from bastards on that side." Lisbette de Baertmakere had willed that her estate be liquidated and a rent bought for her natural child. The child's guardian argued that the rent, which was hereditary, was unnecessary, since the child was inheriting the mother's property anyway. But the magistrates ruled the testament valid, since the mother had also directed that the rent would go to a chantry if the boy died without issue, while otherwise the money would revert to her legitimate heirs.[7]

Since records were poorly kept, even some members of the local aristocracy were uncertain whether they were legally married to each other. Inevitably there was confusion about the legal standing of the children of such unions. The heirs of Simon de Rijke in 1355 contested the validity of Simon's marriage with Lisbette Mortemans and thus the legitimacy and capacity of her child to inherit. The considered judgment of the city clerks was that their consciences told them that "Lisbette honestly was more legal wife than not," and the clerks accordingly could not adjudicate. The *scepenen* ruled that the child was legitimate until someone could prove the contrary. While a bastard child could inherit from a maternal grandfather, the latter's legitimate heirs might contest this if the mother was not still alive. In 1360 the *scepenen* first allowed but then disallowed the seizure of a share of the estate of Jan Van den Hecke by Michiel de Pachteneere on behalf of his daughter. De Pachteneere's child was his legitimate daughter by the bastard daughter of Jan Van den Hecke. The legitimate heirs carried the argument "that if the child's mother were alive, she could not be an heir, and the property could not descend to her by law; thus since it could not come to the mother from her father, so it should not come to her child on her father's account."[8] Some puzzling cases even suggest that bastards might be excluded from their mothers' estates. In 1391 Mergriet de Backere, wife of Jacob Roelins and with her husband, willed 20 lb. gr. to her natural daughter by Meester Zeger de Backere, "from maternal affection, since she cannot inherit any property from her."[9] It is possible that the mother had been disinherited by her own kin; and particularly since she had later married, her inheritance would be affected, although this did not hinder legitimate children of remarried mothers from inheriting from them.

Certainly marriage and the passage of time would affect the estate that a bastard might inherit from his or her mother. In 1371 Merkin, the legitimate daughter of Jan Van den Weghe, inherited 4 lb. (80s.) gr. from her mother, Kateline de Boene. The mother had previously had two bastards, and Jan Van den Weghe had been holding their property, 50s. for a girl and 74s. for a boy. Although these differences are substantial, the legitimate child would inherit half the mother's common property with the father and would thus naturally have a larger estate than her bastards.[10] Bastards thus inherited whatever the mother possessed in her own right when she died, and any gifts from the natural father, but nothing from the mother's later husband.

Since a grant to a bastard would be permanent only if the bastard had legitimate children of his own, a second generation was needed to make the bequest final. Boudin de Quinkere of Zwijnaarde, south of Ghent, agreed to leave his entire estate to his adult bastard Heinric in return for lifetime support, with the usual provision of reversion to the legitimate heirs if Heinric died childless. Heinric then died, but after siring a legitimate son, who in turn died a minor; the widow and her new husband argued successfully that his birth meant that the legitimate heirs of his grandfather were not entitled to the reversion of his estate.[11]

One of our best examples of the complexities of bastardy and its impact on inheritance involves Merkin, daughter of Matte Van Zeverne, allegedly by Heinric, son of Heinric Veleven. The girl's potential heirs denied her illegitimacy, claiming that Matte had had a husband when Merkin was born and that her declaration was the only evidence of Heinric's paternity. Matte had apparently coached the child to say that Heinric was her father, but the heirs retorted that such a detail was impossible for Merkin to know, which should be obvious enough to anyone who stops to think about it. Hence the *scepenen* ruled that the child was without prejudice until she reached her majority, when a court would determine paternity. Heinric's heirs were to hold 4 lb. 10s. gr. at *pensioen,* and the mother would support Merkin with the income.[12] Why the court would have more information about Merkin's paternity later than soon after the fact is unclear, unless perhaps it hoped to detect a physical resemblance between the mature woman and either the alleged father or the mother's husband. Since there was some money from the estate of Heinric Veleven, he apparently thought that he was the father, and it is at least possible that the magistrates were leaving open the possibility of ruling her bastard or legitimate depending on which would be most advantageous for her financially.

Testamentary bequests to bastards might have limitations or conditions similar to those for legitimate children. Many testaments were oral. When death seemed imminent, the family and parish priest would gather at the scene, and some deathbed bequests or acknowledgments of debt were recorded by the oaths of witnesses. When a bequest to a bastard, made to clear one's soul, was part of one's confession to the priest, the latter would record what he had heard in a document under his personal seal and give it to the heirs. Since most oral testaments were made before witnesses, they occasioned little controversy. Hence in 1363 Lye sHerts had to sue the heirs of her late paramour Lodewijc Van den Woelpitte, who had made bequests to their child and to her "for God and services." She proved her case with witnesses to the testament, which was evidently oral. In 1362 Jan de Meyere Van Maelte willed 30 lb. gr. and personal effects to Lisbette Van den Damme and Annekin, his child by her. But since he conceded that enforcing this against his legitimate heirs might be troublesome, he also willed 10 lb. each to the count of Flanders, the abbot of St. Pieter's, and the city of Ghent to help the beneficiaries, a clear statement that the city charged for its legal services in such cases. The father had died by 1367, and members of his clan became guardians of this boy and for a legitimate child also named Annekin. Only from 1372 do we have an estate probated for the bastard, and it includes only 15 lb., since the rest of the bequest had gone to his mother. The money was held by his legitimate half-brother, who was paying him 1 lb. gr. in *pensioen*, appreciably less than the usual 10 percent. His mother was supporting him with the income. The estate of the legitimate child, which was listed one week later, was much larger. It was rare for a father to will so much to a bastard that he would seriously affect the property of legitimate children unless he had a grievance against one of them.[13]

The bastard thus did not lack legal rights but was nonetheless vulnerable. A legitimate child could be disinherited only for cause; a bastard had no such safeguard. A bequest to bastards that limited the mistress but raised the possibility of turning children into tattlers was that of Gillis Van Beverne to his three children by Lisbette de Droeghe. He left them a large amount of cash on condition that if any of the children reached majority "and conduct themselves improperly, in disgrace to and defiance of their friends," the money would revert to those children "who conducted themselves appropriately and acted on their friends' counsel." The mechanics of enforcement are unclear, but the clan definitely had a role in preserving its own good name through the conduct of its bastards as well as of the legitimate children. Gillis Van Beverne also kept the mistress under control by giving her 9 lb. gr. that technically belonged to their children; but the money would be hers to keep if Gillis never ordered her to release it to them.[14] In 1376 Jan Bullaert annulled a donation which he had earlier made to his son, who must have been a bastard, since the special gift was necessary, and transferred it to the son's bastard daughter, who took her father's family name. But he also empowered his kindred to take back the money and hold it for her until they thought she would conduct herself properly if she ever got the money and misbehaved. There were also conflicts over priests' bequests to their bastards. In 1373 the priest Thomaes Uten Berghe willed his house to Mergriet Fraytops "for services." He had died by 1380, when his legitimate heirs—all of them in the female line and with their husbands—unsuccessfully contested the bequests to Mergriet and her two adult sons, one of whom had followed his father's holy calling. The liaison was clearly of long-standing. The predicament of an illegitimate daughter is shown clearly with Betkin de Duutsche, who was willed 5 lb. gr. by her natural father Jan on condition that she abide by the wishes of her guardian, whose identity was presumably known before the father's death, and the guardian's son. The girl was defenseless, for in 1377 her money was being held by her father's widow and the stepmother's new husband, who were supporting her. Yet their willingness to do so in the absence of a blood tie and hence legal obligation suggests affection for her.[15]

In most cases there was little if any difference in the way a father would treat bastard boys and girls in his will. As with legitimate children there may have been a slight disposition to favor girls, probably because they were less likely to find a profitable trade. There are some cases of clear favoritism of a son, as when Daneel Van den Boemgaerde willed his two bastard daughters 25 lb. gr. jointly and the same amount to one son. The admonitions to behave as the clan directs is common in bequests to both legitimate and illegitimate children by persons not their parents. But the language of one paternal donation to a bastard suggests an exceptional degree of dependence. In 1377 Ghiselbrecht de Grutere, one of the richest men of Ghent, willed 60 lb. gr. to his adult bastard Jan, but he "admonished Jan to serve Ghiselbrecht's heirs well and loyally for his entire life-time. He will remain bound and subordinated to them, as is appropriate, and Jan has consented to this."[16] The words "serve" and "subordinate" are simply not found with legitimate children, who received more general ad-monitions to behave themselves as the clan thought appropriate. The im-plications are obvious: a legitimate child would eventually inherit some-thing from its father anyway, but a bastard would not.

The mother was ordinarily appointed guardian of her illegitimate chil-dren, but the father seems frequently to have been chosen overseer in cases where he did not simply renounce all interest in his bastards. Jan Stoffe apparently sired three bastards by two mothers. In 1368 he was overseer of two, who had inherited 6 lb. 4s. gr. from their mother, Lisbette de Bru-were. The guardian was Willem de Bruwere, a maternal kinsman, and Stoffe pledged to support the children with their maternal inheritance undiminished. He also willed them 4 lb. gr. from his own property. He had died by 1378, after fathering another bastard daughter, who had 6 lb. gr. from her mother and 10 lb. from Stoffe. Proof that the mother or her family normally furnished the guardian of bastards is the case of the chil-dren of Gillis Van Westergem. A guardian was named in 1360 for a natural daughter named Callekin and in 1363 for three legitimate children. An es-tate was probated in 1374 for two of those named here; the third evidently had died. Another guardianship under Joos de Meester was established in 1364 for his two natural children by Zoetin de Meester. We are never told what property the bastards had, but they were clearly under a regimen different from that of the legitimate children, whose guardian came from the father's side.[17]

Relations with the father and his clan were obviously extremely com-plex. A mother could hardly conceal an illegitimate child, but the male could easily deny paternity. Thus the mother ordinarily raised the child, even if there was no property. Mothers sometimes took their paramours to court over their obligations toward the bastards, but most of our evidence of paternal involvement are cases in which the father, however reluctantly, admits paternity and concedes some financial liability toward the child or children, although most of these engagements take effect only at the fa-ther's death.

Fathers and their kin could become upset if the mother were negligent. Jan Van der Vesten left 4 lb. gr. to his natural daughter Callekin on condi-tion that she remain with his clan, which furnished the guardian, even after the mother had been acquitted of or served her punishment for homicide, and on condition that the mother not live with another man.[18] Some men tried to renege on agreements to provide for their bastards, but the *scepenen* normally considered these binding contracts.

The story of illegitimacy is clearly involved with that of prostitution, but the extent of that involvement is difficult to determine. Jan Van Audenarde sired a bastard by one Mergriet de Culstreker, whose name, which means "Margaret the Buttockstroker," leads one to suspect a prostitute who failed to take precautions. Some males as well as females seem to have carried on a family tradition of promiscuity. Two men named Jan Van Wassenhove, the sons of Inghelbrecht and Boudin respectively, left bastards by different mistresses.[19]

Some fathers did become guardians of their bastards. The guardian of Annekin de Voghel, who took his mother's family name, was Arnoud Steeland, who was either the boy's father or paternal grandfather of the same name. The priest Hugh Van der Most was also the guardian of his own bastard. The father rather than the mother sometimes handled custody arrangements for the bastards. Some fathers were not above using custody of the child as a weapon against the mother. Willem Arents agreed in 1391 to surrender his bastard to the mother on condition "that she will support the child without his cost and will never again come by day or night before Willem's house and try to make conversation, disturbance, or conflict." He agreed to show this courtesy to her. What makes this case peculiar and probably abnormal is that the mother had apparently surrendered the child to his father, then wanted him back.[20]

The more prominent the father's clan, the more likely it was to be able to exercise rights over illegitimate children. In 1362 Mergriet Van der Capellen became guardian of the two bastards of her brother, Ser Pieter Van der Capellen. The older boy, Annekin, was apprenticed to a furrier in 1365, but only on condition that his mother agreed to leave him for the entire three-year term and "not take him back or release him from the contract." The mother was holding Annekin's money under the support undiminished formula three years later. She was clearly involved in Annekin's upbringing, and the boy may have been living with her, although his paternal aunt was his legal guardian. A similar case involved the daughter of Staes Boye, whose father bequeathed her 50 lb. gr. in 1381. He evidently died in late 1387, and Jan Boye became guardian and the girl's mother overseer.[21] Since so much property was involved, the issue was probably that the money would revert to the paternal line if the child died without issue. The mother was more likely to be the guardian when the *staet* was of less value.

Bastard children seem to have been subjected to the same peculiar custody arrangements that affected legitimate children. Pieter Van Beveren, evidently the guardian, had been holding 15 guldine belonging to Annekin, bastard of Zoetin Van Berghine, but as of April 1, 1375, when the child was "about five years old," he surrendered the money to Zoetin, who agreed to support him until his majority. We are not told that the guardian had been raising the infant, but the transfer of money makes it probable. Lievin de Sceerre was the guardian of Willem Coelman's three natural children in 1361; when the *staet* was furnished the following March, the unnamed mother was to support one boy with the interest on money held by Pieter Coelman; the fate of the second child is unclear, and the third is not mentioned in the *staet*.[22] In a similar case a man with no apparent blood relationship to the mother became guardian of a bastard, while the father was overseer, held money from the boy's maternal estate, and promised to teach him his trade and support him. The money was to revert to the maternal kindred if the boy died; but it is clear that they had no trouble accepting this father, Lievin Van Axel, who was the scion of a prominent butcher family. A new guardian was appointed in 1359. By then the father was Ser Lievin, suggesting that his father had died and he had become the leader of his clan. The boy was emancipated in 1362 and is called "Lievin Van Axel the bastard." He thereupon launched a career in street combat.[23]

There seems to be little doubt that bastards' fathers were thought to have legal and moral obligations toward them, but a necessary precondition of such obligation was for the man to admit paternity. Unless the mother could prove that he was the only male with whom she had had sexual relations, there would be little that she could do if he contested it, and a few cases survive in which the man denies the allegation. Jan de Mulre was told by the *scepenen* in 1363 that if he wished to have information from Aechte Pijnaerts about her child, he had to go to the church court. The lady was on her right thereafter "for all that the dean awards for her bad reputation and disgrace." The parties were to take their disputes over costs of childbed and child support to a secular court. Some hesitation by the natural father is shown in the case of Lievin Mannaert. His two legitimate children inherited substantial properties from his wife, whose estate was probated March 20, 1358. In 1361, while never explicitly admitting paternity, he acknowledged that from March 1, 1358, he had owed a life annuity in grain to Kateline Akets, who in turn would support her daughter Merkin until her majority, and also would pay half the costs of supporting her son Liefkin for the next four years. In return for this she acquitted Lievin Mannaert of all claims. Lievin thus did not want to admit paternity but could not deny that he had had sexual relations with the lady and was paying a price to keep her silent.[24]

More often the man admitted culpability, although sometimes after initial hesitation. In 1350 Mergriet Van den Eeke was awarded 2s. gr. in arrears of what the saddler Willem de Groete owed her for childbed costs, together with 3s. gr. annually for the child's life. We have seen that this amount was insufficient, but it might have been enough if the mother or her relatives contributed a like amount. In a more edifying case of 1391 Jan Bloume pledged to support his daughter, who took his name. She was six months old, and he pledged to provide her complete support in food, drink, clothing, and shoes, and other necessities for the next six years. The parents would support her at common cost thereafter. Since the term is "support her," rather than "have her supported," the parents were probably living together and expected to continue doing so. The six-year term is peculiar; perhaps they expected the mother to be working and bringing in an income by that time. When the natural father died after admitting paternity, his blood heirs were responsible for fulfilling his bequests to his bastards unless they had grounds for a legal challenge. The heirs might also be responsible for the mother's childbed costs as an expense incurred by the father. Widows were not liable for any donations of their husbands to bastards unless they expressly agreed to share costs.[25]

The obligations of fathers to support their natural children are shown nicely in two cases of 1380. When Jan Roetstoc willed 12 lb. gr. to his natural daughter by Mergriet Van den Moure, he ordered the girl's mother to be compensated for her trouble and support costs, presumably by the father or his heirs. Ellin Van den Pitte actually made a contract with his former maid, by whom he had a child. He agreed to support the child and act as its father without the mother's cost. The girl had been in the service of his late wife, for which he also pledged compensation; she was leaving or had left his service, and he was honoring his duty to support his illegitimate child.[26]

Fathers' obligations to support their bastards continued until maturity, although such assistance could be commuted. But the form taken by most paternal bequests is very suggestive of standards of sexual morality and customs. The standard was for the father to will the bastards a decent amount, while their mother would get either nothing or a small re-membrance "for services."[27] Fathers probably valued their bastards, who were blood relations, more highly than their mistresses, but they may also have been motivated by the fact that the women had their own property and kin. We also do not know what provisions men may have made in private charters for their paramours.

Many of these arrangements suggest a continuing liaison, particularly when bequests are to be shared by children born later to the same mother. Hence Heinric de Muelre willed 6 lb. gr. to Beatrise Uten Houke if he predeceased her. If she died first and had children by him, the gift would go to the children in equal shares. The carpenter Jan de Peister willed 25 lb. gr. to his bastard Annekin, who took his family name, but the bequest was to be shared with any children whom he might have subsequently by the same mother, if this much remained in his estate when he died. He clearly was unable to marry the woman for some reason, but he considered her and her children his family and was evidently leaving nothing to his legiti-mate kin.[28]

Some men had permanent housekeeping arrangements with mistress and bastards while continuing to have relations with their wives. In late 1372 the tanner Ghiselbrecht de Scouteete left six bastards by one mother but no legitimate children. The liaison was clearly of long-standing, and two of the girls were still under tutelage in 1383. His widow contested his substantial bequests to them, but the testament was upheld in 1375, and the oldest illegitimate son was destined for his father's profession through ap-prenticeship to another tanner. While Ghiselbrecht de Scouteete may have been separated from his wife, Jan Casteleyn was raising two families. In 1380 he willed 2 lb. gr. to each of his bastard sons by Lisbette Van Erpe. Noting that Lisbette was pregnant by him again, he raised the amount to 3 lb. gr. in 1382 and included the same amount for the unborn child. Casteleyn's wife died in 1384, leaving three legitimate daughters by him, and he became their guardian. The term "love child" is not a modern invention, for it is found in the fourteenth-century texts, suggesting that unions that produced natural children were generally the result of un-guarded affection or of love that could not be sanctioned by the marriage laws of the medieval church.[29]

By no means all of our cases involve hot-blooded youths or concupis-cent older men with younger women. Lisbette Craymans was half-owner of a house near the Béguinage of St. Lisbette by 1335. She bought out the co-owners in 1344. Since the diminutive is never used for her name, she was presumably at least in her twenties by 1335. In 1359 she sold the house to Jacob Bette; but on October 31 of that year Bette in turn gave the house in alms to Merkin, his daughter by Lisbette, while giving Lisbette rent-free residence in the place for life with Merkin. The land tax books show Lisbette Craymans paying through 1383, with no mention of either Jacob Bette or Merkin. From 1346 she is called *joncvrouw*, normally a title of respect reserved for mature women, in the tax records. She thus must have had a single illegitimate child in her forties by one of the most prominent men of the city.[30]

Concubinage was probably inevitable in a society that placed such restrictions upon marriage and divorce. But there are considerations that suggest that bastardy and concubinage were generally accepted far beyond the extent statistically demonstrable. Several wives, for example, joined with their husbands in setting up endowments for the husbands' bastards, although, of course, some husbands may have used physical or psychological coercion to get their wives to agree to use their own funds. Some wives attach conditions to their bequests, suggesting reluctance to make them, while others show genuine affection, suggesting that the natural child was familiar to them, perhaps living in the same house as a member of the family. While many bastards were the fruits of the man's premarital liaisons, as we have seen, some childless wives seem to have accepted the fact that their husbands, desiring children—a fact relevant for the overall notion of children and their desirability at this time—would sire bastards by other women and that there was nothing especially remarkable in this. A widow might even become the guardian of her husband's illegitimate children, and nothing could have forced any woman to assume that responsibility had she not desired to do so. In such cases the widow clearly thought of the youngsters as her own children.[31]

But while some wives accepted their husbands' bastards, and a few husbands their wives', there is also some evidence of hostility on the part of the spouses, usually coming out only after the death of the bastard's parent. Although the widow was not bound to honor her husband's bequests to his bastards, since these funds were to come from his heirs' half of common property, she was entitled to compensation for half of what he gave as a marriage portion to a bastard daughter. Bastards could find that their claims on the estate of their natural parents were admitted in principle, but that the heirs might dispute liability among themselves for the actual payment, particularly where sons-in-law became liable for payments to their wives' bastard kin. The mistress and her bastard were vulnerable vis à vis the widow and the legitimate heirs, and litigation sometimes could last for lengthy periods. Gillis de Mulre had died by January 20, 1382, when his two legitimate daughters were assigned guardians. On March 16 Mergriet Bernaerts sued the widow and heirs for various parcels of property and money that she claimed to have loaned Gillis, as well as for substantial monetary damages and child support that Gillis had promised. She accepted a settlement that included commutation of the child support in August, but litigation continued. In January 1383 the heirs were ordered to give her the money that Gillis had transferred to her under his seal, but she in turn was to return various chattels and personal effects. Despite the likely antagonism, widows were sometimes entrusted with the money or rents that their husbands willed to their natural children.[32]

There seems to have been surprisingly little housekeeping as experimental marriage. Most concubinage either resulted from the standard causes—lust on the part of one or both and perhaps economic dependence with the woman—or from an impediment to marriage, such as priesthood, separation from a hostile spouse, or occasionally entailment of an estate on condition that one remain single. Gifts made to a bastard whose parents later married could be valid if the child wished it but had to be renounced if he wanted to share in the regular division of his father's estate. Although most natural children would benefit from the father marrying the mother, there could be motives against it. A case of 1349 has bastards consenting to their father marrying their mother, although he claimed to be doing it to make them his legitimate heirs. They pledged to make no claims against him regarding their mother's estate.[33] If the father had less property than the mother, the children could actually lose if he married her, since he would acquire dower rights over her estate, which otherwise would have passed directly to the children.

Another indication that bastardy carried mainly a legal and proprietary but not a moral or social stigma is that so many women of the upper classes had paramours and bastards. Nomenclature does not help much here, for even extremely prominent people had namesakes with no blood tie. But some cases can be documented clearly. That men of the upper classes would seek liaisons should occasion no surprise, but they often sought out women of their own social milieu.

Some cases are shown by the amount of property involved. In 1390 Jan Toete willed 25 lb. gr. to his natural daughter by the daughter of Jan Damman vor tGravensteen, a prominent spice dealer who was a member of one of the most distinguished lineages of the city. The bastard daughter of

Gerolf Ser Simoens by Lisbette Van den Zomple had two wealthy parents; her father willed her the enormous sum of 80 lb. gr. In 1368 Daneel de Coyere, a retainer of the lord of Lovendegem, made provision for his three bastards by three different mothers, one of them the daughter of Ser Jacob de Pape. Heilzoete Mayhuus, presumably of the shipping family, was the mother of two girls by Jurdaan SerSanders.[34]

The heirs' reasons for caution in dealing with bastards were not necessarily the result of hard-heartedness, particularly when the decedent also left legitimate children. Meester Maechlein Van St. Baefs, of a family prominent since the thirteenth century, died in late 1355 or early 1356, leaving a will, two legitimate children, a woman who claimed to be his wife, and a bastard son. A preliminary arrangement settled all claims except those of the bastard, and when the arbitrators took up his case in early 1357 they stated that they did not wish to deprive him of all property, but that they feared that the estate would escape the family if he died without issue "and for other reasons too long to write." They nonetheless secured 33 lb. par in rents for him, specifying reversion to the father's side if he died childless, something which would have been harder to enforce had he been given cash.[35]

Bastards almost always received less money in wills than the legitimate children got through regular division of the estate. In 1381 Jan de Meyere of Zegelsem willed 10 lb. gr. to each of his two bastards. One had died without heirs by 1396, and the survivor acquitted the bequest since his father now had "many legitimate children" for whom he had to provide, and a new arrangement had been made for the bastard. How typical this case is can only be surmised, but on June 11, 1361, Ser Pieter Van den Damme, a prominent dyer, gave 60 lb. gr. to his son Arend for services rendered for as long as he had been able to do so, which probably means that he had worked since adolescence, and which he still performed for his trade and household. In return the son would pay the father a substantial life annuity; the older man was apparently retiring from business. Almost as an afterthought Ser Pieter willed 3 lb. gr. to his bastard.[36]

Since bastards were less likely than legitimate children to have adult champions, they were perhaps more subject to fraud and abuse, although very little direct evidence has survived. In a flagrant case Jan Lichtvoet agreed in 1351 that the natural children of his brother Philips would pay him 6 lb. gr. and in return get everything else in his estate. He was dead by 1355, and the guardians of the children were their cousin, Jan Liehtvoet the younger, and their brother-in-law, Arnoud Zelle. These men apparently had swindled the older Lichtvoet by representing to him that there was less in the estate than was actually the case and pocketing the difference. They were sent on pilgrimages; yet Zelle continued to be the guardian of Liefkin Lichtvoet as late as 1360.[37]

When men sought refuge from domestic unpleasantness in illicit house-keeping arrangements, their emotional preferences were naturally reflected in their wills. Jan Van der Wostinen had a liaison for many years with Aechte de Meyere. In 1366 he willed 10 lb. gr. to his two bastards by her and smaller amounts to his sister and her two daughters. These children may have died, for in 1377, without mentioning them, he willed 30 lb. gr. to a third bastard by Aechte. He evidently did this on his deathbed, for on November 14, 1377, a guardian was appointed, apparently from the father's side. On December 20 the widow's son, Jan de Hodeverre, and the legitimate heirs sued Aechte for numerous properties, including a house that Van der Wostinen had given to her. The *scepenen* acquitted her of all claims except those concerning his personal effects. The 30 lb. bequest to the youngster was enough for a comfortable living allowance, although like most people in Ghent she suffered a loss of income during the war of the 1380s.[38] Her father had apparently left most of his property to her rather than to his legitimate heirs.

That bastards were considered an integral if somewhat legally disadvantaged part of the family is shown by the treatment of some adult bastards. Minor children, legitimate and natural alike, would ideally be treated affectionately, but one also detects a certain reserve in these records, perhaps because of the likelihood of early death. Yet parents and particularly fathers also respected their children as co-workers, a natural consequence of the early use of children as laborers. There is more evidence at Ghent of fathers treating their minor children as near-equals than of mothers leaning on the judgment of adult sons. We have seen that some fathers willed property to their bastards on grounds that they had been kinder to them than their legitimate children. In 1379 Pieter Moeraert gave to his adult bastards, one of them a married woman, 20 lb. gr. each because "they loyally helped Pieter to acquire his property with their labor, as good children."[39] Both bastards and legitimate children were used as domestic servants. Some bequests were large enough to suggest more than a desire simply to acquit one's soul, but rather strong affection, particularly when the natural children were adults who had proven themselves loyal.[40] The emotional bonds linking fathers with their adult bastards are shown in the case of Gillis Truebe. In 1383 he willed 4 lb. gr. to his bastard daughter and her husband, who in return agreed to care for him during his illness. He also left 12 lb. gr. to his bastard son under the same terms, but he added the proviso that Gillis's own property would pay expenses. While it is possible that the son was being favored over the daughter, it is unlikely that she would have agreed to support him under those circumstances. She probably had received a marriage gift that has not survived in the record, and the extra bequest to the son was intended to equalize, as was standard practice with legitimate heirs. In a similar case of 1382 Lievin de Vos of Oosterzele, who was prominent at Ghent, willed 40 lb. gr. and all his weapons and equipment to his bastard Gillis, in return for "many good services and serious labors of trips which Gillis had had to make outside the city during these wars for his father, and he had sustained great anxiety, fear, and danger in life and limb" and had remained faithful to him and had never been rewarded.[41] This bastard was evidently the father's main support, and it was in the father's power to reward him accordingly. There are enough cases of this nature to suggest that many fathers did not view their bastards simply as inconvenient reminders of incontinence, but as children valued as much as the legitimate offspring. We hear little of the attitude of women toward their adult bastards, probably because the legal bond of the mother was less complex than that of the father. Most surviving cases suggest affection, although there are exceptions. There are occasional glimpses of the regard that could develop between bastards, even those placed in a menial position, and their legitimate siblings. When Willem de Houveneere died in 1390, his children were old enough to be heard by the *scepenen,* for they told of the many services that Betkin, their father's bastard, had performed for him and their stepmother. In recognition of this the magistrates awarded Betkin a small amount from the property of the legitimate children. She is called Betkin when the document begins, but thereafter the adult form Bette, suggesting that she had probably been an indiscretion of the father's youth who had been forced to serve him and those children who had had the good fortune of generation only after the paternal wild oats had been sown and reaped.[42]

Part Three

Pride and Lineage

Chapter Nine

Clans at Peace

F amily history is ultimately genealogy, which is extremely difficult to trace in medieval Ghent, as we have seen. Given names tend to run in families, so that unless one person is called "son of" another, it is sometimes impossible to tell whether different documents refer to one or more people. The Flemish habit of identical names even extended to giving two children by different spouses the same name when both children were alive.[1] One does wonder how anyone knew who was calling whom in some of these establishments. Second, terminology for in-laws frequently merged with that for the blood kin, although separate words existed. Persons who are clearly parents-in-law will be called "our parents,"[2] while "father" is sometimes used when the person can only be a stepfather.[3] In-laws were considered family members who were expected to assume the amities and hostilities of the other clan. "Brother" can mean either half-brother or brother-in-law.[4] Although words did exist to distinguish in-laws, there is no separate terminology to distinguish children who shared both parents from those who shared one. This fact, together with the complications of remarriage, results in parents often not having the same patronymic as their children. Although the name changes of females make it especially difficult to trace them, kinship ties through the mother were no less keenly felt than were the paternal, and under most circumstances the clans on both the maternal and paternal sides shared property equally. Hence many relationships described in the records that seem to have no family tie may actually refer to cousins or descendants in the female line.

Titles can sometimes indicate order of priority within clans. "Ver" is used frequently for women but does not seem to have denoted a legal standing. One finds it for dowagers, usually for mature widows, occasionally for younger widows. "Meester" indicates a master of arts, such as a clerk or a physician. It is not ordinarily used as a title to indicate mastership in a guild, although it is occasionally found in this context. "Der" is used for men in holy orders, but it also indicated the senior male of an extended family, even if the person was young. On December 5, 1356, the guardian of Simon Braem's children acquitted their mother of Simon's estate. The *scepenen* simultaneously emancipated the eldest son Jan, who then became "der Jan" in the same document as the senior male of his kindred.[5] But "der" also seems to have been used as a general title of respect and veneration. It evidently conferred no additional powers on its bearers.

We do not propose to contribute to the historiographical debate over the relative importance of the nuclear and the extended family in medieval Europe. It is clear that both were critical. We have seen that while the nuclear family was the basic social unit, few nuclear families survived intact for more than a few years. We have seen that the clan intervened in the affairs of the nuclear family only infrequently as long as both husband and wife were alive. The only exceptions involve cases in which the property of the entire clan might be affected by the poor judgment of a member. But the clan did intervene to protect orphans and widows and to protect themselves from any irresponsibility by clan members which might bind the rest. Once the conjugal family was severed by death or separation, the clan could usurp the domain of the surviving spouse over the children. In-laws were considered part of the extended family circle. The clan exercised social functions which only recently have been assumed by governmental agencies.

Considerations other than the high death rates and frequent remarriages made the nuclear family a less self-contained unit than tends to be the case today. First, wetnurses were used by those who could afford them, although we have little direct information on this point for Ghent. Second, boys became apprentices, usually in their teens, and most guilds did not allow the father to be his own son's master, although some stepfathers were. The plethora of half-siblings and stepchildren meant that most persons felt kinship with a far greater number of individuals and nuclear families than do their modern counterparts.

Some of the most prominent families of the city lived in large complexes of houses that sheltered several generations. Even when families did not do so, it was common for older relatives especially to reserve a room or apartment in a house for themselves while leaving the bulk of the property to their descendants. But there are enough cases of aged parents making special arrangements to be cared for by their children or other kin to show that they could not expect lodging unless they paid for it. At the same time, that real estate was divided according to strict rules meant that relatives, and particularly parents, might own a share of a residence, most of which belonged to a younger couple, and they could not be evicted from their own property.

Most of our evidence that an extended family occupied the same residence comes from the urban aristocracy. In 1373 Jan Damman up de Leie was living in the same house with his daughter and her husband; the lady owned half the house. There were two generations of the Gommaer family and several in-laws in the complex "de Buc" in the Hoogpoort. A more complicated case involves the elder and younger Jan Houtscilt. The father was widowed by 1362 and divided several properties in and around the Nieuwpoort, in St. Jacob's parish, with his son and daughter. Houtscilt's mother still lived in one of these properties. The son's discretion was evidently suspect, for his father reserved the right to eject him if he misbehaved, and his guardian and overseer agreed, giving him only the income from his properties on which to live. Jan Houtscilt the younger made an evidently childless marriage. In 1375 he and his wife disposed of several properties in return for rents for their two lives, but they agreed to keep a complex that included their residence and three other houses diagonally across the street. In 1359 the moneychanger Clais de Wayere and his two adult brothers, the carpenters Jan and Melis, were occupying a single house in the Donkersteeg, near the financial center of Ghent. They owed 25 lb. gr. secured on the house, suggesting that they had borrowed the money to buy it and that the debt was actually a mortgage.[6]

In the fourteenth century as now, the care of aging relatives, particularly parents, gave concern to conscientious adult children. Many problems described in this section had relevance for elderly men as well as women. But men were in a better position to save their earnings during their working years, and some foundations, such as the Weavers' Hall, were open to elderly guildsmen but excluded their wives.[7] Priests sometimes willed gifts to their mothers, to be deducted from their estates before other heirs divided the remainder. Lay children might also agree to care for their aged parents on these terms. A common form was for an old woman to surrender her property to her child and spouse or to will them a set amount before other heirs divided the estate in return for lifetime support.[8] Some women sold their houses but reserved lifetime use of parts of them. Mergriet Van Scerdruwe did this, keeping for life an apartment in the upper story and free access for all her friends to visit her. The buyers were also forbidden to rent or resell the house without her consent, but all restrictions on them ended at her death.[9] Some women lived in inns; in 1378 Jehane Ruwaerts and her innkeeper were fined for carrying weapons at night. Some women moved to more modest lodgings as they got older. In 1369 Mergriet Van den Pitte was paying a land tax of 10s. on a house in the Struserssteeg, but by 1383 she had surrendered this to another woman and moved into the adjacent house, which owed only 6s. and was presumably smaller.[10]

The legal disabilities of married women sometimes rendered them incapable of providing for their parents as they would like. Jan Verpeerensone and his second wife, Kateline Van den Steene, had supported her aged and indigent father, Ghiselbrecht Van den Steene, for many years. The source claims that father and son-in-law got along well. But Kateline, stating that she acts to secure continued support of her father after her own death, willed her stepson 10 lb., while her sister Mergriet agreed to give Jan Verpeerensone 1 lb. annually to help support him. It seems clear that Kateline was dying and that Jan, his protests of good will to the contrary, intended to turn the old man out unless he was paid for keeping him. The labor of caring for a mother could have a cash value, although there is no reason to think that it was ordinarily conceived in those terms. In 1391 Gerard Van Roden agreed to support his mother for life "and to do to her all that a good child ought to do for his mother" in return for all her property.[11]

Particularly because of the high death rate and frequent remarriages, which blurred clan lines and degrees of responsibility, there was some jockeying among children and in-laws over the care of aged kinswomen. Arnoud Bergaert had apparently been supporting his widowed mother but was bothered by the fact that his sister and her husband, Jan Van Bost, held some of the old lady's property. In 1361 they turned the money over to Arnoud, who agreed to support his mother for life and to return all her property to her estate before division when she died. Such cases, however, are balanced by examples of obvious affection, particularly apparent where an old person feels abandoned by his or her other relatives and singles out one who has treated him or her well. In 1357 Jan Ser Roelfs rewarded his daughter Lisane, who had provided more support for him than his other children, particularly during illness and time of need, by giving her his residence in the aristocratic Lange Munt and then resuming life use of it himself, a common way of avoiding having property divided among heirs whom one wanted to exclude while reserving it for one's own lifetime.[12]

Other support arrangements provide variations on these basic themes. Some careful parents specified that they would be supported "according to [their] status." In 1366 Jan de Blende agreed to support his aunt or pay her an annuity in lieu of it. At this time she also had an apartment in his house, and he willed her an additional 40 lb. gr. The nephew may have been the older of the two. Support arrangements sometimes had the aspect of an estate settlement before death. When the widow of Jan de Wielmakere gave all her property to her daughter and son-in-law in return for lifetime support, not only did the other children consent, but one brother took the opportunity to sell to his sister all his property from their paternal estate, an obvious way to simplify the settlement when their mother eventually died. In 1389 Yde Herdincx sold her daughter a house in return for a life annuity in grain and life use of the house, in which the daughter and her children were not living at the time, although they reserved the right to do so if they paid half the tax. Prudent women made certain that they would not be left defenseless if there were personality clashes. The widow of Gillis Van den Rietgavere surrendered to her daughter and son-in-law all her dower rights on the daughter's property and all her own property in return for lifetime support; but if they could not get along together, the younger couple would keep the property and pay her a life annuity of 4 lb. gr., which was certainly enough for a single elderly person.[13]

The division of labor in the fourteenth-century home meant that care of the aged or indigent relative fell mainly on the wife. Two years after settling her husband's estate the widow of Pieter de Winter surrendered to her son Jan and his wife a cash settlement and chattels in return for lifetime support. But the money was to be refunded immediately if either Jan or his wife predeceased her. The implication is clear: if the son died first, his widow would have no motive to care decently for her mother-in-law, but the old lady did not want to leave her money with her son if his wife died, presumably because a man could not care for her as well as a woman.

Housewives could be victimized by support arrangements not involving other women. Willem Van den Maelgavere, evidently a middle-aged bachelor, sold a house to Gillis Van Overtheet while keeping an apartment and access to water and facilities. Gillis and his wife even agreed to handle his laundry. If Willem ever married and went elsewhere to live, he might sublet his rights on the apartment and the laundry service, but only to "as appropriate a person as himself."[14]

Some children did not want to have an impecunious mother alive to disturb their felicity in the hereafter. Jacob Hoye, "having God before him and thinking of the salvation of his soul," willed his mother 10 lb. gr. because she was "old and sick and could not get around to take care of herself." Sons might also arrange for persons outside the clan to care for their mothers, usually renouncing their share in a cash sum or the mother's entire estate to finance it. The support might take the form of an allowance for life, with which the old lady would presumably arrange her own living accommodations.[15]

Some of the bondage in which maids found themselves seems to have resulted from the desire of elderly masters to insure their continued comfort. Gertrud, the wife of Jan Quintins, willed her share of their common property to her niece, Meere de Wullewerker, a case in which one wonders whether the family name is actually a profession. The bequest was made for services that the girl had done and would do in the future for Gertrud and her husband, day and night as a good maid is supposed to do. If the language is not empty rhetoric, and "good people" were to attest whether she was actually performing her appropriate services, maids were on call at all times. In 1390 Jan de Zomer and his wife gave to the wife's daughter a house in which Jan's mother would have an apartment. The girl presumably would take care of the old lady. In 1390 the aunt of Sophie, daugher of Jan de Pape, who was marrying Michiel Van der Zickelen, willed her all her property in return for lifelong support, but Michiel reserved the right to renounce the arrangement if Sophie predeceased her aunt.[16]

The care of the elderly devolved in principle on their blood relations, but we have seen that this could be complicated even when there were adult children, and matters became extremely delicate in their absence. Successive transfers of the same property could reduce an old lady to penury, but her rights could not be ignored. In 1354 Mergriet Van Huesdine declared that she had no rights on a house which Willem Arnoutssone had just bought and had no property in it except a bed, old chests and chairs, and ten torn pillows. In return for this declaration Willem allowed her to live in the house as long as she wished. Unattached women of all ages are found living alone in apartments or houses throughout the city. Lisbette Steppe, to cite only one example, lived in one-sixth of a house adjacent to her father's, but it was a separate residence. The presence of female lodgers had its risks for landlords. Jan de Bastaert Van den Nokere was sent on a pilgrimage in 1363 as the landlord of the hostel where Jane Van den Nokere, presumably a kinswoman, had been raped.[17]

Brothers were evidently expected to provide for sisters who had no other source of income. Although blood payments went in law to the male kinsmen, some special dispensations were made by clans for females deprived of support by a killing. Some elderly bachelors and their maiden sisters lived together and had common property. Brothers and their wives sometimes cared for elderly sisters, but this does not invariably mean indigence. Persons of both sexes too poor to care for themselves could be provided for at the various hospitals and "Holy Ghosts" of the city. Surprisingly, in view of the brutality attending the civil strife of this age, the city seems to have been willing during the 1380s to use the confiscated assets of political fugitives to care for their indigent female relatives.[18]

Almost certainly most children took care of parents who survived into old age. Many of the surviving cases concern old people who arranged to have nieces, nephews, or grandchildren support them. We often cannot tell whether this is being done because closer kin refused to do so or because there were no closer relatives. Occasionally an adult child is acquitted by other heirs of the estate of the deceased parent, which would only have been necessary if the older person had been living in the child's home. The elderly seem to have maintained their own establishments when possible until they became physically or mentally incapacitated. A case that would be quite pathetic were it not for the suggestion that the old man had considerable property involves Zeger Boudinssone Zegaerts. In 1386 he surrendered all his property to the two sons of his brother Goessin Zegaerts on condition that they support him for life. We are not told whether Goessin Zegaerts was still alive or whether either of his sons was married. They pledged to support their uncle without selling any of his property, suggesting that it was producing a substantial income. Zeger concludes by saying that he did this "because of the good trust and affection which he has found and still daily finds in his nephews Zeger and Clais, and he has had to be living with someone, and his other heirs cannot and will not do it for him."[19] We are not told whether the nephews were his closest living relatives, but it is clear that the old man felt rejected.

When younger family members did not feel capable of caring for a collateral relative or did not care to do so, they made arrangements with others. Kateline Abelin and her husband Staes Onredene, for example, surrendered to Zeger Van Meeren her share of her aunt's estate, in return for which Zeger would support the lady or have her supported and pay the debts on the estate.[20] The case shows clearly that the niece was apparently the closest heir but not the only heir, since she did not stand to inherit the aunt's entire property. But it was she who had the obligation of supporting her, and rather than do so directly, she surrendered her share of the property.

An elderly couple who were approaching desperation but still intended to "go out with heads held high" were Jan Van Berghine and his wife Beatrise Croec. Their son Jan, a prominent mercer, was already an adult by the early 1360s. He had died in early 1386 with his affairs in such disarray that his parents had renounced his estate to his widow. The parents thus must have been at least in their seventies when they described themselves in 1391 as aged and "scarcely able to get about and manage for themselves." Beatrise's niece had lived with them and served as maid for more than twenty-two years, and she now pledged to stay for the rest of her life. In return the couple made her a substantial bequest on condition that she "behave according to their counsel so that Lisane [the niece] and her friends may have honor."[21] The old couple could count on nothing from their son's estate, desperately needed help, and had turned to their niece, upon whom support devolved in principle in default of children, even though her services had to be compensated.

When siblings were alive, they were preferred to nieces or nephews for support, and sisters to brothers. In 1378 Clais Quaetsot surrendered all his property to his sister Mergriet and her husband in return for some spending money and lifelong support in his illness.[22] Grandchildren might also support the elderly. In 1366 Lievin Sluetel and his wife pledged to do "all that good children" should for his grandmother, a pledge secured on all property that he stood to inherit from her. While most cases in which clan members agree to special provision for relatives involve an old person who would be cared for by his or her descendants or collateral relatives, the old might also care for the young. In 1372 Gillis Van Coudenbrouc pledged in return for 6 lb. gr. to support his nephew for life, but he agreed to return

2 lb. to the nephew's wife if he died during the coming year. The situation suggests a person who was not expected to live long and whose wife, perhaps burdened with other domestic responsibilities, simply could not cope with him.[23]

The extended family thus acted as a charitable group that fostered the welfare of its members. We have noted the role of the clan in the upbringing of children. A related question is the extent to which kinsmen followed or tried to follow the same profession and pass the father's trade on to the son. We have better information on this question for the middle classes than for the upper. It seems likely that the sons of financiers and rentiers inherited enough property of particular kinds from their fathers that a choice of business in the modern sense was not really open to them unless they chose to liquidate all assets. But statute evidence and some demographic material against which the laws can be tested have survived for several guilds.

There seems no doubt that the statutes of the fifteenth century show that most guilds with great political influence were making mastership hereditary or at least limiting very severely the enrollment of persons who were not sons of masters. Scholars have shown a regrettable disposition to draw conclusions for the fourteenth century from this evidence.[24] But fourteenth-century texts suggest that all guilds except the butchers and fishmongers were still open to outsiders. It is certainly true that virtually all guild statutes that have survived from the fourteenth century give preference to the sons and occasionally the daughters of persons already masters in the same guild, and there is a clear tendency to close ranks after 1385. Most guilds were defining "freedom" by that time as enjoyed only by children born after the father became a master; although other children could enter the trade, they would be treated as outsiders. But for most of the fourteenth century the favoritism of heirs generally took the form of a low entry fee and in some cases a shortened term of apprenticeship.[25]

The notion that heredity of profession within the clan was the norm is weakened by other considerations. First, at least eight guilds were still admitting bastards in the fourteenth century: the brewers, the tailors, the haberdashers, the tanners, the saddlers, the graytawyers, the painters, and the shippers.[26] Second, numerous texts refer to "have him taught a trade" without specifying which one.[27] Persons with the same name are found in totally different professions; and while this fact alone does not necessarily mean that they were relatives, one may presume that they were kinsmen when they are found in a document as heirs of the same person, when they have business dealings together, or when they are both involved in the same surety or as principals in one act of violence.[28]

It is perhaps less than astonishing that kinsmen would matriculate in guilds of a similar nature.[29] But some are found in professions so different that no amount of family tradition or learning of skills around the house can explain it. To give only a few cases, the tailor Willem de Witte in 1370 was sustained in his demand that the boatman Willen de Witte help him pay a damage claim, since they had pledged "fraternal association."[30] A sawyer and a cheesemaker who are both named Jan de Zomer are in the same debt recognition. The scribe Heinric Van den Steene was a relative of the wheelwright Jan Van den Steene. Members of the Louf family were variously butcher, baker, and tanner, and the butcher and the baker were brothers.[31]

The same person could also exercise strikingly divergent professions. Although it is possible that some of these may be persons emancipated in a guild through their fathers but then choosing a different profession at maturity, the language suggests the contrary, and some guilds prohibited dual matriculation. In 1390 we find Willem de Paeu simultaneously "baker and boatman."[32] Jan Van der Eeken is called a shearer in references through 1372; but in that year he used a brewer as surety, and by 1381 he was called a brewer himself.[33] He was able to change occupations without surrendering his rights in the shearers' guild. There is also at least one brewer who became a baker.[34]

Prominent families frequently had members in different guilds. The brewer Stevin Valke was the son of the pursemaker Arnoud Valke, while their kinsman Willem Valke was a smith.[35] Some members of the Goethals family were carpenters, others brewers.[36] The Van Hijfte included bakers, brewers, and barristers.[37] Some families enjoying hereditary rights as butchers had members who were brewers, notably the Deynoots and the Meyeraerts.[38]

Our conclusions concerning the transmission of mastership within the family in law and in fact may be summarized with the example of the brewers, one of the largest nontextile guilds of Ghent in the fourteenth century. The brewers were developing traditions of hereditary mastership before 1400, for they were compiling lists of masters by the early 1360s and by the 1380s were automatically admitting only those sons born after the father became a master brewer. They limited the number of new enrollees who were not sons of masters to three annually in 1422 and to one in 1443.

But the guild statutes can be checked against three lists of master brewers from the fourteenth century: one, compiled from older originals through early 1362, named living brewers and those recently deceased who had sons who might claim mastership; a second list is dated 1363; and a third is from 1394–95.[39] There are gaps, for some brewers entered the guild after 1363 and had died without sons before 1394, but there is only one error, in the 1362 list, which cannot be explained by the time lag. It is thus possible for us to examine the extent to which the brewers were a hereditary group in the fourteenth century.

The list of 1362 contains 158 names with 130 patronymics. Thus 21.5 percent of the brewer families had more than one member in the guild. But although there is only a brief period between the establishment of this list and that of 1363, the total number of masters in 1363 is 237, an increase of 50 percent, while the total number of patronymics in 1363 is 187, an increase of 43.8 percent; thus 26.7 percent of the families of 1363 had more than one member in the guild. The different bases of compilation make comparison of these two lists difficult, but the number of brewers was definitely increasing in the 1350s and 1360s, and the guild was showing a slight tendency to concentrate within the same families.[40]

Of great interest also is a comparison of individuals between the lists. Of the 158 persons in the first, only 84 are found in that of 1363, a decline of 46.8 percent, while there was a 30.8 percent decline in the number of families.[41] Only one father and son are simultaneously listed as enfranchised in the list of 1362, but nine are found in that of 1363, suggesting growing preference for the descendants of brewers.

The lists of 1363 and 1394 were both intended to be complete lists of masters. There were 214 in 1394, a decline of 9.70 percent since 1363. The lapse of time renders a comparison of personal names meaningless, since many naturally would have died. But if the guild were becoming markedly more hereditary or oligarchical, one would expect to find patronymics continuing. Yet of the 187 family names of the 1363 list, only 67 are still present in 1394. Of the 157 patronymics in the list of 1394, 90 are thus new since 1363; 57.32 percent of brewer families had thus joined the guild during the previous thirty-one years. One suggestion of closure, however, is that 36.3 percent of the families listed in 1394 had more than one member in the guild, a figure nearly 10 percent higher than that of 1363. The distinction between masters' children and outsiders who were received first appears in the guild book in 1385, when six insiders and twenty-five outsiders became master brewers. The distinction between children born before and after the father had become a master first appears in 1386, and the ratio between newcomers who were of brewer families and who were outsiders had been reversed. The list of 1394 thus seems to have been the basis upon which the guild would thereafter restrict new entries; indeed, in 1396 seven sons of a single prominent master matriculated.[42] But the example of the brewers, which can be elaborated only because of the survival of the magnificent guild book, proves clearly that most fathers did not pass their trades down to their sons in Ghent during the fourteenth century.

What is probably a rather typical case of how family ties could influence profession and political affiliation is that of Gillis Van den Spieghele, who is in none of the lists of master brewers but was already an official of the guild by 1366. His father may have been a weaver, for his paternal guardian had been a weaver named Van den Spieghele. The guardian, however, chose to have him learn the trade of his stepfather, the brewer Maes Van den Zandberghe. Evidently with loans from Maes he established a brewing business in the Lange Munt and bought a complex of adjacent properties. He was *schepen* of *gedele* in the weaver-dominated magistracy of 1382–83, which suggests that he had maintained ties to the profession of his paternal kin. He had died by December 1383, and Maes Van den Zandberghe became guardian of his children and is called their grandfather. That his clan could have put him into his father's profession had they so chosen cannot be doubted. But they did not do so, and although he did follow a family profession, his stepfather was a more influential figure in his life than were his blood relatives.[43]

The clans of fourteenth-century Ghent thus provided charity and established a number of social controls that did not seriously impair the autonomy of most of their more responsible members. But the network of clans was something less than an archetypal peace association. The kindred pacified conflicts among its members and defended them against the adherents of rival clans. We turn next to this more public sphere of action of the extended families.

Chapter Ten

Clans in Conflict

e have seen that the extended family could restrict the autonomy of the nuclear family. Property might be divided, orphans raised, and women situated only with the consent of the kindred. Yet the mechanism of this involvement is often unclear. When two kinsmen quarreled, judgment was supposed to reside with the clan in principle, only going to the *scepenen* if the relatives disagreed. Whenever kinsmen brought an action to the magistrates without going first to the arbitration of their relatives, the *scepenen* invariably remanded their case to the "kin and friends."[1] In the disposal and inheritance of property the "kindred and friends" seem to have had a rather free hand to suspend the ordinary rules of law. But this was only true when the nuclear family was broken. Jack Goody and Jean-Louis Flandrin have seen the conjugal couple in northern France emancipating itself from the constraints imposed by the lineage only in the sixteenth century.[2] This emancipation had occurred in Ghent by the fourteenth century for people who were in their first marriage. Death and widowhood, the presence of orphans, and above all remarriage created circumstances under which kindreds could limit the discretion of individual family members, but not of entire conjugal families.

Since the magistrates insisted on prior arbitration within the family before accepting a case between relatives, we find some dramatic and rather formal proceedings at the home of a principal.[3] In a dispute over the payment of a dowry in 1389 the *scepenen* ordered it taken first to the clan, then to outside arbitrators, and only then to the city council if the arbitrators split.[4] The paucity of the records shows in itself that most clans usually functioned in this manner; but that family members occasionally sought the help of the magistrates before going to the kindred shows that the principle was not absolute or even clearly established at this time.

In cases of doubt the kindred decided in principle who should inherit. They might award portions of an estate to someone not mentioned in a testament or legally entitled to a share. When Diederic de Scaermaker died in 1381, his and his widow's estates were examined by various kinsmen from both sides and two priests, who found that the assets of the estates barely surpassed liabilities. They nonetheless awarded 1 lb. gr. to Diederic's aunt, who was apparently younger than her nephew, for she is stated to have lived with him since her childhood. The kin and friends were consulted about the value of particular items, sometimes using the services of professional appraisers.[5] When one kinsman in need sold property to another, representatives of the clan usually witnessed the transaction and consented to it. This is less invariably true when the case concerned the sale of dower rights or an attempt by kinsmen to consolidate portions of an estate, leaving full owership of certain parcels to particular individuals.

The clan was normally consulted on the proper course of action if something seemed wrong. The evidence of a *retrait lignager* principle, by which family members would have the opportunity to offer the same price as an outsider before property could be alienated, is nonetheless inconclusive. The potential heirs of both parties had to consent to a collusive agreement. Their consent was not required for donations to bastards, probably because the bequest normally reverted to the legitimate line if the bastard died without issue. But the heirs were normally asked to consent to donations to charitable foundations, for these were not recoverable.[6]

We have seen that the clan was involved in the distribution of the blood price and that it could determine whether a woman would get something from it. The kindred and friends could freeze the assets of a newly married couple whose discretion was suspect. In 1353 Fransois Van den Veere and his wife Kateline Craenkins acquitted her guardian but pledged not to sell or encumber their land "until they have legitimate heirs of their bodies or by the wishes of the majority party among Kateline's kinsmen and friends." Siblings also had the right to prevent the alienation of property among themselves or even to threaten loss of property to stop a brother or sister from marrying, although one suspects that this was normally exercised only when preconjugal lunacy was suspected. Such restrictions only were possible, however, when the siblings' property was still undivided in the common nest. Once an estate was divided, alienations by one party would not affect the others. Marriage was clearly a crucial step, and we have seen that making the wrong marriage could be disastrous not only for oneself but also for one's entire kindred. A man's wedding gift to his wife became property transmitted through the female line, but a gift from the woman's father to her and her husband was only half hers. Even if she died before her father had transferred legal title to the property, he still owed half the amount to his son-in-law.[7]

The principle of family solidarity and collective liability was very well established, particularly in cases of violence but also in economic matters. The Van den Kerchove clan had such an extended idea of clan solidarity that they once forced Jan Basijn to swear that he was not a kinsman of another Jan Basijn who had given them offense.[8] While kinsmen could renounce their relatives' debts, they could not do so if they had any intention of eventually inheriting from the estate.

Clan members were expected to support one another. In 1357 Jacob, son of the late Arend Bergaert, left his surety to pay the costs that he had incurred in street brawls. He asked the "guardians and overseer of his mother" to use her property to repay the "boys" who had vouched for him. Why the mother had guardians is unclear, but they agreed that from grace, and not because they were legally obligated to do so, they would loan him enough to cover his costs, but this had to be repaid to his siblings from his share of her estate when she died. The clan as a whole declared that none of the mother's property would be extended to help any of her other children for any reason. Families thus were clearly expected to help wayward members even if there was no legal obligation.

Other cases reinforce this point. Pieter Van Adeghem had incurred heavy debts, whether through business misfortune or wasting his money we are not told. His father Heinric and his uncles Lievin and Jacob Everboud had come to his assistance, but they had sold all his property to recover their losses, and Pieter Van Adeghem now recognized the legitimacy of these alienations. He still owed a debt of 52 lb. 10s. gr. to one uncle, a figure so large as to suggest that the original debt must have been overwhelming, and he agreed to pay it from the first property that he might acquire. His father also agreed, without mentioning consent of the kindred, that any unpaid remainder might be taken from his estate when he died. He was assuming his son's debts as his own by this procedure.

Both the uncles but particularly the father were showing considerable affection for the young man when their financial interests might have been served better by cutting him off.[9]

But family members were also capable of taking firm action to safeguard the interests of prudent or innocent kinsmen against wastrels. In 1388 the priest Jan Van West made substantial bequests to the several children of his brother Jacob, reserving the incomes of all the property for his lifetime, because of the "improper conduct" of the brother who would otherwise have been his heir.[10]

A primary function of the kindred was obviously the acquisition and preservation of property for its members. There does not seem to have been vast variation in the methods used by kin groups as opposed to others in acquiring property. We are thus concerned primarily with inheritance, the preservation of what has been acquired. There was a considerable difference in inheritance laws among the Flemish communities, and not only on minor points. What we describe for Ghent does not necessarily hold true for the rest of Flanders. When Callekin, daughter of Jacob Van Mourseke, died at Damme, her mother and brother were heirs of half her property according to the laws of Damme. The brother then sold his rights on the estate to Pieter Colpaert, who claimed that Willem Wenemaer of Ghent had taken property belonging to the girl. Wenemaer responded that he need not return it, since Callekin had inherited property only from her father, her mother was still alive, and according to the custom of Ghent property reverted to the side of origin. Colpaert protested that since Callekin was a citizen of Damme, her mother and brother had a right to share the estate there, although not in Ghent, and the *scepenen* of Ghent sustained this argument.[11]

We have seen that inheritance at Ghent was absolutely partible, with no special rights for males or for eldest over youngest, though Flemish customs in other areas or towns favored the sons. Women at Ghent thus seem to have been in a particularly favorable situation. On March 9, 1363, the sons of Gillis Libbe sued their sisters over land left by Gillis at the village of Huise, claiming that it went entirely to the sons according to the custom of the place where the land was located. The ladies responded that the division should be according to "where the hearth was split," and their father had died in Ghent as a burgher. The *scepenen* of Ghent awarded half the estate to the sisters.[12] The division into halves by sex is only because there was an equal number of brothers and sisters, not to women and men receiving an equal share in principle. While partible inheritance undeniably helped women and fostered individual rights, it could make it very difficult for families to hold substantial properties together for several generations. This fact may help to explain the penchant of the upper classes of Ghent for land investment; however minimally profitable, the rents from the land were easily divisible. We have also found that the property of children was normally kept undivided as long as all remained at home in the "common nest," but that it might be split into equal shares when all children had reached their majority. Despite this some adult siblings preferred to leave their properties together and take their share of the income.

Siblings inherited only from that side on which there was a blood relationship, although they might have dower rights on the property of affinal kin. But while the rules for division were very precise, it is hard to apply mathematical formulas to the documents which we have. First, the costs of parties in settling the estate and in any litigation were paid before any division was made. The decedent's testament might subtract still more. Dower rights of surviving spouses were a complication, particularly when the survivor remarried and had children. Children of a later marriage had rights on the property of the parent's children by the previous spouse or even on the dowry of a first spouse, together with rights in the parent's share of common property held with the first marriage partner. Property that a spouse had inherited during the marriage was considered to come exclusively from that person's side; it was not common property, which was divisible. Hence in 1377 the *scepenen* awarded the widow of Jacob Van Loe only dower, and not ownership of half and dower on the rest, on the land which her late husband had held at Hijfte, since testimony showed that he had inherited it from his mother. The same principle holds true for property that one spouse had acquired by means other than inheritance before the marriage. In 1357 the claim of the sons of Jan Van der Ellen against their stepmother was sustained that their father had owned certain properties before he had married her. It accordingly went to his heirs. If he had given any of them to his wife during their marriage, this was invalid; for while prenuptial arrangements were legal, "man and wife cannot according to the law of the city give property to each other during the marriage."[13]

When one adds to these considerations the fact that nomenclature is imprecise and that we are often not told the degree of relationship of collateral kin who inherited, one has a mammoth historical problem on one's hands. Hence when the estate of Boudin Van den Kerchove was being divided in 1355, the magistrates ruled that Raes Van den Kerchove would have half of all chattels, of land bought during Boudin's marriage, and all land which Boudin had owned before his marriage, since he was "Boudin's whole brother, paternal and maternal sides." He would share all other property with the Blandin family, who were kindred of the decedent on the maternal side only and were thus entitled to half of what he had inherited from his mother's family.[14]

The complexity of inheritance customs caused problems even for real estate. The house was inviolable; depending on the context, the word can mean a building or a clan. The head of the clan was ordinarily the party of recourse when buildings were involved,[15] since few pieces of real estate were owned outright by anyone because of the partitions. There had to be rules for what happened when a house with space for only one nuclear family was owned by several persons. Some principal heirs tried to buy out the others, but this was not always possible. We have seen that different generations tended to live in different parts of the same complex. The large numbers of *staten* which mention no real estate, or which do mention it but say that it is all rented out, show that fourteenth-century Ghent had a fair number of apartments inhabited by single persons, most often women, and small nuclear families, leaving aside the question of those unable to keep a decent roof over their heads.

Although it was unusual, houses were occasionally divided physically among heirs, but this was possible only with very large houses, often those that were used as businesses as well as residences. It usually meant that the heirs could not get along, for rents were normally higher when a property could be rented integrally. In an obviously exceptional case of 1350 the estate of Mathijs Van Meeren was being divided between his widow and their son Jan. The widow claimed that Jan had the documents concerning Mathijs's debts. He denied this but refused to swear to it. The arbitrators predictably ordered him to produce them, meanwhile sequestering all chattels in their present places. Their action suggests that the debts on the estates of decedents were normally paid through the sale of chattels, a suspicion strengthened by the statement that if the son were allowed to remove his half of the chattels, he might escape his and his mother's joint obligation to pay the debts. Since it was apparently not possible for them either to continue to hold the house jointly and each take half the income, or to give some of the real estate to one and the rest to the other, each party was ordered to get a carpenter and several neighbors as appraisers "and divide into halves, and whatever chattels are in each half will remain there."[16]

A case suggesting convenience and business rather than disagreement involves the "Pollinaessteen" on the Koornmarkt, where most properties were businesses, although some doubled as residences. In 1391 three-quarters of this property belonged to Jan Ghiselins and Jan de Coc Van Ayeghem, while the rest belonged to Jan Van den Hulle, who is stated to have chosen the cellar for his share, a fact clearly showing division into apartments. The house needed repairs, and the parties agreed to a proportional division of the costs; each was not made responsible for paying only what affected his own part directly. A good example of the problems and possible solutions is afforded by the Casteel Wandelaert. In 1354 Philips Van Roden owned five shares, while Jan Van Gavere and Willem Van Hemelrike jointly owned seven. Since they were the majority shareholders, they claimed that "they should be able to purchase or rent the house according to the appraisal of the *erfscheeders* or others." Philips Van Roden denied this on grounds that he owned five shares outright, while the others had only 3½ shares individually. The *scepenen* sustained this argument and agreed that he might rent the house, but the part that he did not use was to be placed at the disposal of the other owners for the same price. Thus individual shareowners might not pool resources to outvote a larger individual owner, and the person who held the largest share could decide what to do with it and had the right either to use it himself, to sell, or to rent. Four years later the parties also disagreed over whether the land on which the building was located should be divided, and again the *scepenen* ruled that there could be no physical division unless all parties agreed.[17]

On balance, the rights of surviving spouses to half the common property and to dower rights on the decedent's estate seem to have posed a greater threat to the stability of family property than did partible inheritance among the children. The financial interests of children and their widowed parents were clearly not always the same. The widow and son of Hugh de Buc were living in the same house in 1372 when they quarreled over provisions of a maintenance agreement for the mother, who evidently had her own apartment. The settlement also provided that the son's wife begged her mother-in-law's forgiveness and reserved the older woman's right on grounds of her half interest in the house to eject her if she created further discord between mother and son.[18] That in-laws too might have different monetary interests is not surprising. Apart from the isolated mother-in-law problems, however, there is little direct evidence in the records of Ghent of hostility of sons- and daughters-in-law toward the parents of their spouses.

An interesting if almost certainly atypical case is afforded by Dankaert Steenaerd, who was accused of leading his young son-in-law Pieter de Veldein into wicked ways. We do not know who brought the matter to the *scepenen,* but it was presumably Pieter's clan. Dankaert had abused Pieter's "youth and lack of judgment" to induce him to agree to property transactions that the magistrates now annulled. A man could thus be married and presumably emancipated and still have his business dealings invalidated on grounds of his youth and inexperience.[19]

Although in-laws sometimes squabbled over property, they were considered as much a part of the family in principle as blood kin. This is particularly true of sons- and fathers-in-law because of their role in the guardianship of women. The husband of an older daughter would no more have an interest against her siblings than would a brother, for all profited as the assets of the common nest grew. Hence, when the two guardians of the daughters of Pieter Van der Donct quarreled over who had been supporting the girls, the *scepenen* adjudicated the matter but then replaced them with the now responsible male of the family, the husband of the presumably older daughter.[20]

Despite the lack of direct evidence, one suspects that there was considerable hard feeling beneath the surface between in-laws and siblings over inheritances. The *scepenen* in 1378 admonished the children of Goessin Rijm to behave like kinsmen, not like strangers who try to divide everything down to the last penny. One becomes accustomed to the law, whatever it may be. Still, one cannot help wondering about the impact that haggling over the right to keep one's clothing would have on personal relations with one's children and in-laws. In 1376 the heirs of Jan de Scermere's wife allowed Jan to keep his clothing, which was valued at 28s. gr. But since they had been entitled to 14s. gr., they were to receive that amount from his estate if he had more children. Such a point was made of it that it was obviously an extraordinary concession. Estates were ordinarily probated on the assumption that the surviving spouse would owe his children or other heirs of the late spouse half the value of his clothing, for which a cash amount would usually be added to the value of the estate as appraised.[21]

The nature of domestic relations and of the nitpicking that could take place among heirs is shown by the case of Heinric Van der Kuekenen. Emancipated in 1357, he had married by 1359 and was dead by January 1360, when the widow and his heirs were battling over his substantial property. The heirs had to pay his charitable bequests, but the *scepenen* ruled illegal his gift to his wife of her clothes and his bed, donations made "because of his great debts to her of which she had been ignorant." She even had to sue the heirs to get the property coming from her side and her dower rights on Heinric's estate. In 1383 Gillis Stoute, as sole heir of his brother Jan, sued the heirs of Jan's daughter over her marriage portion, claiming half of it because "it was more proper for him to have it than for it to go to a foreign side, and he should not be deprived of his half simply because his niece had survived her mother." The other side argued that when the mother died, the daughter had inherited half the common property notwithstanding the marriage portion, and custom is that "when the bed is divided [i.e., one parent had died], whatever had been given freely as a gift is not to return." The *scepenen* devised an even more complicated solution: the maternal heirs were to get the marriage portion, while reserving that any land coming from the father's side would revert there. Any land purchased during the marriage would be divided with the maternal heirs.[22]

The heirs had an exact idea of the liabilities of each kinsman, but their methods are sometimes hard to determine exactly because of the crudity of their calculations. When Ghiselbrecht SerSanders left 70 lb. gr. to his two bastards in 1387, his heirs determined their extent of liability. The relationship of each heir to the deceased is not specified, and the total amount paid falls 4 lb. 4d. short of being 70 lb. However, the widow and heirs of Sanders SerSanders were to pay 19.25 percent; the heirs of Simon SerSanders and the widow and heirs of Clais SerSanders 13.43 percent apiece; Busscaert Van Munte 12.5 percent; Gerem SerSanders 9.25 percent; Philips SerSanders 16.25 percent; the widow and heirs of Daneel SerSanders 5.82 percent; and Jan SerSanders and the knight Wouter Van Herzele 2.11 percent apiece. How one should interpret some of these figures is pure conjecture. Since the heirs were also to pay the support of the bastards until the bequests were paid, some of these amounts may have been adjusted to reflect who was lodging them, although the contrary is implied. Sanders SerSanders was probably a brother, for his share is nearly one-fifth and is considerably higher than those of the other heirs. A clearer statement of the principles of division of an estate is that of Clais SerSanders, probated in late 1388. The widow surrendered her rights of dower on several rents in return for a life annuity of 3 lb. gr. Of this sum, four heirs were to pay 18.75 percent apiece and one 25 percent. Simon SerSanders, who paid 25 percent, had been in the group with Clais SerSanders in the Ghiselbrecht SerSanders case in paying 13.43 percent; those paying 18.75 percent were Philips and Gerem SerSanders, Busscaert Van Munte for his wife, and the widow of

Sanders SerSanders, Busscaert Van Munte for his wife, and the widow of Sanders SerSanders.[23] A comparison of these two cases and the percentages paid suggests that Simon and Clais were brothers; hence Simon was heir of 25 percent of Clais's estate; but both were nephews in the same degree of Ghiselbrecht. The three SerSanders and the wife of Busscaert Van Munte were paternal uncles and aunt of Clais SerSanders and got jointly 75 percent of his estate. Philips SerSanders, as guardian of the bastards of both Ghiselbrecht and Jurdaan SerSanders, the latter of whom was the legitimate father of Clais, was the half-brother of Ghiselbrecht and brother on both sides of Jurdaan and hence uncle of the late Clais. Gerem SerSanders and the wife of Van Munte, who were in the same relationship to Clais, were evidently first and second cousins of Ghiselbrecht and paid a correspondingly lesser share of his bequests. Sanders SerSanders was the brother of Ghiselbrecht and Clais's uncle. The distinction seems to be that Ghiselbrecht's estate was inherited by one full brother (Sanders) and one paternal half-brother (Philips), who jointly paid exactly three-eighths of his bequests to his bastards if one counts their amounts as percentages not of 70 lb. gr. but of what was actually spent. The rest of the estate descended not to uncles but to increasingly distant cousins, and the property was thus more fragmented, while Clais's estate was inherited by a brother, three uncles, and an aunt. The half-sibling relationship meant a difference of 10 percent in the inheritance.

But an attempt to apply these percentages to other inheritances fails completely. The clan settled matters, and only the presence of two documents separated by a brief time enables us to see how the SerSanders handled the estates. It is plain that our subjects knew very well who was related to whom, however difficult it may be for us to figure it out from the records which they left. An interesting case bearing on the chronology of mortality, the rights of the maternal heirs, and ascent versus descent of property is the estate of Jan, son of Jacob Van Mayeghem. He died leaving a widow and his mother, but no children, and his father had also died. Jan Sateleere claimed to be the closest male relative of the maternal side, although Jan Van Mayeghem's mother was still alive. He argued that the mother had given her son a marriage gift after her own husband's death; accordingly the property should revert to her side, and he should take precedence over her, "because all inheritance of good debt should go downward and not revert according to law." The widow of Jacob Van Mayeghem claimed that since her husband was already dead when she endowed her son, it should revert entirely to her as nearest heir. She also demanded a *staet* of her son's property from the latter's widow, but the younger woman refused on grounds of having already bought out the rights of her husband's paternal kin. Only the mother's argument was sustained; she was awarded half of her late son's estate, and his widow had to furnish a list of his property; the son's widow was unprejudiced against those with whom she had dealt from his paternal kin.[24] The claim of the male from the mother's side is interesting mainly in that it was raised at all, for it is a transparent attempt to get some property through a legal technicality. The issue between mother- and daughter-in-law was more serious, hinging on the fact that the mother was a widow when she made the marriage gift and that her son apparently had no property other than this—one wonders what had become of his paternal inheritance—and that as such the mother was entitled to half of his property. The other half went to the widow, while his paternal kindred had no rights at all to it. The usual rule that property did not revert to a parent unless both were still alive and married to each other did not apply in such a case as this.

As is true of modern inheritance law, much depended on who died first. Kateline Van Valenchiennes died eight days before Whitsuntide 1368, while her husband Clais de Scouteete died between then and August 1. Kateline's daughter argued on these grounds that the heirs of her step-father Clais should have no share of her mother's estate. If he had died first, part of his estate would have gone to her as common property; thus when she died, her heirs would have inherited something that actually came from him, while this would not be true if she died first, for they would have had only her share of the common property. This argument was evidently sustained.[25]

A case illustrating several of these principles involves the brothers Heinric and Jan Van den Scatte, who evidently died within a few months of each other in 1358 and 1359. Jan was apparently childless, while Heinric left four children. Heinric's estate was divided by Jacob Rabau, apparently a maternal uncle. The oldest boy, also Heinric, had to pay his mother 18 lb. gr. as her share of a debt of 45 lb. previously awarded by the *scepenen* of *gedele;* the widow's share was thus 40 percent, while her four sons divided 60 percent equally. On three separate occasions the guardian of Heinric's children acquitted the widow of their uncle Jan of his estate. The version of May 23, 1359, has the woman pledging to pay the children "a share corresponding to the settlement which Jan de Mersman has made toward the widow for the share of the estate inherited by his wife, sister of Jan Van den Scatte, from her brother." The version of May 27, 1359, has the sister getting 39s.6d. gr.

from the estate, while the nephews and niece got 5 lb. 18 s. gr., or exactly three times the share of the sister.[26] Once again there seem no fixed percentages to which a relative of a given degree would be entitled.

A curious case of the mid-1360s suggests that if a married woman died while both her parents were alive, they would inherit at least part of her property even if she had children; the principle of upward reversion "if the bed were whole" normally applied only if the decedent had no children as heirs. Jan Van Zielst was sued in 1364 by Heinric de Blauwere for claims on the estate of Jan's late wife Kateline. Jan refused to answer, since his wife had been dead for over ten years. Her father had been alive when she died; he and his wife had arranged the marriage for her. Although nothing is said about mother surviving daughter, the father did for a year and a day and more. Under the law of the city, her property was to go to her father under these circumstances; but the estate had passed to other heirs since no claim was raised within the year and a day. What makes this case more curious is that Jan Van Zielst and his wife, Kateline de Mey, had a daughter, Nanne. In an undated text of 1366–67 the girl is stated to hold 3 lb. 10s. gr., and her guardian was Jan de Mey, the blue dyer. She was emancipated on September 9, 1367, which is logical enough for someone whose mother was dead by 1353 or 1354. Evidently still unmarried, she acquitted her stepmother of her father's estate in 1376.[27] The daughter was a maternal heiress of her mother; but since both her grandparents had been alive and married to each other when the girl's mother died, they had been their daughter's paternal heirs. Without this condition the granddaughter would have become a paternal heiress of her grandfather and received her mother's entire estate.

Most of our information concerning the internal solidarity of the clan comes in connection with deeds of violence. Peacekeeping forces were hopelessly inadequate to deal with the tinderbox presented by guild hostilities and family feuds, particularly the latter.[28] For clans to take matters into their own hands was an inalienable right, and going to the authorities was an act of transgender pusillanimity. Competing clans were expected to arrange matters among themselves. Only when the count's bailiff or the city gendarmes actually stopped a fight and took someone into custody did the public police enter at all. The *scepenen* remanded some acts of violence to the kindred for judgment, although usually only when the antagonists were from the same clan or one party admitted his guilt and agreed to accept the verdict of the victim's kindred. But public legal authority was so weak, even in theory, that when a person was executed by a public court, his kindred were entitled to compensation from the clan of the man who had prosecuted him, a situation that had ended in England long before the Norman conquest.[29] That a killer was executed did not free his clan from the responsibility of paying the blood price to the kindred of the dead man.[30]

The kinsmen and friends had a duty to come to a kinsman's aid; bold was the man who fared abroad without his relatives. In 1385 the kin of Joos Van Cattenbeke asked that Jan Van Buxstale be punished for Joos's death. Jan testified that Joos and another man had assaulted him at night and had raped his niece. He had had to call three times to neighbors, a standard formula of Flemish criminal procedure, and finally had had to kill Joos in self-defense. The suit, however, was quashed not on these grounds, but because Joos Van Cattenbeke had called three times for help from his own kin. Since they had not appeared, presumably because they were not close enough to the action to hear him, they had no right to complain about what had happened to him.[31]

While the *scepenen* tried to tone down the level of violence and sometimes enforced arbitration, they never denied the principle that the clans had the right to commit offensive and defensive violence. Even collusive agreements to commit homicide were enforceable in the courts against persons who later tried to renege. Any kinsman or suspected kinsman was fair game. In 1360 Jan de Kersmakere was severely injured and mutilated by the Van Riemeland party. They agreed to pay him 8 lb. gr. in compensation, but only if he swore—as he did—that Pieter de Kersmakere, who had kidnapped the brother of the "Van Riemeland children," was not his relative.[32] The Van Riemeland clan had evidently gone on an orgy of bloodletting against anyone named de Kersmakere, a common name meaning candlemaker, without finding out whether they were even relatives of their enemy, let alone his accomplices. There is no hint that anybody, including the magistrates, thought that they had behaved reprehensibly as long as they compensated Jan de Kersmakere for his injuries. The entire matter was settled by arbitration and merely recorded with the *scepenen*.

Much violence was perpetrated by kinsmen. While liability for violent deeds is now owed primarily to the state and scarcely at all to the relatives of the injured party, the reverse was true in fourteenth-century Ghent, but with a twist. The blood price went not to the decedent's nuclear family, but to the males of the extended family. If the dead man had a son, he received the *montzoen,* as we have seen, and a share of the *maagzoen.* If he had no son, the money would go to his brother, failing him to the oldest nephew, or failing him to an uncle. There is no notion of upward reversion. Unless special circumstances led the magistrates to award a special indemnity to parents, they got nothing. Neither, as we have seen, did the widow and daughters. The *zoen* was a blood price, not innocent victims' compensation. It compensated the males of the clan for the loss of one of themselves, not the nuclear family for the loss of a breadwinner.

The *montzoener* was not simply a profiteer. He had the primary responsibility for arranging the blood price or, failing that and if insult were given to the clan by an unacceptable offer, of continuing the vendetta and possibly falling victim to continued hostility himself. The primary obligation to atone a death obviously fell upon the accused killer, or failing him and in addition to him, his brother. When Lievin Van Campine murdered the miller Arnoud Van Raesseghem, his brother Pieter on his own initiative tried to force their father's tenant farmers to contribute to the atonement, but his father had refused to consent. As was common in such cases, the *scepenen* did not rule, since this could mean execution of the guilty party. Arbitrators ordained that the father should pay part of the blood price, despite his own reluctance, and secure a life annuity for his guilty son. The actual perpetrators may have been dead or exiled, for the thrust of this complaint is of Pieter against his father. The arbitrators admonished Pieter that after this compromise "he and his father should love and honor each other as is proper between father and child."[33]

But the sources are not entirely consistent about the extent of the responsibility of clan members in homicide actions. Innocent persons were not technically bound to offer atonement; that was the responsibility of the guilty party. But, in fact, innocent kinsmen did offer the blood price, whether out of a sense of responsibility to the clan of the murdered person, as they claimed, or from fear of retaliation by the other side. In the suit of Willem de Raed against Jan Van der Mersch on account of the latter's kindred, the *scepenen* acquitted Jan, for they could not legally force a man to help his kinsman pay the blood price; but if as a kinsman Jan wished to pay anything to help, "as one relative should do voluntarily for another," Willem might collect it.[34] The implication is clear: while they could not force him to pay, he would do so voluntarily if he were a decent man.

There could be complications when one party or side of the clan stayed out of a homicide atonement. Gillis Van der Biest assumed responsibility for the death of Daneel Saudenis, but his paternal kindred had purged themselves as innocent parties before the victim's clan. Thus Gillis's maternal kindred agreed to join him in the atonement, tacitly admitting responsibility, and agreed to pay "as much more than half the blood price as the principal owes." Since declaring one's innocence usually meant offering a payment lighter than would have been expected otherwise—malice did increase the tariff—one assumes, since this was a highly unusual proceeding, that in most cases both the maternal and paternal kindred admitted complicity and helped atone the deed. The more usual form is for the blood price to be given, together with the identity of the principal perpetrator and the victim. Usually, although not invariably, the *montzoener* is also named. Both parties furnished sureties, but often different guarantors are listed for the maternal and paternal sides.[35]

As would be expected, many murderers were themselves killed later. In 1372 Zeger Van Lake was the principal killer of Jan Van der Erloe, paying 30 lb. gr. His brothers were his sureties and evidently paid part of the blood price. Zeger was killed in 1375 by persons who are not mentioned in connection with the earlier assassination. His blood price was 40 lb. gr., and his brother was the *montzoener*. The kinsmen and friends of Zeger Van Lake were quarreling over the distribution of the *maagzoen* by the following summer, and the *scepenen* emphatically stated the principle that those members of the four quarters of the clan who had not contributed to paying Van Lake's fine for killing Van der Erloe were not entitled to a share of the blood price paid for Van Lake's own death.[36]

Much of the factional infighting in Ghent during the fourteenth century seems to have divided the city along clan lines. Some families of the upper classes had uniforms or colors by which their retainers were known. But political issues, notably the question of the relations of the city with the count of Flanders, could also divide families. During the civil war of the 1380s the city government confiscated the property of comital partisans who had fled, then sold it at far less than its market value as a means of raising money. While this property was often sold to persons who had no demonstrable family tie to the person whose property was seized, there were cases in which one family member benefited from another's loyalty to the count.[37]

Our general impression is that most homicides in Ghent during this time were committed by persons who had enough property to pay the blood price, albeit usually with help from the kindred. In 1370 Staes de Hamer was an accomplice of the brewer Jan de Scouteete, who was principal in a homicide and an assault. Staes was sent on a distant pilgrimage; but here as ordinarily the document states that the principal killer was to pay on behalf of himself and his helpers, which would imply that Staes was responsible for part of the blood price. The atonement was promulgated on August 4, 1370. By December 23 Staes de Hamer had evidently asked his kindred for help in paying his share and had been turned down. The *scepenen* noted that "Staes can hardly do this without the help and grace of his kin and friends." Thus they asked them to help him "insofar as kin or friends help their kinsman and should do it out of grace, insofar as you would want help or assistance from your kinsman, which we promise you in equal or even greater measure."[38] The use of "we promise" suggests that the magistrates were merely repeating a pledge given them by Staes, but a more graphic example could hardly be imagined of the extent to which the city government supported the notion of moral responsibility to the clan to help, even if there was no legal liability.

Physical violence in both its terminal and transitional forms was an activity that did nothing to tarnish the reputation of a gentleman. The heirs of a late wife were bound to help her widower pay for any homicide that he had committed or had agreed in principle to atone during the marriage, since the lady had owned half of their common property. The suit of Wouter de Kindere against his late wife's heirs, alleging that they were liable for half the manslaughter fine which he owed, was quashed, but only on grounds that he had committed the deed before his marriage and had not arranged the atonement during his wife's lifetime. Children thus became liable to the extent that they had inherited common property from their mother. In such cases the father might become their legal guardian, for no one seems to have thought that an imputation of homicide compromised his fitness to act for his children. Hugh de Spoermakere held the maternal estate of his children in 1387, despite the fact that his children were "in profit and in debit" for a homicide that he and his late brother had committed. The children, however, were also owed half of any compensation that the father was able to collect for his own injuries from Jan Fierins, since all these deeds had been committed during the life of the wife and mother.[39]

In-laws' liability was even greater when the wife was still alive. Men were entitled to help from their in-laws in bringing offenders against their own clans to justice, and this obligation was legally enforceable. The family obligation to help members who had to pay a blood price extended even to cases in which the kindred had urged the perpetrator to stop misbehaving. In a case decided by arbitrators and recorded by the magistrates in 1369, Heinric Van Heedevelde sued his brothers Jan and Ghiselbrecht over the amount that each owed in an atonement made with Arnoud Van der Borch, who had apparently injured Heinric severely, paying him a fine of 10 lb. gr. Testimony showed that against the wishes of his brothers Heinric had returned to the place where he had been wounded and injured someone there, leaving him for dead, a deed which cost 3 lb. gr. Rumor circulated at this point that Heinric had died of his own wounds. Thereupon one Pieter Van der Straten and his wife returned to the place to avenge what they thought was Heinric's death; Pieter was killed and his wife severely injured, and all this cost the Van Heedevelde clan 20 lb. gr. for Pieter and 5 lb. 10s. gr. for his wife. Heinric was to apply to all of this the 10 lb. gr. that he had been awarded for his wounds, but if he had managed to collect anything else from the kinsmen and friends, he could keep this in compensation for his injuries.[40] These are enormous sums of money in terms of the purchasing power of the time. The issue seems to have been not whether the kindred should contribute, but whether Heinric should bankrupt himself to pay for his own malicious mischief, and the answer was definitely no, for not only did he keep everything above the 10 lb. gr. that he collected from his clan, but money that was collected from his castle at Marke by his brothers was to be returned to him, not used to compensate them for their damages on his behalf.

The complexities of relationships within the clan are shown in the division of the blood price. Particularly when, as often happened, the decedent was a young man without legitimate children, the monetary plum of the *montzoen* might be disputed among rival claimants. In 1361 Wouter Van den Bochoute and Heinric Reyniere both claimed to be the *montzoener* of Zeger, son of Brecht Van den Dorpe. Wouter based his claim on the fact that his mother was the aunt of Zeger's father. Reyniere's claim was more complicated. He was the oldest male of Brecht's paternal clan, for his mother and Brecht Van den Dorpe had been siblings. He thus claimed to be the closer relative, even though Wouter was the older man, and this claim was sustained. The *montzoen* thus descended in principle in the paternal line, and the age of the claimants, which was at best difficult to determine, was irrelevant. Distant relatives could acquire considerable property in this way. In 1378 Andrieskin, son of Jan Ghuse, was the *montzoener* of Jan de Roede, evidently his maternal uncle. Following the principle that an affine is a member of the family, the boy's father substituted for his wife as receiver of the *maagzoen* from the paternal side. But the issue would change when the *montzoener* died, and the *maagzoen* was shared equally with the kindred of the maternal side. In 1352 the maternal heirs of Ghiselkin, late son of Heinric Van den Colcte, demanded a share of the *montzoen* that the boy had received from his father, since it was now part of Ghiselkin's estate. This argument was disallowed, but only on grounds that the mother was still alive and all of the boy's property had come from the paternal line.[41]

The rules for division of the blood price could be relaxed by internal agreement of the kinsmen and friends. A younger son was normally entitled only to his share of the *maagzoen,* which went to all four branches of the kindred, while his older brother as *montzoener* received half the total blood price, but sometimes the younger boy was given more. A separate wardship was established for a minor who was a *montzoener.* He and his siblings received a second guardian for inherited property.[42]

According to law the *maagzoen* was to be divided with each brother apart from the *montzoener* receiving twice as much as a first cousin, who receives twice the amount of a second cousin, who in turn receives twice the amount of a third cousin. Distribution was by the four bilateral branches, two each from the father's and mother's sides.[43] Yet the surviving records of distribution are impossible to correlate with these principles. The historian of the family thus cannot deduce degree of kinship through a *maagzoen* award. An unusually clear case is that of Oste Van Gheetscure, whose *zoen* was 50 lb. gr. A division was specified, but the total shares, including deductions for costs, only come to 47 lb. 10s. gr. If we assume that someone who got 2 lb. 10s. was omitted from the document, the costs become 10 percent of the total blood price paid. No *montzoener* is named in this case, but Jan Van Gheetscure received the largest amount, 7 lb. or 14 percent. We are not told his relationship to Oste, but Kateline, Oste's daughter, received 4 lb. (8 percent) despite her sex, while her children received 6 lb. (12 percent). Arnoud Uten Wulghen and his children got the same amount as Kateline's children; we are not told his relationship, but if he was a brother, he and his children received less than Kateline and her children together. Siblings were not necessarily treated equally, which vitiates our attempt to impose a system on the figures, for the two sisters of the decedent and their children got 2 lb. 10s. and 3 lb., respectively, while Annekin, his brother's child, got 1 lb. 10s. The *maghen,* by whom we assume the more distant kinsmen, received 8 lb. (16 percent), with each of the four quarters getting 2 lb. Since nieces and nephews are provided for in the individual shares, the *maghen* are probably more distant cousins.[44]

Although kinsmen stood together against threats from outsiders, internally the clan was hardly an archetypal peace association. Spouses battled each other and their children, and there were occasional in-law problems. In trying to determine the incidence of violence between members of the same family the historian encounters all of the problems already mentioned in connection with family history at Ghent at this time, notably the fact that unless a relationship is stated or the patronymic is identical—and the latter is not an infallible guide—one cannot know whether the fighting is between collateral relatives or persons of no family tie. The historian can only cite examples of infrafamily violence and try to deduce their implications, but no patterns can be discerned. Arbitrators between warring parties are sometimes called "common kinsmen," but this need not mean a close relative.[45]

In early 1363 Jan Van Bassevelde paid the unusually low blood price of 2 lb. 10s. gr. for killing Clais Puls. That summer Pieter Puls killed Gillis Van Vlachem, who in turn wounded his half-brother, Wulfram Puls; Pieter Puls, the uncle of both the killer and the victim, stood surety for both sides. At least one case of intrafamily violence was probably due to an extremely quarrelsome relative. Ghiselin de Vlaminc was involved in numerous acts of petty violence between 1368 and 1379. His wife left him in 1374. In 1380 his death was atoned by Zeger de Vlaminc, probably a relative, and the *montzoener* was his brother Jan de Vlaminc.[46] The Van den Herweghe family evidently had a certain penchant for brawling. In 1364 Jan Van den Herweghe was killed by Jan Van den Colcte, while in 1377 Bertelmeus Van den Herweghe was killed by Boudin Van Belle and his accomplices. In the summer of 1378 Willem Van den Herweghe in turn atoned the death of Pieter de Leenhere. The names of sureties and principals give no indication of whether these deeds were connected with one another; but the *montzoen* of Pieter de Leenhere descended to a child, Zegerkin de Leenhere, who is not stated to have been his son. If the child died, however, his property was to go to his maternal heirs, not the paternal, suggesting that the Van den Herweghes were probably paternal kinsmen of the Leenheren, unless he had been *montzoener* as the son of a sister of the decedent.[47] A man who killed his kinsman was naturally deprived of his normal share of the blood price. In 1372 Jan Gheenssone paid 15 lb. 10s. gr. for the death of Matheus Gheenssone. He would ordinarily have received 2 lb. gr. from the *maagzoen,* but it went instead to the decedent's two daughters. Here as normally the *montzoener* was the brother, still a minor, of the dead man, while his two daughters received something only by grace of the kinsmen and friends.[48]

A Termination

The historian of the western European nuclear family in the "early modern" period will find many interesting points of detail in this description of conditions in Ghent during the fourteenth century, but the overall picture presented will occasion little surprise except among those to whom "medieval" means "backward." Just as twentieth-century America is governed by the principles of an eighteenth-century constitution, so fourteenth-century Ghent was ruled by a twelfth- and thirteenth-century constitution. Adaptation of the general principles to developing actual practice meant that the fundamental laws of medieval Ghent had limited applicability to domestic life. The position of women in law was one of strict subordination to men. In fact, women exercised considerable behind-the-scenes power over their men and are frequently found in the business world, either as partners of their husbands or sons or acting independently. The medieval theologians were markedly unsuccessful in their attempt to banish physical passion between the sexes from the Christian experience. While it is true that clans arranged many marriages, this occurred primarily among wealthy families that stood to lose a great deal through the common property rights acquired by spouses over each other's assets. Persons with less property married for reasons of mutual attraction. While many women were victimized by their legal disabilities, others seem to have overcome

207

them. More depended on individual abilities, personalities, and attitudes than on the legal framework.

The power of the clans was unquestionably greater in the fourteenth century than later. The individuality of both men and women was severely circumscribed by the power of the extended family. The clan's rights were minimal as long as the conjugal family remained intact; but when husband or wife died, the lineage immediately gained rights over the children and over the free disposition of property by the surviving spouse. The clan safeguarded the property rights of its members from outsiders and from wastrels within the family. The city government normally deferred to the clan in disputes arising between relatives, taking action only when the leaders of the kindred could not agree or the losing party appealed their judgment. The clan functioned most conspicuously as a "peacekeeping" force, for in an age of weakened state control accompanied by heightened levels of violence the blood feud between clans was resuscitated. The growth of the modern state apparatus at both the local and regional levels would circumscribe the clans' power; they were a much less significant social force by the sixteenth century.

Children were under obvious legal disabilities in their relations with their parents, their clans, and outsiders. But there can be no doubt that the conjugal family and the clan took their responsibilities toward children extremely seriously and expended considerable time, effort, and money in raising them properly. That what the clans often thought was in the best interest of the child does not conform to modern notions of proper child-rearing begs the question. They acted, as most modern parents act, to the best of their ability and understanding. Children were valued, cherished, and protected by those in authority over them.

Hence we consign to the rubbish heap of history the notions that "childhood" was suddenly "discovered" in the modern age; that the conjugal family in preindustrial Europe was an economic rather than an emotional unit; that human affection and sexual attraction had little place in marriage; and that women were either systematically oppressed or were protected beings enveloped in an ether of Marian chastity.

This book is finished. The human history of which it is symbol continues. If this work has been able, even on a limited and local scale, to demonstrate the undying continuum of human experience, it will have served its purpose.

Notes

ADN: Archives départementales du Nord, Lille

ARA: Algemeen Rijksarchief (General Archives of the Realm), Brussels

BB: Boek van den blivene

BR: Gentse Baljuwsrekeningen (Accounts of the Bailiffs of Ghent)

EP: G. Espinas and H. Pirenne, eds., *Recueil de documents relatifs à l'histoire de l'industrie drapière en Flandre,* 4 vols. (Brussels: Commission Royale d'Histoire, 1906–1924).

G: Stadsarchief te Gent, Ser. 330, registers of *scepenen* of *gedele*

HMGOG: *Handelingen der Maatschappij voor Geschied- en Oudheidkunde te Gent*

K: Stadsarchief te Gent, Ser. 301, registers of *scepenen* of the *Keure.*

RAG: Rijksarchief te Gent (State Archive of Ghent)

Rek. Gent 1280–1336: Julius Vuylsteke, ed., *Gentsche Stads- en Baljuwsrekeningen, 1280–1336* (Ghent: F. Meyer-Van Loo, 1900)

Rek. Gent 1336–1349: N. de Pauw and J. Vuylsteke, eds., *De Rekeningen der stad Gent. Tijdvak van Jacob van Artevelde, 1336–1349,* 3 vols. (Ghent: H. Hoste, 1874–1885)

Rek. Gent 1351–1364: Alfons Van Werveke, ed., *Gentse Stads- en Baljuwsrekeningen (1351–1364)* (Brussels: Commission Royale d'Histoire, 1970)

Rek. Gent 1376–1389: J. Vuylsteke, ed., *De Rekeningen der stad Gent. Tijdvak van Philips van Artevelde, 1376–1389,* 2 vols. (Ghent: Ad. Hoste, 1893)

SAG: Stadsarchief te Gent (Municipal Archive of Ghent)

WD: Stadsarchief te Gent, Ser. 156, Register no. 1: Wysdommen der dekenen

Z: Stadsarchief te Gent, Ser. 330, *Zoendincboeken,* bound with registers of *scepenen* of *gedele*

Introduction

1. Compare conclusions of D. Nicholas, "The Population of Fourteenth-Century Ghent," HMGOG, n.s. 24 (1970): 97–111, and Walter Prevenier, "Bevolkingscijfers en professionele strukturen der bevolking van Gent en Brugge in de 14de eeuw," in the *Album Charles Verlinden* (Ghent: Story, 1975), 269–303.

2. A. Verhulst, "Neue Ansichten über die Entstehung der flämischen Städte am Beispiel von Gent und Antwerpen," *Niederlande und Nordwestdeutschland . . . Franz Petri zum 80. Geburtstag* (Cologne and Vienna: Böhlau, 1983), 1–17; A. Verhulst, "Die Frühgeschichte der Stadt Gent," *Die Stadt in der europäischen Geschichte. Festschrift Edith Ennen* (Bonn: Röhrscheid, 1972), 108–137.

3. Note particularly the classic works of Henri Pirenne, *Histoire de Belgique,* 3d ed. (Brussels: Lamertin, 1922), 2: 28–135, and *Early Democracies in the Low Countries: Urban Society and Political Conflict in the Middle Ages and the Renaissance* (New York: Harper and Row, 1963).

4. Prevenier, "Bevolkingscijfers," 278, arrives at 60 percent. For a number of reasons not relevant to the present discussion, I think that this figure is too high for the textile workers.

5. D. Nicholas, "Structures du peuplement, fonctions urbaines et formation du capital dans la Flandre médiévale," *Annales. Économies. Sociétés. Civilisations* 33 (1978): 501–527.

6. Georges Bigwood, "Gand et la circulation des grains en Flandre, du XIVe au XVIIIe siècle," *Vierteljahrsschrift für Sozial- und Wirtschaftsgeschichte* 4 (1906): 397–460; D. Nicholas, "The Scheldt Trade and the 'Ghent War' of 1379–1385," *Bulletin de la Commission Royale d'Histoire* 144 (1978): 255–261.

7. J. A. Van Houtte, *Bruges, essai d'histoire urbaine* (Brussels: La Renaissance du Livre, 1967), and the literature cited. For a more recent study that notes the impact of the Bruges market on Flemish interior trade, see D. Nicholas, "The English trade at Bruges in the last years of Edward III," *Journal of Medieval History* 5 (1979): 23–61.

8. D. Nicholas, *Town and Countryside: Social, Economic, and Political Tensions in Fourteenth-Century Flanders* (Bruges: De Tempel, 1971).

9. For example, Pirenne, *Early Democracies*, 176–177; *Histoire de Belgique*, 2: 64–74.

10. Frans Blockmans, *Het Gentsche Stadspatriciaat tot omstreeks 1302* (Antwerp: De Sikkel, 1938).

11. Paul Rogghé, "Het Gentsche Stadsbestuur van 1302 tot 1345. En een en ander betreffende het Gentsche Stadspatriciaat," HMGOG, n.s. 1 (1944): 135–163.

12. Paul Rogghé, "Het Eerste Bewind der Gentse Hoofdmannen (1319–1329)," *Appeltjes van het Meetjesland* 12 (1961): 1–47.

13. Hans Van Werveke, *Jacob Van Artevelde* (The Hague: Kruseman, 1963); Paul Rogghé, *Vlaanderen en het zevenjarig beleid van Jacob van Artevelde,* 2 vols. (Brussels: H. Steyaert, 1942); a less idealized portrayal of Van Artevelde is found in D. Nicholas, "Artevelde, Jacob van, kapitein van Gent," *Nationaal Biografisch Woordenboek* (Brussels: Koninklijke Academiën van België, 1972) 5: cols. 22–35. For a discussion of the Van Artevelde myth in history, see Patricia Carson, *James van Artevelde: The Man from Ghent* (Gent: E. Story-Scientia, 1980).

14. A. Verhulst, "L'Économie rurale de la Flandre et la dépression économique du bas Moyen Age," *Études Rurales* 10 (1963): 68–80; A. Verhulst, "Bronnen en Problemen betreffende de Vlaamse Landbouw in de late Middeleeuwen," *Agronomisch-Historische Bijdragen* 6 (1964): 205–235; D. Nicholas, "Economic Reorientation and Social Change in Fourteenth-Century Flanders," *Past and Present* 70 (1976): 23–24.

15. Quoted in J. C. Holt, *Robin Hood* (London: Thames and Hudson, 1982), 185.

16. C. Erickson and K. Casey, "Women in the Middle Ages: A Working Bibliography," *Mediaeval Studies* 38 (1976): 340–359.

17. For example Frances and Joseph Gies, *Women in the Middle Ages* (New York: Barnes and Noble, 1978).

18. Eileen Power, *Medieval Women,* ed. M. M. Postan (Cambridge: Cambridge University Press, 1975), 53–75. Miss Power died in 1940; this book was compiled from her lectures.

19. *Histoire Mondiale de la Femme,* publiée sous la direction de Pierre Grimal (Paris, 1965).

20. *Recueils de la Société Jean Bodin* 12: *La Femme* (Brussels, 1962).

21. Shulamith Shahar, *The Fourth Estate. A History of Women in the Middle Ages,* trans. Chaya Galai (London and New York: Methuen, 1983).

22. V. Vanderhaeghen, ed., *Het Klooster Ten Walle en de Abdij den Groenen Briel. Stukken en Oorkonden* (Ghent: C. Annoot-Braeckman, 1888); C. P. Serrure, ed., "Oorkonden betrekkelijk het Karthuizers-Klooster bij Gent . . . 1308–1483," *Vaderlandsch Museum voor Nederduitsche Letterkunde, Oudheid en Geschiedenis* 4 (1861): 325–362; A. Dubois, ed., *Documents relatifs à l'hospice St. Laurent à Gand, publiés par les soins de la Commission administrative des hospices civiles de cette ville* (Ghent, 1867); Elza Luyckx-Foucke, "Het Krankzinnigengesticht St. Jans-ten-Dullen te Gent," *Hospitalia* (Mar., 1942); Luyckx-Foucke, "Het Sint-Aubertus-Gesticht up Poortakker," *Bijdragen tot de Geschiedenis en de Oudeidkunde* 18 (1943): 77–96; D. de Coninck and W. Blockmans, "Geschiedenis van de Gentse Leprozerie 'Het Rijke Gasthuis' vanaf de stichting (*ca.* 1146) tot omstreeks 1370," *Annalen van de Belgische Vereniging voor Hospitaalgeschiedenis* 5 (1967): 3–44; G. Maréchal, "Het Sint-Annahospitaal te Sint-Baafs te Gent," *ibid.*, 4 (1966): 31–50; L. Van Puyvelde, *Un hôpital du moyen âge et une abbaye y annexée: La Biloke de Gand. Etude archéologique* (Ghent: Van Rysselberghe and Rombaut, 1925); Jean Béthune, ed., *Cartulaire du Béguinage de Saint-Elisabeth à Gand* (Bruges, 1883); J. B. Béthune and A. Van Werveke, eds., *Het Godshuis van Sint-Jan & Sint-Pauwel te Gent, bijgenaamd de Leugemeete. Oorkonden* (Ghent: C. Annoot-Braeckman, 1902); Paul Rogghé, "Het Alinshospitaal te Gent," *Appeltjes van het Meetjesland* 16 (1965): 132–145; P. Rogghé, "Gent in de XIVe en de XVe eeuw. Geloof en Devotie, Kerk en Volk," *ibid.*, 20 (1969): 194–217.

23. Of Herlihy's numerous works, see those cited below, together with "Land, Family and Women in Continental Europe, 701–1200," *Traditio* 18 (1962): 89–120; "Women in Medieval Society," Smith History Lecture, 1971 (published Houston: University of St. Thomas, 1971); and "Life Expectancies for Women in Medieval Society," in *The Role of Women in the Middle Ages,* ed. Rosemarie T. Morewedge (Albany: State University of New York Press, 1975), 1–22.

24. A particularly excellent collection of articles, several of which had been published previously in scholarly journals, is *Women in Medieval Society,* ed. Susan Mosher Stuard (Philadelphia: University of Pennsylvania Press, 1976).

25. Peasant parents at Montaillou had a deep if somewhat ritualized affection for their children in the late thirteenth and early fourteenth centuries. Emmanuel Le Roy Ladurie, *Montaillou: The Promised Land of Error* (New York: Random House, 1979), 210–11.

26. Philippe Ariès, *Centuries of Childhood: A Social History of Family Life,* trans. Robert Baldick (New York: Knopf, 1962).

27. *The History of Childhood,* ed. Lloyd de Mause (New York: Harper and Row, 1974).

28. On the subject of children outside the patrician environment, see Barbara Hanawalt, "Childrearing among the Lower Classes of Late Medieval England," *Journal of Interdisciplinary History* 8 (1977): 1–22. For a psychoanalytical approach

based on seventeenth-century texts, see David Hunt, *Parents and Children in History: The Psychology of Family Life in Early Modern France* (New York: Basic Books, 1970).

29. Edward Shorter, *The Making of the Modern Family* (New York: Basic Books, 1975). The cover bears Ariès's encomium: "It is truly excellent . . . a powerful synthesis presented with a logical rigor and grace rare among historians."

30. Lawrence Stone, *The Family, Sex and Marriage in England, 1500–1800* (New York: Harper and Row, 1977).

31. Jack Goody, *The Development of the Family and Marriage in Europe* (Cambridge: Cambridge University Press, 1983).

32. David Herlihy and Christiane Klapisch-Zuber, *Les Toscans et leurs familles: une Étude du catasto florentin de 1427* (Paris: Presses de la Fondation nationale des sciences politiques, 1978). Note also Christiane Klapisch and Michel Demouet, "A uno pane e uno vino: The Rural Tuscan Family at the Beginning of the Fifteenth Century," *Family and Society. Selections from the Annales . . .* , ed. Robert Forster and Orest Ranum (Baltimore: Johns Hopkins University Press, 1976), 41–74; C. Klapisch, "Household and Family in Tuscany in 1427," in Peter Laslett assisted by Richard Wall, *Household and Family in Past Time* (Cambridge: Cambridge University Press, 1972), 267–281.

33. David Herlihy, "Family Solidarity in Medieval Italian History," in *Economy, Society, and Government in Medieval Italy: Essays in Memory of Robert L. Reynolds* (Kent: Kent State University Press, 1969), 173–184.

34. See the discussion of this subject by Jacques Heers, *Family Clans in the Middle Ages. A Study of Political and Social Structures in Urban Areas* (Amsterdam: North Holland, 1977); and Diane Owen Hughes, "Urban Growth and Family Structure in Medieval Genoa," *Past and Present* 28 (1975): 3–28.

35. Richard A. Goldthwaite, *Private Wealth in Renaissance Florence* (Princeton: Princeton University Press, 1968); R. Goldthwaite, *The Building of Renaissance Florence: An Economic and Social History* (Baltimore: Johns Hopkins University Press, 1980), 103–108, 111–112; R. Goldthwaite, "The Florentine Palace as Domestic Architecture," *American Historical Review* 77 (1972): 977–1012.

36. F. W. Kent, *Household and Lineage in Renaissance Florence: The Family Life of the Capponi, Ginori, and Rucellai* (Princeton: Princeton University Press, 1977).

37. Paolo Cammarosano, "Les structures familiales dans les villes d'Italie communale, XIIe-XIVe siècle," in *Famille et Parenté dans l'Occident médiéval. Actes du Colloque . . .* , ed. Georges Duby and Jacques Le Goff (Rome: École Française de Rome, 1977), 182–194.

38. Georges Duby, *The Knight, The Lady, and The Priest: The Making of Modern Marriage in Medieval France* (New York: Random House, 1983), which supersedes his *Medieval Marriage: Two Models from Twelfth-Century France,* trans. Elborg Forster (Baltimore: Johns Hopkins University Press, 1978); G. Duby, "Lineage, Nobility, and Chivalry in the Region of Mâcon during the Twelfth Century," in *Family*

and Society, ed. Forster and Ranum, 16–40; G. Duby, *The Chivalrous Society* (Berkeley and Los Angeles: University of California Press, 1977).

39. Peter Laslett, *The World We Have Lost,* 3d ed. (New York: Scribner's, 1984).

40. J. Hajnal, "European Marriage Patterns in Perspective," in *Population in History,* ed. D. V. Glass and D. E. C. Eversley (London: E. Arnold, 1967), 101–143.

41. For this general discussion, see Peter Laslett, *Family Life and Illicit Love in Earlier Generations* (Cambridge: Cambridge University Press, 1977).

42. Jean-Louis Flandrin, *Families in Former Times. Kinship, Household and Sexuality in Early Modern France* (Cambridge: Cambridge University Press, 1979).

43. See works cited by Laslett in *Family Life,* 47–48.

44. E. Le Roy Ladurie, "Family Structures and Inheritance Customs in Sixteenth-Century France," in *Family and Inheritance: Rural Society in Western Europe, 1200–1800,* ed. Jack Goody, Joan Thirsk, and E. P. Thompson (Cambridge: Cambridge University Press, 1976), 37–70; E. Le Roy Ladurie, "A System of Customary Law: Family Structures and Inheritance Customs in Sixteenth-Century France," in *Family and Society,* ed. Forster and Ranum, 75–103, both after Jean Yver, "Les deux groupes de coutumes du Nord," *Revue du Nord* 25 (1953) and 26 (1954).

45. Cicely Howell, "Peasant Inheritance Customs in the Midlands, 1280–1700," in *Family and Inheritance,* ed. Goody et al., 112–155, notes that there is some evidence of the Parisian system in England, but unigeniture was more usual.

46. Laslett and Wall, *Household and Family in Past Time, passim.*

Chapter 1. The Fruits of Frailty

1. Moenin was a diminutive form of Symoen. SAG, G 5,1,f. 3v; G 6,2, f. 20r; G 4,5,f. 48v; G 1,4, fos. 2r. 5v.

2. SAG, K 1, f. iiir.

3. SAG, G 3,3, f. 17r; G 1,4, fos. 2r, 5v; K 10,1, f. 8v; K 10,2, f. 52v; K 11,2, f. 53v; K 12, f. 29r; G 8,3, f. 14v; K 6,1, fos. 18v, 48r.

4. W. Van Iterson, "Vrouwenvoogdij," *Tijdschrift voor Rechtsgeschiedenis* 14 (1936): 421–452; 15 (1937): 78–96, 175–190, 287–387.

5. SAG, K 5,1, f. 8r; G 5,1, f. 63r; G 3,1, f. 39v; G 3,2, f. 12r; G 5,1 f. 6v.

6. See D. Nicholas, "Crime and Punishment in Fourteenth-Century Ghent." *Revue Belge de Philologie et d'Histoire* 48 (1970): 289–334, 1141–1176.

7. An exceptional case of 1380 has the death of Kateline Van den Doerne simply forgiven, since the man responsible had already been exiled for the deed. In no other cases involving women was the blood price renounced. SAG, Z 6,5, f. 1v.

8. Fewer women than men were recorded as committing crime in England at this time, but the proportions are still substantially higher than in Ghent. See Barbara Hanawalt, "The Female Felon in Fourteenth-Century England," *Viator* 5 (1974): 253–268, reprinted in *Women in Medieval Society,* ed. Stuard, 125–140.

9. ARA, BR 1371, f. 21; BR 1376, fos. 3, 19; BR 1373, f. 1.

10. For one case in which childbed death seems probable, compare SAG, G 4,5, f. 10v with G 5,2, f. 47r.

11. SAG, G 8,3, fos. 36v, 40r; G 8,4, fos. 80r, 81r; G 9,1, f. 62r; K 11,2, fos. 52r, 61r.

12. SAG, G 4,4, f. 48r; G 4,5, f. 66r–v; G 5,1, f. 69r; Z 5,1, f. 13r. A new *staet* was provided in 1374, showing some decline in the value of her rental property in the intervening years, but additional land had been bought for her with the profit of her rents; G 5,4, f. 46v.

13. SAG, G 2,3, f. 37v. The age of legal majority, however, was twelve. See ch. 7, and n. 26.

14. SAG, G 6,1, f. 1r.

15. Laslett, *World We Have Lost*, 2d ed. (New York: Edward Arnold, 1971), 84–93.

16. SAG, G 6,1, f. 12v; K 5,2, f. 29 r–v; G 1,1, f. 55r.

17. Thomas Kuehn, *Emancipation in Late Medieval Florence* (New Brunswick: Rutgers University Press, 1982), 20–21, notes that emancipation under civil law made a male a paterfamilias and a woman a materfamilias, but he does not elaborate on the practical impact of that distinction.

18. SAG, G 5,5, fos. 4v, 12r; K 3,1, f. 38r; K 13,1, fos. 43r, 53v; G 9,1, f. 69r; K 7, f. 30b r.

19. SAG, G 2,2, f. 29v; K 11,2, f. 8r; G 8,1, f. 57v.

20. SAG, G 7,3, f. 59v; G 8,2, fos. 46r, 49r, 87 r–v; G 8,4, f. 52v; K 10,2, fos. 105v, 115r, 130r; K 11,1, fos. 5v, 91r, 108r; K 12, f. 29v.

21. SAG, G 6,1, f. 19r.

22. In Mediterranean Europe the girl normally received only her dowry. Shahar, *Fourth Estate*, 177.

23. SAG, K 4,1, f. 26v; K 2,2, f. 17r.

24. SAG, K 10,2, f. 2r; K 1, fos. 117r, 247r; Z 5,5, f. 19v.

25. SAG, K 1, f. 110; K 11,1, f. 108v; K 1, f. 52r; RAG, SN 118, f. 114r; SAG, K 3,2, f. 3v; K 12, f. 83r; K 7, f. 2r.

26. RAG, charter of St. Michiel's church, Apr. 25, 1361; SAG, K 1, fos. 14r, 104r, 13r, 21r.

27. SAG, K 7, f. 35r.

28. Jack Goody, "Inheritance, Property and Women: Some Comparative Considerations," in *Family and Inheritance,* ed. Goody et al., 25.

29. SAG, G 6,1, fos. 20v, 22r; Ser. 152, no. 4, f. 53v; Ser. 152, no. 5, f. 64r.

30. For examples of consent given, see, among many others, SAG, K 1, f. 229v; K 2,2, f. 44r; K 4,2, f. 23r; RAG, charter of St. Michiel's church, Sept. 21, 1388; see also SAG, G 4,5, f. 40r; G 7,5, f. 26r; K 2,2. fos. 29v, 43r.

31. SAG, K 6,2, f. 57v.

32. SAG, G 7,4, f. 42r; G 8,1, fos. 34v, 74v; K 13,1, f. 48r.

33. SAG, K 1, f. 232r; K 4,1, f. 33v.

34. SAG, K 2,1, f. 14r; K 7, f. 30b v; G 5,5, f. 41v.

35. SAG, K 3,2, f. 42r; K 4,2, f. 40v; G 5,4, f. 41v; G 5,5,f. 19r; G 8,2, f. 37r; G 8,3, f. 64r; G 9,1, f. 15r.

36. SAG, G 4,3, f. 18 bis; G 4,2, fos. 18v, 19r; G 7,5, f. 15r; Z 4,4, f. 3r; G 6,4, f. 21r; G 7,5, fos. 33v, 43v; G 8,1, f. 6r; G 7,5, f. 15r.

37. SAG, K 2,2, fos. 41r, 42r, 91–1.

38. SAG, K 4,1, f. 29v; K 3,2, BB, f. 3v; Z 5,2, f. 7v; K 3,2, fos. 42v, 44r; G 5,1, f. 52v; K 10,2, f. 48r; K 11,2, f. 51r; K 13,1, f. 42r.

Chapter 2. What Man Puts Asunder

1. SAG, K 1, BB 1353, f. 143r; Z 2,2, f. 7r; Z 6,2, f. 12r; Z 6,5, f. 6v.

2. SAG, Z 6,4, f. 7v; Z 1,3, f. 11v.

3. SAG, K 11,1, f. 54v.

4. See, for example, SAG, G 7,5, fos. 10r, 46r, 47v; G 8,1, fos. 5v, 37v, 61 bis v, 63v, 60r, 74v; G 8,3, fos. 24v, 26v; G 8,4, fos. 6r, 50v, 51v, 63r; G 9,1,f.48v.

5. SAG, G 2,2, f. 24r.

6. Monique Vleeschouwers-Van Melkebeek, "Aperçu typologique des principales sortes de registres produits par l'officialité de Tournai au moyen âge, avec des notes sur le registre de sentences de Bruxelles (1448–1459)," in *Bronnen voor de Geschiedenis van de Instellingen in België. Handelingen van het Colloquium te Brussel 15.–18. IV. 1975* (Brussels, 1975), 430–431. In contrast, of 122 cases in a marriage litigation register in rural Cambridgeshire, eighty-nine involved clandestine unions. Consanguinity and affinity, those twin pillars of iniquity so despised by the moralists of the church, were less frequently used as grounds for annulment than bigamy. See Michael M. Sheehan, "The Formation and Stability of Marriage in Fourteenth-Century England: The Evidence of an Ely Register," *Mediaeval Studies* 33 (1971): 228–263.

7. SAG, K 5,2, f. 44r; K 6,2, f. 58r.

8. SAG, G 1,1, f. 1r; G 1a, f. 34r; G 1,2, f. 39r; K 1, f. 115v; G 2,1, f. 11v; *Rek. Gent 1351–1364*, 186.

9. SAG, G 7,3, f. 27r; K 6, f. 26r.

10. SAG, G 5,4, f. 28r; G 7,4, f. 4r.

11. SAG, G 8,3, f. 24r.

12. SAG, G 7,5, fos. 46r, 51v; G 8,2, f. 88v; G 8,3, f. 76r; G 2,5, f. 1r; K 3,2, f. 33r; G 7,3, f. 33v; G 7,4, fos. 16v–17r; K 9,1, f. 29r; Ser. 152, no. 3, f. 28r; Ser. 152, no. 4, f. 26v. Another case illustrating the dangers of failing to finalize a separation is the claim of Lisbette Van Worems against her husband Jan de Knijf for property which he had acquired since they had separated de facto, but not de jure; SAG, G 2,4, f. 9r. Note also Reynoud Hughenzone, whose wife had to pay his claims on property which she had inherited; SAG, G 2,5, f. 37r.

13. SAG, K 12, f. 72r.

14. The Kateline Platijns here is not the same as Callekin, daughter of Jan Platijn, who was evidently orphaned during the plague of 1368 and was still under
wardship in 1385 and evidently had no connection with the Overakkers. She may
have been a niece of the Kateline Platijns of our case; SAG, G 3,4, f. 1r; K 4,2, f. 4v;
K 8,1, f. 20v; K 9,1, f. 12r; K 10,1, f. 27r; K 13,1, f. 8r. Jan de Wannemaker, separated
from his wife in 1384, had also fathered a bastard by his maid by Apr. 1391; SAG, K
9,2, fos. 36v, 39r.

15. SAG, G 7,2, f. 41v; G 7,3, f. 62v.

16. SAG, K 11, 2, f. 65r; K 12, f. 32v; K 13,1, f. 6v.

17. SAG, K 1, f. 3r.

18. See SAG, K 11,2, f. 11v; K 11,1, fos. 37r, 100r, for examples.

19. SAG, G 2,1, f. 25v.

20. SAG, G 1,1, f. 53v; G 1,2, f. 11v; G 1,3, f. 35r; G 1,4, f. 1r; K 4,2, f. 32v; G 6,1, f.
4v; G 6,5, f. 18v.

21. SAG, K 10,2, f. 82r; K 11,1, fos. 37v, 106v; G 8,3, f. 75v; K 11,2, fos, 14r, 64v,
75v; G 8,4, f. 50v; G 9,1, f. 66v; K 11,2, f. 10r; G 9,1, fos. 10v–11r; K 11,2, fos. 13v, 14 r–
v; G 8,4, f. 50v; K 11,2, f. 64v; K 12, fos. 23v, 33r; G 9,1, fos. 44r, 48v; G 9,2, f. 15v.

22. SAG, K 1, f. 188r; G 2, 4, f. 22 r–v.

23. Jan de Mey separated from Kateline, daughter of Philips de Schachtmaker,
in May 1377. There was one child, and the marital assets were divided into thirds.
Three years earlier Kateline had been given three years' possession of her father's
house, and the term was expiring just as they separated. SAG, K 6,1, f. 44v; K 4,2,
f. 20r.

24. SAG, K 10,1, f. 55r; K 2,2, f. 33v.

25. SAG, K 3,1, f. 32v; K 9,2, f. 22r; K 6,2, f. 58r; K 8,1, fos. 10v, 11r; K 12, f. 29r.

26. SAG, K 1, f. 27v. For another case suggesting this principle, see G 7,3, f. 16r.

27. See, for example, the case of Willem Uten Hove, SAG, K 1, fos. 1v–2r.

28. SAG, Ser. 152, no. 3, fos. 9v, 11v.

29. SAG, G 1a, f. 16r; K 7, fos. 3v, 44v; K 13,1, f. 6r; K 5,2, f. 10r.

30. SAG, K 6,2, f. 31r; K 10,2, f. 92r. See also the case of Mathijs Van den
Wincle, K 13,1, f. 54r.

31. SAG, K 5,1, f. 19v; G 8,2, f. 37v.

32. SAG, K 1, fos. 176r, 250r.

33. SAG, K 4,1, f. 1v; G 1,4, f. 11r; G 1,1, f. 36r; G 3,1, f. 23v; G 4,1, fos. 18r, 27r; G
4, 2, fos. 14v, 50r; G 4,4, fos. 9v, 14r. A similar settlement was made between Jan de
Wannemaker and his wife Kateline Leeuwaerts, who had separated before 1384. As
a supplementary agreement in that year Jan was to pay her 14 lb. gr. and take their
joint residence and all chattels and furnishings. SAG, K 9,2, f. 36v.

34. SAG, K 2,1, f. 2v; K 5,1, f. 11r; G 4,1, f. 17v; K 6,2, fos. 57v, 42r, 48r, 58r; G 6,4,
f. 29v; G 7,1, f. 3v; K 8,1, f. 30v; G 7,4, f. 77v; *Rek. Gent 1351–1364*, 659, and SAG,

Ser. 400, 9,f. 234r, for the references to Jan de Pottere as a moneychanger; those to Aechte de Pottere are SAG, Ser. 400, 9, fos. 254v, 295v, 318r; Ser. 400, 10, fos. 4r, 40r; *Rek. Gent 1376–1389,* 5, 63, 255, 317. For the house in the Kouterstraat, see RAG, charter of St. Niklaas's church, July 7, 1381.

35. SAG, G 1,1, f. 38r; Z 1,4, f. 1r; G 1,3, fos. 31r, 32r. Jacob de Costere, in turn, murdered Frans Louf, whose family included tanners, in 1361 and was himself killed in 1376 by Jason Sausier. We do not know whether the succession of killings had any connection. SAG, Z 3,1, f. 10v; Z 6,1, f. 20v.

36. SAG, K 7, fos. 22v, 31v, 38v; K 9,1, f. 24r; G 8,1, f. 70r; G 8,2, fos. 30v, 68v; K 12, f. 12r; G 4,5, fos. 23v, 36r; K 5,1, f. 9r; G 6,2, f. 31r; K 6,2, f. 32r.

37. SAG, K 2,1, f. 34r; Z 5,5, f. 13v; G 6,5, f. 11r; G 1,1, f. 25v; K 4,2, f. 2r.

38. ADN, B 1566, f. 10v; SAG, K 1, fos. 185r, 185-1, 216-3, 257r.

39. ARA, BR 1374, f. 1; BR 1377, f. 1.

40. SAG, G 3,4, fos. 27r, 47r; Z 3,4, f. 15v.

41. SAG, Z 2,2, f. 13v; K 3,1, f. 6v; G 3,3, f. 13r; K 3,1, fos. 9v, 39v; G 4,5, f. 17v; G 5,2, f. 33v; K 3,2, fos. 30r, 32v; Z 6,1, f. 21v; K 6,2, fos. 31v, 32v, the property division at the separation; G 4,5, f. 17v; K 3,1, f. 39v; K 3,2, f. 30r; K 4,1, f. 20v; G 2,5, 12r; Z 6,4, f.2r, the story of the attempted murder. Both Jan and Mergriet were from brewer families. Jan sold his brewery and moved to a house across the street in 1382. He and his wife are mentioned together in 1385 as heirs of Lisbette Van Coudenbrouc, suggesting that he had not renounced her property when they separated; SAG, K 8,3, f. 36r; G 7,5, fos. 49r, 59r.

42. SAG, Ser. 400, 10, f. 39v; G 2,3, f. 39v; Z 3,3, f. 5r; G 3,3, f. 42v; G 3,5, f. 27r; Z 4,5, f. 9r; K 4,1, fos. 30v, 36v; K 4,2, f. 27v; K 6,2, f. 51v.

43. SAG, G 9,2, f. 5v; G 8,4, f. 77v; K 11,2, f. 66v.

44. SAG, G 3,5, f. 5r; G 4,4, f. 38r; G 6,2, f. 7v; G 5,3, f. 1r; Z 5,2, f. 7r; K 3,2, f. 44r.

45. Zoetin and Jan Van Libertsa had an adult daughter, who renounced the estate of Simon de Pape when he died in 1384. The girl's parents were both dead by early 1387, the mother apparently first, for Jan Van Libertsa left a widow named Kateline Paridaens. SAG, G 5,1, f. 60v; K 7, f. 43v; K 6,1, f. 30r; G 6,3, f. 52r; Z 6,5, f. 1v, the attack on Van Libertsa in 1380; G 7,4, f. 82r; K 10,2, f. 52v; G 3,1, f. 18r; G 4,2, f. 1r; G 6,1, f. 41v; G 8,2, f. 53r.

46. SAG, Z 2,3, f. 9v; Z 1,3, f. 5r; G 1,3, f. 14r; Z 1,3, f. 7r; G 1,5, f. 40r; K 1, f. 241r; Z 3,2, f. 11v; K 3,2, f. 23r.

47. Aechte's mendacity continued. In 1373 she lost a suit against the abbot of Eename, in which she claimed that she owned half a mill while the abbot argued that he had bought out her rights for a life annuity. Recordkeeping was sloppy, and she evidently thought that she could get away with a transparent lie in the presumed absence of documentation; SAG, G 4,4, f. 31v; G 6,1, f. 7v; G 2,3, f. 28r; G 3,4, f. 17v; G 4,1, fos. 2r, 7v, 20r; K 4,1, f. 37v; Z 2,4, f. 1r; K 2,2, f. 45v.

48. For his career, see SAG, Z 2,2, f. 14v; Z 3,5, f. 6r; Z 4,2, f. 9r; Z 6,3, f. 19v; Z 6,1, fos. 4r, 13r; Z 6,2, f. 17r; Z 6,3, fos. 14v, 15v; Z 4,4, f. 5v. The marital separation is given K 4,2, f. 8v.

49. SAG, G 1,1, f. 16v.

50. SAG, K 1, f. 184v; G 2,5, f. 7v; G 4,5, f. 43r; G 4,4, f.48r.

51. SAG, G 1,3, f. 22v; K 6, f. 55r; G 6,4, f. 29v; G 7,2, f. 32r; G 8,1, f.11r; G 8,3, f. 15r; G 8,4, f. 68r; K 11,2, f. 23v.

52. This is another case of deliberate timing of a separation decree. The estate of the wife's mother, Kateline Rijnvisch, was being settled through most of 1374. On the day the final settlement was promulgated, Nov. 4, 1374, her daughter and Fransois Van den Boengaerde announced their property division. Why the objection regarding guardianship of Meuskin was not raised earlier is not clear. By 1390 Fransois Van den Boengaerde was fathering bastards by Zoetin Vierjaers. SAG, K 5,1, f. 9r; G 5,4, f. 21r; K 5,1, f. 8v; K 12, f. 44r; G 6,4, f. 34v; G 7,1, f. 13r; G 8,1, f. 74r.

53. SAG, K 7, fos. 34v, 37v.

54. SAG, G 5,2, f. 6r–v; G 2,1, f. 23v; K 4,1, f. 8v; G 6,1, f. 48r; G 7,1, f. 35r; G 7,2, f. 17v.

55. For the Van der Houven references, see SAG, G 9,1, fos. 26v, 36v, 32r; G 8,4, fos. 75v, 68v; G 7,3, f. 67v; G 8,4, f. 17v; G 8,2, f. 26r; G 6,2, f. 19v; G 7,4, f. 65v; G 8,1, 63v. For Jan de Bitere, see K 10,1, f. 8v, where he is called "Meester Jan," a sign of status and distinction; G 5,1, f. 32r; G 5,2, f. 15r; G 7,1, f. 6r; G 8,4, f. 68v; G 4,5, f. 58v; G 4,1, fos. 5v, 24r.

Chapter 3. What Man Joins, Let Not God Put Asunder

1. Walter Prevenier, ed., *De Oorkonden der Graven van Vlaanderen (1191–aanvang 1206). 2. Uitgave* (Brussels: Commission Royale d'Histoire, 1964), 27.

2. A. E. Gheldolf, ed., *Coutume de la Ville de Gand*, 1 (Brussels, 1868), 450–452.

3. ARA, BR 1372, f. 1; BR 1376, f. 3; BR 1377, f. 3.

4. Shahar, *Fourth Estate*, 83; Goody, *Development of the Family and Marriage*, 24–25.

5. SAG, G 7,4, f. 30v.

6. SAG, G 3,5, f. 21r; G 6,5, f. 6r.

7. SAG, K 2,1, fos. 12r, 19r, 16a.

8. SAG, G 3, 1, f. 26r; K 5,2, fos. 15r, 38v, 22v, 46r; K 10,2, f. 76v. She had lost her mother by late 1360. Since the sources of the mid-1370s mention three adult brothers, she was probably the daughter of a second wife who died young, perhaps at her birth, and hence would have been in her mid-teens by 1375. Van der Wostinen was playing with fire, for the Heinmans were involved in several homicides during these years. We hear nothing more of the pair until 1387, when Lisbette Heinmans, as Van der Wostinen's widow, bought a share of a house adjacent to her residence.

9. Kateline and her sister were emancipated in 1351, while Jacob and his brother

only acquitted their father of their maternal estate in 1360. By June 1372 Kateline was married to Heinric Borluut, whose brother Jan had been the guardian whom she acquitted in 1351. She thus evidently married a younger man, than a much older man when the first died. SAG, K 3,2, f. 34v; G 1,2, f. 9r; G 3,1, f. 33r; K 2,1, fos. 9r, 17v.

10. *Rek. Gent 1351–1364,* 434; SAG, K 1, f. 230r; G 3,1, f. 47v; G 4,1, f. 6r; G 4,2, f. 9r; G 4,3,f. 38v.

11. SAG, K 3,1, f. 16v; G 3,3, fos. 18v, 47r; G 3,5, f. 10v; G 5,3, f. 9v; K 2,1, f. 2v.

12. SAG, K 10,2, f. 45r; G 7,2, f. 13r.

13. SAG, G 6,2, f. 47r; G 7,4, f. 39v; G 8,3, f. 58v; G 8,4, f. 2r; K 11,1, f. 78r.

14. SAG, K 10,1, fos. 6r, 28 r–v; K 11,2, f. 66v; K 12, f. 11r; G 7,5, f. 9v; G 8,1, fos. 5v–6r, 38v; G 8,3, f. 59v; RAG, charter of St. Pieter's abbey, Nov. 22, 1375.

15. SAG, K 9,1, f. 8v; K 10,2, f. 88v; K 11,2, f. 10v; K 12, f. 69r.

16. SAG, G 7,4, fos. 17r, 25v; K 10,1, fos. 28v, 55v. For another case involving the cooperation of another woman with the girl, note the seduction of Celie, daughter of Jan Ser Maechleins of St. Baafs, by Lievin Van Sloete in 1372; SAG, G 2,1, f. 15v; G 2,2, f. 10v; K 1, f. 240r; G 3,5, f. 23v; G 4,4, fos. 26r, 43v; G 4,5, f. 72v; G 5,2, f. 58r; K 3,2, f. 34v.

17. SAG, K 1, f. 2r.

18. SAG, K 6,2, f. 52v.

19. N. de Pauw, ed., *De Voorgeboden der stad Gent in de XIVe eeuw (1337–1382)* (Ghent: C. Annoot-Braeckman, 1885), 52.

20. SAG, Z 6,1, f. 13-1; Z 4,5, f. 10v.

21. SAG, Z 4,1, f. 13v; G 1,5, f. 9r.

22. SAG, Z 6,2, f. 19v; Z 5,2, f. 9v; ARA, BR 1379, f. 1; SAG, Z 3,4, f. 3r; Z 3,5, f. 14r.

23. SAG, Z 4,2, f. 8v. See also SAG, K 1, BB, f. 145r.

24. SAG, Z 4,2, f. 3v; Z 5,5, f. 6r; ARA, BR 1382, f. 3.

25. ARA, BR 1377, f. 3; SAG, Z 1,3, f. 13v.

26. The Willebaert brothers were both hostellers. Although Jacob later became eminently respectable, he evidently had a hot temper, which got him into trouble when he was young; see below, p. 148. Daneel seems to have had a bad reputation. He was involved in some fracases in 1358, and by 1361 he owed considerable money at the cloth halls. He went bankrupt in the late 1360s. Both parties soon married other people, and the sources mention no further contact between the families. Daneel Willebaert had married Aleit, daughter of Jan Borluut, by May 1363. By Mar. 1361 Kateline Kindekin had married Wasselin Van den Pitte, who survived her in an evidently childless marriage. She died between June 10 and Oct. 6, 1382. Her testament, full of pious donations to charity, and her career after 1358 give no hint of her youthful indiscretion. SAG, K 1, f. 179r; K 3,2, f. 21r; Z 2,4, f. 5 bis; K 1, f. 257r; K 2,1, f. 24v; K 3,2, f. 18v; Z 2,3, f. 8v; K 3,1, f. 30r; K 4,1, f. 19v; G 3,1, f. 46v; G 7,3, f. 21v; G 7,2, f. 29 r–v.

27. ARA, BR 1377, f. 3; SAG, K 10,2, f. 2r.

28. SAG, Z 6,3, f. 11r–v.

29. SAG, Z 2,4, f. 9r–v; Z 4,1, 2v.

30. SAG, Z 3,1, f. 2v. We are not told that the girl was a Beguine. If she was not, that she was out alone at night in itself suggests a fair degree of freedom of movement for women.

31. SAG, Z 1,2, f. 12v; Z 1,2, f. 8v.

32. SAG, Z 6,2, f. 18r. The term used for her injuries is *quitsinghen ende smerte*, which ordinarily means that the perpetrators did not initiate hostilities. Had they done so, *mesgripe* would be the normal term, and they would have been sent on pilgrimages, rather than being sentenced to pay her compensation. She did not, however, have to do penance for her own faults.

33. SAG, Z 6,4, 8r. Clappaert was married; his wife settled his estate in 1383; G 7,4, f. 19r.

34. SAG, Z 6,4, f. 8r; G 4,4, 49v; Z 6,3, f. 3v.

35. Young Clemencie is probably not the girl born in 1365, whose name was Griele, although names for very young children are occasionally transposed in these sources. SAG, K 2,2, f. 8v; Z 4,1, f. 14r; K 4,1, f. 25r; K 8,2, f. 6v.

36. SAG, Z 5,5, f. 9r.

37. SAG, Z 4,3, f. 11r; G 5,1, f. 21r.

38. SAG, Z 5,5, f. 10r.

39. SAG, K 7, unnumbered folio inserted.

40. Burghers of Ghent who committed crimes outside the city usually chose trial at the site of the deed, for fines according to the *Keuren* of the villages and small towns were much lower than in Ghent. The *scepenen* of Ghent sometimes sent notification to the rural magistrates inhibiting a trial once it had begun, and no village would dare to resist; see Nicholas, *Town and Countryside*, 72–73. Hence in 1379 Jan Pauwels, accused of rape before the *scepenen* of Ghent, was allowed to choose trial outside the city; SAG, K 7, f. 54r.

41. SAG, K 5,1, f. 34r; Z 6,2, f. 20v; Z 6,3, f. 9v; G 6,3, f. 27r; G 6,2, f. 47v; Z 6,3, f. 22v; G 8,1, f. 66v.

42. SAG, G 5,4, f. 15r.

43. She did in fact marry legally, to the prominent Gentenaar Sohier Walraven, and sold her rights on Veys's estate to his kin in 1388; SAG, K 3,2, f. 7v; G 8,3, f. 61r; G 5,2, fos. 53r, 62r.

44. SAG, K 1, f. 126r; Z 1,3, f. 6r; K 8,2, f. 21v; K 8,3, f. 25v; Z 5,2, f. 27v.

45. SAG, G 7,3, fos. 38v, 40v; K 6, f. 31v; G 3,1, f. 9r.

46. In 1373 the wheelwright Daneel de Temmerman willed 24 lb. gr. to Adelise, daughter of Heinric de Pape of Bailleul, and her daughter by him for loans and goods received; SAG, K 4,2, f. 3v.

47. SAG, K 3,2, f. 21v; K 5,1, f. 24v; K 8,3, f. 34r; K 10,1, f. 23v; K 6,2, f. 47v; K 7, f. 46r. Waelkin was evidently a bachelor, for he had no other children. If either lady

gave birth to a male, he would get the *montzoen;* SAG, Z 1,1, f. 5v.

48. SAG, K 1, f. 134r.

Chapter 4. Freedom in Bondage

1. The case of Ghent suggests far more deviation from legal norms than seems to have been the case at Ragusa, where aristocratic women were found in business, but to a limited extent. Even here, however, the city statutes consign women a purely domestic role. See Susan M. Stuard, "Women in Charter and Statute Law: Medieval Ragusa/Dubrovnik," in Stuard, ed., *Women in Medieval Society,* 199–208.

2. For the relative wealth of the parishes of Ghent, drawn from a list of 1327 enumerating the persons who could be taxed in case of emergency, see Nicholas, "Structures du peuplement," 514–516.

3. E. M. Meijers, *Het Ligurisch Erfrecht in de Nederlanden.* III. *Het Oost-Vlaamsche Erfrecht* (Haarlem: H. J. Tjeenk Willink en zoon, 1936), 32–50.

4. In a case of 1386 a husband was apparently arguing that the fact that his wife had gone insane and thus could not make a binding contract prevented him from disposing of common property. While the magistrates rejected this particular argument, there were clearly some customary limitations on the husband's discretion. SAG, K 10,2, f. 18r.

5. See case of Godeverd de Wayere, SAG, K 4,1, f. 23r.

6. See, for example, SAG, K 11,1, fos. 9v, 63v. The same problem could arise when the husband had stood surety or in connection with debts incurred during the wife's minority; G 8,4, f. 7r; G 9,1, f. 56v. The wife's heirs could also be bound; G 8,3, f. 25r.

7. SAG, K 1, f. 157r.

8. For that matter it is surprising enough that Van den Kerchove, who was raised in the Mayhuus household, did not know the true state of affairs. SAG, G 8,4, f. 45r; G 5,5, fos. 33r, 41v; G 6,3, f. 36v; G 6,2, f. 31v.

9. See, for example, the case of the daughter of Jacob Van Artevelde, who sold her father's property at Baardonc and mortgaged his real estate complex "de Vos" to pay the enormous debts of her husband, Jan de Scoteleere; N. de Pauw, ed., *Cartulaire historique et généalogique des Artevelde* (Brussels: Hayez, 1920), 324–326.

10. SAG, G 4,4, f. 39r, case of Philips Uten Dale; K 1, f. 114r; K 7, f. 29b r.

11. SAG, G 7,3, f. 6r; K 3,1, f. 4v; G 4,5, f. 47v.

12. See SAG, K 6,2, f. 51r; K 5,1, f. 38r; G 3,5, f. 6r; K 11,1, f. 48r; K 5,2, f. 50r; Z 2,3, f. 4 bis; K 1, f. 142.

13. SAG, K 1, fos. 54v, 55r. 67v; K 5,1, f. 3r; G 8,5, f. 3v; G 4,5, f. 28r; G 1,2, f. 30r; K 10,2, f. 20v.

14. SAG, G 6,4, f. 9r; K 9,1, f. 23v.

15. SAG, K 1, fos. 23r, 10r, 109r; G 7,4, f. 10r; K 11,2, f. 14r; K 13, 1, f. 66r.

16. SAG, K 1, f. 215–2; Z 1,2, f. 4v.

17. SAG, G 2,5, f. 48v, for one example.

18. SAG, G 2,4, f. 42v.

19. SAG, K 3,2, fos. 15r, 25r; K 4,2, f. 5r. Most of the creditors acquitted the couple on Oct. 3, 1373. They must have inherited property to pay off the debt so quickly.

20. When Kateline, daughter of the meyer of Zegelsem, was assaulted, the guilty parties accepted her father's arbitration. Her surety for good behavior was her brother, but she subsequently gave personal consent to this arrangement; SAG, Z 3,2, 10v. In another case that is perhaps more instructive, Everard Van den Wincle and his wife had taken the entire estate of Lisbette de Blasere as heirs. Lelye Beerevelt claimed a share of the estate, represented by her legal guardian Jan Hoernic. Costs on Lelye's behalf done by Van den Wincle and his wife were annulled, since Lelye had not been present to consent to them, and this without apparent reference to Hoernic's role; K 1, fos. 120r, 124v.

21. The husband was dead by 1387, and she was being pursued by several men who had been damaged as his sureties. SAG, K 10,1, f. 18v; K 9,2, f. 23r; K 10,2, fos. 46r, 115v; K 11,1, fos. 2r. 4v.

22. SAG, K 1, fos. 122v, 213r, 232r; G 1,5, f. 1v; K 8,2, f. 22r; K 1, f. 154r; K 10,1, f. 26r. The wife of Jan Van der Wostinen, who apparently was physically unable to move about, joined others, presumably relatives, in acting for him in 1385; G 7,5, f. 31r.

23. SAG, K 12, f. 59v; G 2,5, fos. 7v, 16v.

24. SAG, K 13,1, f. 2v; G 4,1, f. 22v; G 7,4, f. 83v; K 10,1, f. 6v; K 13,1, f. 2v; G 7,5, f. 56r; G 8,1, f. 3v; K 10,2, fos. 78r, 79r, 124v, 107v; K 11,1, fos. 41v, 73r, 97v, 55r; K 11,2, f. 63r; K 12, f. 19v; K 13,1, f. 61r.

25. No kinship is stated, and the document only makes sense if we assume that an artisan was entering the priesthood in mid-life and wanted to pass on his business; SAG, K 11,2, f. 75r.

Chapter 5. Bondage in Freedom

1. SAG, G 2,1, f. 4v.

2. De Pauw, ed., *Voorgeboden*, 104.

3. In 1361 Jacob Godewale and his wife claimed damages from Michiel de Vlaminc and unnamed, armed companions for expenses incurred by the wife, who was evidently in charge, although the reference can also be interpreted to mean that she threw the roisterers out. The Godewales were apparently small operators, for they never posted bond as hostellers. SAG, K 1, f. 236v.

4. *Rek. Gent 1336–1349*, 2: 543, 545, 547, 554. Her surety in 1342 was her brother, Justaas Rijm.

5. *Rek. Gent 1336–1349,* 2: 546; 3: 9; SAG, G 2,4, f. 37r; G 2,5, fos. 9r, 49r; Ser. 93 bis, no. 7, f. 14r. For the chantry, see RAG, charter of St. Bavo's abbey, Mar. 4, 1358.

6. *Rek. Gent 1336–1349,* 2: 560; 3: 9, 406.

7. References in SAG, Ser. 301, books of receivers for 1372, 1373, 1365.

8. *Rek. Gent 1351–1364,* 434; SAG, G 1,3, f. 7v; G 1,4, f. 17v; G 1,5, f. 35r; G 4,4, f. 35r; K 6,2, f. 34v; Z 3,5, f. 13r; G 7,4, fos. 19r, 51r; K 10,2, fos. 19v, 116v; K 11,1, f. 30v; K 11,2, f. 7r; K 7, f. 24v; K 3,1, BB f. 1r.

9. SAG, G 8,1, f. 58r; K 2,2, f. 37r; K 8,3, fos. 6r, 25r; K 4,2, f. 7r; K 5,1, fos. 38v, 43r; K 5,2, f. 37r; K 9,2, f. 15v; K 10,1, f. 32r; G 8,1, fos. 58r, 79r; G 8,2, f. 11r; K 12, f. 55v; K 13,1, f. 7v; K 11,1, f. 80v.

10. SAG, K 1, f. 67v.

11. The sergeants were still trying to get their money in 1366, and the count himself authorized them to proceed against her and her new husband; SAG, K 2,2, fos. 22v, 58–1.

12. SAG, K 9,1, f. 7r; G 7,3, f. 62r. The word is *prijsterigghe,* which cannot refer to a man.

13. SAG, K 6,2, f. 51v; K 8,3, fos. 16v, 32r.

14. In 1386 a debt was paid to Kateline Van der Zickelen at Ter Zickelen, the biggest bank in Ghent, owned by her family; SAG, K 10,2, f. 26r. In 1387 a debt was owed to Gillis Zoete's widow, due at the hostel of Simon Van Roeselare in Den Ham, either to her or to Simon in her name; SAG, K 10,2, f. 112v.

15. *Rek. Gent 1351–1364,* 184.

16. SAG, Ser. 301, 5, Book of Sureties for 1375–76, f. 2r.

17. *Rek. Gent 1336–1349,* 3: 406; *Rek. Gent 1351–1364,* 432, 496.

18. SAG, Ser. 301, 2, behind Jaarregister, f. 3r; Ser. 400, 9, fos. 233v, 254v; *Rek. Gent 1376–1389,* 4, 170.

19. *Rek. Gent 1336–1349,* 3: 445; *Rek. Gent 1351–1364,* 247, 251.

20. *Rek. Gent 1351–1364,* 23, 90. We do not know the basis on which the fees were assessed on the moneychangers.

21. SAG, Ser. 93 bis, no. 7, f. 14r; *Rek. Gent 1336–1349,* 2: 166, 543, and *passim.*

22. SAG, Z 1,3, f. 8v; On June 2, 1363, he and Celie gave a rent to their daughter, a sister in the leper hospital. His estate was being settled fifteen months later. RAG, charter of Rijke Gasthuis; SAG, G 3,5, f. 5v.

23. SAG, G 3,5, f. 5v. Neither Jan Van der Haghe nor Jan de Wapenmakere, a subsequent husband of Zoetin Amelaken, was a moneychanger or moneylender, although a Jacob Van der Haghe was a moneychanger briefly.

24. *Rek. Gent 1351–1364,* 307–308, 353.

25. SAG, Z 2,1, f. 7r; G 2,2, f. 34v.

26. In that year he was "overseer" of a child; SAG, G 3,1, f. 25r; G 3,2, f. 45r.

27. SAG, Z 3,3, fos. 5v, 12v; Z 4,1, f. 14v; Z 4,5, f. 16v.

28. *Rek. Gent 1351–1364,* 549, 659, and *passim* in later accounts. Jacob Amelaken

was married to Kateline de Hond. He owned grazing land with her family outside the Grauwpoort, an unusual investment of the Amelakens in real estate.

29. SAG, Z 4,5, f. 16v. On his profession, see SAG, Ser 176 no. 1, f. 2r.

30. References in Books of Sureties, SAG, Ser. 301, 2–4.

31. This could mean her sister-in-law, since these terms are not always distinguished, or conceivably the children of her Rebbe sister, perhaps the same Goskin who had fought young Jacob in 1356 and had taken the more distinguished name of Amelaken. SAG, K 5,2, f. 45r.

32. SAG, K 6,f. 53v.

33. SAG, K 5,2, f. 11v; K 6,2, f. 23r.

34. The Amelaken house was apparently on the side of the Vismarkt toward the Hoyaert; see SAG, G 9,1, f. 2v. The material on the Amelakens may be found in various sources: *Rek. Gent 1351–1364*, 23, 90, 307–308, 353; SAG, Z 1,3, f. 8v, the homicide by Jan Amelaken; G 3,5, f. 5v, the acquittal of the estate of Godeverd Amelaken, which merely says that the heirs acquitted Celie without mentioning amounts; Z 1,1, f. 15r; Z 2,1, f. 7r; G 2,2, f. 34v; G 3,1, f. 25r; G 3,2, f. 45r; Z 3,3, fos. 5v, 12v; Z 4,1, f. 14v; Z 4,5, f. 16v; Z 3,5, f. 14r; Z 4,3, f. 2r; G 4, 5, f. 31v; G 5,3, f. 37r; Z 5,4, f. 3r; K 5,1, fos. 18v, 26r; K 5,2, f. 11v, the donation of 5 lb. to Mergriet Mabels; K 5,2, f. 45r, the bequest to her niece and nephew; Z 6,2, f. 8r; K 6, f. 53v, the suit of 1377 between Jacob and Celie; Z 6,2, f. 18r, an assault involving Jan Amelaken; K 6,2, f. 23r, the will of 1378; G 8,3, f. 59v; G 6,4, f. 23r; Z 6,5, f. 8r; G 9,2, f. 55r; G 7,3, f. 36r, the suit of Jan. 17, 1383, between Jan and Jacob Amelaken; G 7,3, fos. 39r, 51r; G 7,4, 4v, the suit of Aug. 1383 between Jacob and Jan's widow; G 7,4, fos. 10r, 35r, the list of the property of Jan Amelaken's widow; G 7,4, fos. 58r, 77v; G 8,2, f. 9r; G 9,1, f. 2v; K 12, f. 64v.

35. SAG, K 4, 26v.

36. SAG, K 9,2, f. 41v. The arrangement was evidently a failure, for in 1385 she confiscated his residence for the amount of the loan; K 10,1, f. 44v. See also G 7,2, fos. 10r, 28r; K 8,3, fos. 33r, 35v–36r; K 9,2, f. 41v; G 7,5, f. 14v; Z 4,3, f. 10v; G 6,5, f. 3v; K 9,2, f. 35v; K 10,2, f. 54v; G 7,3, f. 62v; K 9,1, fos. 9r, 25v, 26r, 27r; K 10,1, fos. 27v, 39r, 44v; G 3,1, f. 52v; G 3,4, f. 53r; G 4,2, f. 8v; K 11,1, f. 57v.

37. SAG, K 6,2, f. 20r; ARA, BR 1380, f. 3.

38. SAG, K 6, f. 60v; K 13, 1, f. 28v; G 2,2, f. 11r.

39. *Rek. Gent 1280–1336*, 329, 752–753, and *passim; Rek. Gent 1336–1349*, 1: 41; 2: 373, 228, 232, 47; 3: 37; and *passim.* See also above, n. 3; *Rek. Gent 1376–1389*, 194–195, 227, and *passim.*

40. She is mentioned in the accounts, for example, SAG, Ser. 400, 9, f. 311r. She is identified in 1378 as Bette, the wife of Jan Bruggheman, "who lived in and took care of the house of the *scepenen* of *gedele*." Z 6,4, f. 2r.

41. ARA, BR 1378, f. 1; BR 1385, f. 3.

42. Willem Cleyne was a notorious brawler, involved in one homicide and sev-

eral assaults, but none of them was against Pieter Boudins. SAG, Z 3,1, f. 12r; Z 3,4, f. 19r–v; Z 5,3, f. 11v; Z 5,5, f. 10r; Z 6,1, f. 3r.

43. SAG, K 1, f. 223v; Ser. 152, no. 5, f. 39r; K 4,2, f. 15r.

44. Shahar, *Fourth Estate,* 4, 196. See above, p. 89 and n. 9. In 1389 the magistrates sustained a claim for payment against the wife of Simon de Clerc, "since she is a merchant woman." She was subsequently ordered to pay Jan Van Langevile for blue dyeing. SAG, K 11,2, f. 29r.

45. SAG, G 8,2, f. 3r; G 4,5, f. 21v; Z 2,5, f. 18v; G 6,2, f. 24v.

46. SAG, G 6,3, f. 23v. The daughter of Jan Baliet was to be taught sewing and tailoring, but this may not have been for professional purposes. Her father was a brewer, and she eventually inherited a share of his establishment; SAG, G 1,5, f. 9r; G 7,5, f. 49v.

47. SAG, G 7,5, f. 31r.

48. SAG, G 6,4, f. 28r.

49. SAG, Z 5,3, f. 4v; Z 4,1, f. 5v; Z 1,4, f. 3v.

50. SAG, K 9,2, f. 21r. This lady was a second wife. Her stepdaugher had married the brewer Heinric Peiteric and thus would have had no use for the bakery except as a rental property. On the identification of Peiteric, see SAG, Ser. 160, no. 6, f. 21r.

51. SAG, G 7,1, f. 35r; G 5,4, f. 30r. On Jan Scatteman, see Z 6,2, f. 3r.

52. SAG, K 3,2, f. 20r.

53. SAG, G 2,4, f. 26r; G 1,5, f. 30r; K 2,1, f. 8r; G 2,5, f. 51r; G 2,4, f. 9v; K 11,1, f. 88v; K 13,1, f. 23r. Boudin de Hond is listed as a master brewer in the guild book, Ser. 160, no. 6, f. 11.

54. RAG, charter of St. Niklaas's church, Oct. 22, 1377, and guild book lists. In fact, the property evidently continued to be used as a brewery, for in 1387 she and her son-in-law, the beltmaker Lievin Van der Sluus, sold their share to Tonis Platijn, who served twice as dean of the brewers. She probably rented it to another brewer in the interim.

55. For example, SAG, Ser. 160, no. 6, f. 13r. The fourteenth century lists of masters date from 1362, late 1363, and 1394. With the obvious gaps it is not surprising that some material involving women is not recorded. In 1376 the widow of Wulfram Van der Mersch kept for her lifetime her husband's heirs' share of the brewery and equipment "Ten Wielkine" in the Lange Munt. The heirs were apparently not brewers, and the widow is not in the lists of masters. SAG, G 6,1, f. 30v.

56. SAG, Ser. 160, no. 6, f. 12r; G 6,2, f. 24v.

57. Laslett, *World We Have Lost,* 8.

58. SAG, K 9,1, f. 12v.

59. SAG, WD, fos. 2r, 45–2, 47, 47–1, 20r.

60. SAG, Ser. 165, no. 1, f. 12r; in 1393 the wife of Jan Van Berlijs was fined for having spoken disrespectfully to the officers of the guild.

61. SAG, G 6,4, f. 16r; Ser. 163, no. 1; male guildsmen were also expected to bring their wives to the annual guild banquet.

62. SAG, WD, f. 47–2. The accused man claimed that the lady was his maid. The guild ruled that she might help him carry the fruit to market, but she could not be present in the stall to sell it and certainly not while the master was absent.

63. De Pauw, ed., *Voorgeboden,* 47, 120. F. de Potter, *Gent van den oudsten tijd tot heden* (Ghent, 1883–1901), 2: 562–563.

64. The wife of Lievin de Brune made candles at her residence on the cemetery of St. Niklaas's church, a logical place; SAG, K 10,1, f. 31r. See also K 11,2, f. 69v.

65. SAG, G 1,1, f. 50v; G 8,3, f. 2r; Z 6,1, f. 4v; Z 6,3, f. 18v; K 11,1, f. 99v; Z 2,4, f. 10r; K 11,1, f. 5v. There is a reference to Mergriete Van der Wostinen, der surgiene, but since she was owed a debt by a male surgeon, this is probably a scribal error in which the same word was written twice; K 11,2, f. 28r.

66. SAG, Z 2,5, f. 14r; K 13,1, f. 37r; K 1, f. 223r; K 8,2, fos. 6v, 33v.

67. SAG, K 8,3, f. 28v.

68. SAG, K 2,2, f. 21v; K 9,1, f. 7r; K 8,1, f. 21r; K 1, f. 219r.

69. A list of around 1349 of weavers who pledged never again to take up arms against the régime includes no women; RAG, Fonds Wyffels, no. 643. In 1349 Jacob Minne acquitted his sister of their mother's estate; she gave him a loom, but this merely means that before the settlement either the mother or sister had owned it; SAG, G 1a, f. 1r.

70. EP 2: 518–19: although the wife of Clais Rabau claimed that she had inherited mastership as the child of a free dyer, the guild argued that women had never had rights to membership.

71. SAG, K 1, fos. 148r, 202r, 237v, 249v; K 2,1, f. 20v; K 8,3, f. 34r; K 11,1, f. 11v.

72. SAG, G 3,5, f. 33r.

73. SAG, G 7,4, fos. 7r, 35r; K 13,1, f. 29v; WD f. 46r.

74. SAG, G 6, 2, f. 37v.

75. SAG, G 1a, f. 2r; G 1,4, fos. 12v, 31r, 32v; K 1, f. 166r; G 1,5, f. 27r; G 2,5, fos. 31r, 27r; G 3,3, f. 16v; K 3,1, f. 17v.

76. When Mergriet Loenine died, the magistrates granted her stall to her two minor daughters rather than to the widower; SAG, K 2,1, f. 28v.

77. SAG, K 1, f. 27r; K 3,1, f. 16r; G 7,5, f. 18r, where reference is made to a debt owed by "the wool ladies." See also above, the case of Aechte Van den Scake. The identity of the *wulhuis* and the cloth hall (*lakinhalle*) is confirmed by the grant of stalls in the *wulhuis* for the sale of white and blue *lakenen,* K 3,1, f. 16r.

78. De Pauw, ed., *Voorgeboden,* 29; *Rek. Gent 1351–1364,* 136; SAG, K 6,2, fos. 3r, 50v; K 5,2, fos. 15r, 40r; K 4,2, f. 34v; K 6,2, f. 2r; Z 4,4, f. 1v; Z 5,2, f. 16r; K 9,1, f. 24r; K 11,1, fos. 8v, 99r; K 12, f. 40r.

79. SAG, Town Charter no. 357.

80. De Pauw, ed., *Cartulaire des Artevelde,* 711–718.

81. ADN, B 1596, f. 18v: "because she was with those banished for rebellion,"

suggesting perhaps assistance to exiles rather than active involvement. Her son Jan Van den Potijser was involved in several deeds of violence, one an assault on a lady for using foul language about his mother. We do not know her maiden name, but no Potijser is listed in the guild book of the brewers. She could have learned the trade from a male relative or from Heinric Spene; on the identification as a brewer, see SAG, Ser. 160, no. 6, f. 12r. See also SAG, G 3,2, f. 34v; Z 4,1, f. 15r; Z 4,5, f. 10v; Z 5,1, f. 10v; Z 4,3, f. 2v; Z 5,2, f. 5v; K 5,1, f. 23r, the sale of the rent; K 9,2, f. 9r. K 9,1, f. 3v. She was still alive as late as 1383.

82. Of many examples, see SAG, K 1, f. 82r, the lifetime use willed of two apartments with a cellar to Kateline Van der Dorent by the guardian of Gillis and Jooskin Addin, SAG, G 5,5, f. 22r; K 1, f. 177r; K 2,2, f. 48v; K 6,2, f. 52r.

83. For one example, see SAG, K 8,2, f. 1v.

84. SAG, G 7,4, f. 35v; RAG, Sint Niklaas 118, f. 48v; SAG, G 3,4, f. 52r; G 4,2, f. 32v; K 10,2, f. 49v.

85. See case of Jan Uten Hove, who willed 12 lb. gr. to his maid for both services and debts, but the gift would go to her heirs only at his discretion if she predeceased him, and it was annulled if she did not stay with him as her master; SAG, K 6,2, f. 52r.

86. RAG, St. Niklaas 118, f. 91v; SAG, K 7, f. 36v; G 4,3, f. 29v.

87. SAG, K 13,1, f. 86r; K 9,1, f. 18r.

88. In 1387 Lievin Van Formelis assigned to Marie Ketels, widow of Mathijs Colvin, 12 gr. per week for her lifetime for services to him. She in turn willed him all her property to repay her and her husband's debts to him, of which he was postponing collection until her death; SAG, K 10, 2, f. 70v.

89. SAG, K 9,2, f. 4v. For similar cases, see Z 3,3, f. 11r; SAG, Alinshospitaal 189, f. 27v.

90. Lisbette Van Zwijnaarde, Jacob's wife, had died by late 1376. By the summer of 1379 the widower was buying a life annuity in grain jointly with Lane de Temmerman, to be delivered to their residence in Ghent. In Apr. 1381 Lane rented from Jacob a house with two outbuildings for her lifetime for 12s. gr. annually. The property was stated to be worth a still higher rent—12s. gr. was quite substantial—but Jacob was giving it to her cheaply because "she had served her whole life" Jacob and his wife for twelve years [*sic*] and pledged now to continue the service for her and Jacob's lifetimes. In May 1384 Lane was suing de Puur's heirs to fulfill these arrangements and other bequests. Those listed here were validated, but several others were disallowed. SAG, K 4,2, f. 7r; G 6,2, f. 14r; G 6,4, f. 6v; K 8,2, fos. 5r, 25r; K 9,2, f. 41r; G 7,5, f. 11v.

91. One suspects long-term housekeeping arrangements in such cases even if no bastards are mentioned. The lady apparently served another priest after Goethals's death, for in 1385 she assigned to her nephew 10 lb. owed her by the priest Pieter Wayberch; SAG, K 3,2, f. 6v; K 10,1, f. 33r.

92. SAG, K 4,2, f. 11r; G 8,3, f. 44r; G 7,2, f. 17r.

93. The fond father's hopes would have been dashed. In 1389, ten years after Jan Priem's death, the boy was sent to France to learn the candlemaker's trade. SAG, K 6,2, f. 55v; G 6,4, fos. 19 v, 26r; G 8,4, f. 73v.

94. RAG, B 1324, f. 9v.

95. SAG, K 9,1, f. 6r. For similar cases, see K 5,2, f. 46v; K 13,1, f. 6v; K 6,2, f. 27v; K 10,1, f. 16r.

96. SAG, Z 2,2, f. 2v. A less severe case involving an adult woman is the "injury and abuse" of Heinric Van den Bunre to his maid, for which he was fined 30 lb. par. He also made claims against her heirs for loans, debts, and services, but the magistrates ruled that his attack cancelled this; SAG, Z 6,4, f. 9v.

Chapter 6. The Nest and Its Occupants

1. SAG, G 2,2, f. 3v; G 9,1, f. 55r.

2. Peter Raedts, "The Children's Crusade of 1212," *Journal of Medieval History* 3 (1977): 279–324.

3. *Rek. Gent 1351–1364*, 269, and *passim*.

4. SAG, Z 2,1, f. 6v; G 3,4, f. 40r; G 7,1, f. 32v.

5. SAG, G 3,1, f. 4v; Z 6,4, f. 16r; Z 6,2, f. 3r; G 9,1, f. 48v; K 11,2, f. 60r.

6. In 1352 the son of Jan de Vos agreed to pay interest on his father's property "just as others pay who hold his money." SAG, G 1,2, f. 53v.

7. See suggestion of this with the children of Pieter Brabants, cases of 1355 and 1362, SAG, G 1,5, f. 28r and G 3,2, f. 40v. Sometimes, however, an older sister would be named before her younger brother, and occasionally the children were named in strict chronological order without sex differentiation. G 5,2, f. 10r and G 6,5, f. 4v; G 6,5, f. 21r; G 7,1, fos. 22v, 23v.

8. For such a case, see SAG, G 3,2, f. 11r. In the region of Meaux in the seventeenth century orphans were to have guardians chosen in a family council consisting of four persons from both the paternal and maternal sides. In practice this often happened only when the surviving parent remarried or when the minor's interests had to be represented at law, such as when inheriting from a person other than a parent. The guardian was usually the surviving parent, often the stepfather at the mother's remarriage. The parallels with Ghent are quite striking. See Micheline Baulant, "The Scattered Family: Another Aspect of Seventeenth-Century Demography," Forster and Ranum, ed., *Family and Society*: 106–07.

9. Goody, et al., *Development of the Family and Marriage*, 263ff.

10. For examples, see SAG, G 4,2, fos. 20r, 22r, 23v; G 1,3, f. 20r–v.

11. SAG, G 2,5, f. 28r: since the children of Jan Van der Wostinen were not present when they were being assigned a guardian, their mother, the guardian, and several other kinsmen were ordered into prison until the children presented themselves.

12. See, for example, SAG, G 2,5, f. 52v, where the guardian's right to relocate the child if the mother remarried is stated explicitly.

13. The legal standing of the guardians is given in the Great Charter of 1297, printed Gheldolf, ed., *Coutume de la Ville de Gand,* 474.

14. On Nov. 19, 1383, the widow of the Ghent captain Philips Van Artevelde offered a division of his estate with his heirs, noting that she was doing so within the time limit, probably because she had barely made it: her husband had died Nov. 27, 1382, at the battle of Westrozebeke. De Pauw, ed., *Cartulaire des Artevelde,* 381.

15. The most obvious example is the plague year of 1368–69. Later references mention *staten* of that year by folio number, but they are not in what survives.

16. SAG, G 6,1, f. 38v; G 5,5, fos. 18r, 25r; G 4,4, f. 12r; G 7,5, f. 38r.

17. SAG, K 1, f. 232r.

18. SAG, G 3,4, f. 39r. Another case notes money "to be invested through the *scepenen* at interest or something else for the child's profit"; G 4,4, f. 17v.

19. Hence in 1361 they agreed to the sale of lands belonging to Copkin Van Erdbuur. But in the *staet* of his property, compiled three months later, his mother was to support him "in the manner the *scepenen* think appropriate." SAG, G 3,1, fos. 50v, 61r.

20. SAG, G 1,1, f. 29v; G 7,3, fos. 15v, 17r; G 1a, fos. 28r, 36v.

21. SAG, G 2,5, f. 57r–v.

22. Gheldolf, ed., *Coutume de la Ville de Gand,* 475.

23. SAG, G 6,3, f. 29r.

24. The property of Marikin, daughter of Hugh Janssone, was heavily encumbered. A *staet* was provided in 1370 on the basis of the guardian's accounting to that point. But at the request of the guardian himself, the magistrates inspected his accounts for the next two years, "since the previous *scepenen* did not receive the accounts, but rather they remained in rough draft until now." SAG, G 5,4, f. 38r.

25. For one such case, see SAG, G 2,5, f. 40r.

26. SAG, Z 6,3, f. 3r.

27. SAG, K 1, f. 191v.

28. SAG, Z 3,3, f. 7v; G 5,1, f. 15r.

29. SAG, G 9,1, f. 52v; G 1,2, fos. 22v, 23r.

30. See, for example, SAG, G 5,4, f. 21r; G 5,5, f. 11r; G 9,1, f. 47v, where the child's grandmother cared for her when her mother remarried.

31. For one such case, see SAG, G 7,1, f. 18r.

32. Note the case of the child of Pieter Sciltman, SAG, G 2,5, f. 64r; G 2,3, f. 17v. Her stepfather was the baker Gillis Coepman. The caution was often warranted. A transparent case of a stepfather trying to swindle a guardian involves the claim for compensation made by Ghiselbrecht de Rantere against his stepdaughter's guardian for allegedly failing to list certain properties in the *staet.* It turned out that de Rantere's wife held the property, and he had to pay damages. SAG, G 4,1, f. 1v.

231

33. SAG, G 6,3, f. 48v; G 6,4, f. 27r; G 8,1, f. 52r.

34. SAG, G 4,3, f. 22v; K9,2, f. 7v.

35. The widow of Jan Appelman was given one year in which to recover her stepson's maternal inheritance, and she was to support him during that time. SAG, G 7,3, f. 1v.

36. SAG, G 6,4, f. 33v; G 7,1, f. 36v; G 7,2, f. 7r; G 7,3, f. 40r; G 8,2, f. 36v; G 8,3, f. 7r.

37. Le Roy Ladurie, "A System of Customary Law," in Forster and Ranum, ed., *Family and Society:* 84.

38. SAG, G 5,4, f. 39v; G 6,3, fos. 33v, 37v; G 7,4, fos. 68r. 70r.

39. SAG, G 6,3, f. 37r; G 3,5, fos. 21v, 22v; G 3,1, fos. 8v, 10v; K 1, 216–5, 239–1.

40. SAG, Z 3,4, f. 21r, undated, bound with 1363–64.

41. SAG, G 4,4, f. 61r; K 3,2, f. 8v; G 5,2, fos. 19r, 44v; K 3,2, f. 40r; G 5,3, f. 26r; G 6,4, f. 24v; G 7,4, 51v; G 8,3, f. 17r.

42. For a case in which a father had given his child to a lady to support for over seven years and was to give her the income of the principal of his property but had defaulted on the entire amount, see SAG, K 10,2, f. 69r.

43. SAG, G 2,2, f. 7v; G 1,5, f. 35r.

44. SAG, G 5,2, f. 30r; G 7,5, f. 10v; G 4,5, f. 8r.

45. SAG, G 2,5, f. 19r; G 5,2, f. 56r; G 5,4, f. 38r; G 9,2, f. 65r.

46. SAG, G 2,5, f. 37r; G 1a, f. 37v; G 3,2, f. 29r; G 8,4, fos. 67v, 68r.

47. There are some references to the practice. When Lievin Metten Ossen was killed in 1350, the blood payments were to be invested and the proceeds used to pay "the women who support and direct the children," who were evidently very young; SAG, G 2,1, f. 38v. The eldest child, Liefkin, only began to act on his own in 1365. See also G 6,3, f. 27r, a case in which money held belonging to an infant whose mother was still alive is to be refunded if she died within a year.

48. SAG, G 6,2, f. 37r; G 5,3, 33v, for another case.

49. SAG, G 2,4, f. 8v.

50. SAG, G 2,2, f. 34v.

51. SAG, G 6,1, f. 19r; G 5,5, f. 35v; G 6,4, f. 16r.

52. SAG, G 7,3, f. 28v.

53. Pieterkin was dead by May 1387. SAG, G 5,2, f. 7v; G 8,2, fos. 17r, 52v.

54. SAG, G 2,1, f. 9r; G 8,4, f. 37r.

55. SAG, G 2,5, f. 10v; G 5,4, fos. 38r, 43r; G 5,5, f. 23r.

56. SAG, G 3,3, f. 40r.

57. The widow of Jan de Bastaert, evidently a weaver, settled his estate in 1352. There were four children. A revised *staet* was given to Annekin de Bastaert in 1357, according to which his mother was to support him with the income of his money and half a loom. But this was changed the following September: the mother was to support him only until Oct. 1, 1358, and thereafter might be free of him if she wished. A new *staet* was given on Mar. 1, 1359, and there is no further mention of

the mother's support. Now called Aechte Storems, suggesting that she had remarried, she was merely acquitted for the paternal estate. SAG, G 1,2, f. 23v; K 1, 115r; G 2,2, f. 21r; G 2,3, fos. 2r, 17v; G 2,4, fos. 17v, 19r; G 4,1, f. 35r; G 4,2, f. 5r.

58. A case showing both this confusion and the extensive rights of a guardian from the father's side vis à vis the mother is the estate of Jacob Hiellaert, whose property was secured by the guardian with two persons, but he also agreed that the mother might *houden* the child *onghemindert* for one year; SAG, G 4,3, f. 40r.

59. For cases in which some of an orphan's money is at *pensioen* while some is to be held undiminished, see SAG, Z 7,5, f. 15v; G 1,3, f. 47v.

60. SAG, G 2,5, f. 2v.

61. SAG, G 3,3, f. 29v; G 3,4, f. 22r; Z 2,5, f. 17r; G 4,3, f. 36r. A similar case of a mother agreeing to provide complete support is the widow of Clais de Brune, G 4,5, f. 3v.

62. SAG, G 3,3, f. 24v; K 1, fos. 21r, 22r. A case suggesting a comparable situation is found when Lievin Van Lokeren and his two adult sisters acquitted their mother of their father's estate and of what the children "had helped to acquire, get, and improve with their own labor" while in the common nest; G 2,5, f. 64v.

63. SAG, G 7,5, f. 23v; G 8,3, f. 52v.

64. SAG, G 1,1, f. 8v. Stone, *Family, Sex, and Marriage*, 97, notes that "friends" in seventeenth-century England were close relatives who seem to have performed most of the functions vis à vis outsiders that the Ghent "friends" of the fourteenth century did, but were less active than the Gentenars within the clan.

65. In 1351 the *maghen ende vrienden* of Annekin Scildeman reported to the *scepenen* that they had invested in merchandising the money which the boy's father had previously held for him; SAG, G 1,1, f. 35r.

66. SAG, K 10,2, f. 118v; G 4,4, f. 55r. Only nine years later was this changed, so that the mother would support him without reference to the "friends," G 6,3, f. 49r.

67. SAG, G 1a, f. 4r, where the father supports the boy while paying an aunt to support the girl; see also G 7,2, f. 1v.

68. SAG, G 5,3, f. 53r; G 5,5, f. 17r; G 4,3, f. 8v; G 8,2, fos. 45v, 46r.

69. Hence the widow of Jan Van den Watere and her new husband continued to support the younger of her two sons, while the guardian supported the older boy and the girl; SAG, G 3,4, f. 35r. Similarly, the oldest son of Clais Rabau was to be supported by his uncle Jacob Masch, while the father supported the other three children, G 4,4, f. 9v; see also G 5,1, f. 63r. In 1386 the widow of the butcher Lievin Van Damiaet agreed to support her two younger children and to have additional income from the oldest boy for his support, since he was getting the proceeds of the family stall in the meat hall; SAG, G 8,2, f. 12v.

70. For such a case see SAG, G 2,2, f. 9v.

71. SAG, G 5,4, fos. 37r, 18v, 28r, 22v. The youngest daughter was the only survivor by 1378, and the arrangement was continued. When the children of Willem

de Paeu lost both parents, the two guardians divided the four among themselves and specified exactly the incomes of which of the various properties would be used for each child's support; G 2,5, f. 45 r–v.

72. SAG, G 1a, f. 30v; G 7,2, f. 24v; G 3,3, f. 44v; G 4,3, f. 25r; G 6,1, f. 17r; G 1a, f. 31r; G 7,1, f. 37r; G 3,2, f. 35r; G 3,5, f. 35v.

73. SAG, G 2,1, f. 32v; K 10,1, f. 3r.

74. On the schools of Ghent during the Middle Ages, see Maurice Heins, "Les écoles au moyen âge à Gand," Extrait de *Flandre Libérale* (Ghent, Dec. 1885); M. H. Voordeckers-de Clercq, "De S. Veerlescholen en de schoolstrijd te Gent tot het einde der XIIIe eeuw," *Collationes Brugenses et Gandavenses* 9 (1963): 382–393; and Paul Rogghé, "De Gentse Klerken in de XIVe en XVe eeuw. Trouw en verraad," *Appeltjes van het Meetjesland* 11 (1960): 25.

75. SAG, G 5,5, f. 19v; G 7,4, f. 55v; G 1,4, f. 10r.

76. SAG, Z 3,5, f. 13v; Z 6,2, f. 8v.

77. SAG, G 9,1, f. 31v.

78. SAG, G 5,2, f. 1 bis; G 1,4, fos. 17v, 13r.

79. Heins, "Ecoles," 14.

80. SAG, G 1,5, fos. 29r. 41r; G 3,3, f. 17r; G 1,4, f. 16–2; G 7,5, f. 25v; G 4,5, f. 2v; K 9,1, f. 17v.

81. SAG, G 3,5, fos. 21v, 22v; G 7,4, f. 78r; G 8,3, f. 10r; G 6,4, f. 25v.

Chapter 7. The Flight of the Nestlings

1. In 1378 the knight Gillis de Pape was holding money for the son and daughter of Pieter Rijm. He was to give *pensioen* on the boy's money, but on the girl's he would give only such courtesy payment as he and the clan thought appropriate, since she had reached her majority. She still bore a "kin" name. SAG, G 6,4, f. 8r.

2. When Lievin Fierins owed a debt, three-quarters of it to orphans, he was to pay interest only on that share. SAG, G 7,3, f. 51r.

3. SAG, G 6,4, fos. 33v, 35v; G 6,5, f. 18v. For a similar case, see SAG, G 8,2, f. 39r.

4. In Mar. 1365 Jan, son of the financially troubled Jacob Borluut, was holding 7 lb. gr. at *pensioen* belonging to Barbere Rabau, but he was to return the money to her uncle by October 1; and he was to return the money and *pensioen* immediately if he sold any property during this time. He was thus far from bankrupt, but he needed cash and did not want to dispose of real estate, which would presumably produce enough income by October to enable him to repay the loan; SAG, G 3,5, f. 23v. That money given at *pensioen* was considered a loan by the taker is shown by the case of the children of Wouter Uten Houtkin. Jan Damman owed them over 9 lb. gr., and he was "to loan out directly on the advice of the guardians" 4 lb. gr. of this at *pensioen* to be used to support one of the children. A later note to the document shows that he simply paid interest on the money himself; G 7,4, f. 9r–v.

5. See Nicholas, *Town and Countryside,* 304–306. For cases of such investment, see SAG, G 5,4, fos. 42r, 44v.

6. SAG, K 11,2, f. 47r.

7. SAG, G 5,1, fos. 68v–69v; G 3,1, f. 44r; G 1,1, f. 35r.

8. For one case where a loan is clearly involved, Zeger Van der Donct took 5 lb. gr. at *pensioen* from Annekin Tuckeland, but in turn surrendered all disposition over his own properties to his sureties, suggesting that he was in serious financial trouble; SAG, G 8,1, f. 73v. In an unusual case, which also shows how *pensioen* could be interest on a loan, the daughter of Hugh Janssone was in such straits by 1371 that she took money at interest from another child, payable from her other property and rents; SAG, G 5,2, f. 23r.

9. SAG, G 5,1, f. 56v; G 6,3, f. 26v.

10. In 1376 Daneel de Coyere was holding 12 lb. gr. belonging to Annekin Loete and would pay 24s. gr. *pensioen,* or 10 percent; SAG, G 6,1, f. 30r. Pieter Van der Kuekinen paid 18 scilde *pensioen* on two years holding of 9 lb. gr. belonging to Callekin, Daneel de Coyere's daughter, a rate possible only if the interest was un-compounded; G 6,3, f. 13r. For other cases showing the 10 percent rate, see G 8,1, f. 12r; G 8,2, f. 10r; G 8,3, f. 24v; G 1,1, f. 39v.

11. SAG, G 8,4, f. 9r, a rate of 12.5 percent.

12. See SAG, G 8,1, f. 15v; G 1a, f. 24r; G 8,1, f. 38v. An apprenticeship contract of 1385 allowed the master to keep the bond money for a three-year term, even if the boy left after the first year, but then he was to return the intrinsic value. He clearly expected to tie up the money in investments from which it could not be recovered quickly. The principle could sometimes work hardship. In 1388 Juris Doedekin claimed 5 lb. gr. from the guarantor of a man who had secured it when Doedekin was an orphan twenty years before and in money of that time, and the demand was sustained; SAG, K 11,1, f. 89r. See also K 11,2, f. 37r; G 5,5, f. 41v.

13. The younger of the two daughters of Jan de Juede was to be supported undiminished with 7 lb. gr., the older with 3 lb; SAG, G 4,5, f. 17r. The older was probably working, and accordingly we have included only the figure for the younger girl in Table 8.

14. SAG, G 5,2, f. 29v; G 7,4, f. 14r.

15. The widow of Clais de Crane held 11s. 3d gr. belonging to her three children, "and she will support them to the best of her ability." SAG, G 3,1, f. 29r.

16. SAG, G 7,3, f. 6r. In 1371 Zeger Vilain was declared to have supported his son Liefkin for 30s. gr. annually. He would do it for the next three years for 3 lb. annually, from which 8s. 6d. would be deducted to compensate him for expenses already incurred; SAG, G 5,1, f. 29r. For a similar case, see G 8,4, f. 62r.

17. See SAG, G 5,1, f. 32v, the case of the children of Wouter de Olslaghere.

18. SAG, G 6,4, f. 28r; G 4,5, f. 14v; G 2,5, f. 37v; G 3,5, f. 33v.

19. SAG, G 3,3, f. 17v; G 4,3, f. 26r. For a similar case of labor compensated by the stepmother, see K 8,2, f. 24v.

20. SAG, G 7,2, f. 28v; G 5,5, f. 6v; G 4,4, f. 11r; G 5,2, f. 35v.

21. Liefkin Hansame was situated with Lisbette de Vlaminc, who received a small amount of his money for one year, but she would also collect the income of his trade (*ambocht*); SAG, G 8,2, f. 14v. Compare G 6,4, f. 35v.

22. SAG, G 6,5, f. 14r.

23. SAG, G 1,3, fos. 32v, 41v, 45v; G 1,4, f. 11v; G 2,1, f. 41–1.

24. For example, SAG, G 4,4, f. 5v; G 1,2, f. 1v.

25. Kuehn, *Emancipation, passim.*

26. SAG, G 2,5, f. 53r; G 3,4, f. 10v. A girl was to be supported "until she reaches age twelve." SAG, G 8,4, f. 56r.

27. SAG, G 6,3, f. 28r; G 7,2, f. 2r.

28. SAG, G 6,1, f. 49r; K 2,1, f. 2v; G 3,3, fos. 18v, 47r; G 3,5, f. 10v.

29. In 1353 Jan de Weert came with four *maghen ende vrienden*, probably one from each branch of his kindred, and asked to be released from tutelage and given his property. The kinsmen testified that they considered him "sufficiently old and wise and mature that he should be released from wardship and installed in his property," and the *scepenen* agreed. SAG, G 1,3, f. 29v.

30. SAG, G 7,1, f. 8r; G 7,4, f. 23v; G 7,5, f. 17r.

31. SAG, G 7,4, 11v. A different version of this arrangement has both sons using the boat to earn their living; the older boy was Pieter, without the diminutive, the younger Heinkin, but both were still wards and needed permission; G 9,1, f. 33v.

32. SAG, Z 2,2, f. 5r.

33. SAG, G 6,5 f. 4v; G 7,5, f. 42v.

34. SAG, G 4,1, f. 2r.

35. SAG, G 4,4, fos. 51v, 52r; G 2,1, f. 13r; G 7,4, f. 12v; G 7,3, f. 38r.

36. SAG, G 1,1, f. 36v; G 2,1, fos. 6r, 28v; G 5,1, fos. 44v, 21r; G 1,4, f. 35r; G 4,1, f. 14r. Alienation of the principal is expressly forbidden in a case of 1352, G 1,3, f. 17v.

37. In 1373 the two children of Volker Van Elverzele were given substantial allowances; but if either child spent more than this, the share of the undivided estate belonging to the other sibling would not be drained to compensate. SAG, G 5,3, f. 27r.

38. SAG, G 2,2, f. 11r. She must have been emancipated at a rather advanced age, for she was married to Jan Kriekersteen by Dec. 1360. Her potential heirs agreed, evidently just after the marriage, that Kriekersteen would keep part of their common property if she predeceased him; K 1, f. 226v.

39. They told Jan Cortoys to render accounts and return all documents to his guardians and also to "seek new lodgings apart from the priest Jacob de Backere and to live in a decent place and buy his provisions according to his status." The costs would be borne by the receivers of his property. SAG, G 2,4, f. 8r.

40. SAG, G 3,2, f. 11v; G 6,2, fos. 6r, 11r.

41. If Annekin Van der Rake died or was taken away from Simon Wasselins,

who had agreed to support him, Simon agreed to take one of the boy's siblings in his place; SAG, G 6,1, f. 33v.

42. SAG, G 8,2, f. 6r.

43. Thus in 1378 Gillis Van Bachten willed 14 lb. gr. to his legitimate daughter because his affection toward her was greater than toward his other children, as he stated publicly. He did it without possibility of revocation "in the hope that she will situate herself virtuously." SAG, K 6,2, f. 55r.

44. SAG, K 2,2, f. 11r.

45. SAG, G 5,1, f. 70v; Z 2,4, f. 8r; G 9,1, fos. 12v, 55r.

46. SAG, Z 5,3, f. 13v; Z 5,4, f. 17r; Z 5,5, fos. 2v, 16r.

47. SAG, G 5,1, f. 13r; G 3,4, f. 16v; Z 3,4, f. 6v; G 3,4, f. 29v.

48. In what was obviously a case of extreme neglect, damages of only 3 lb. par. annually for twelve years were paid to the daughter of Jan Appelman for an accident. The same amount, a total sum of 3 lb. gr., was owed by Mergriet Van der Wostinen for her "carelessness" with the son of Jan Van Wachtebeke, who was injured so seriously that he would never again have full use of his arm. Yet this amount is less than half of what an adult master artisan might hope to earn in a single year. SAG, Z 3,2, f. 8v; G 8,3, f. 53v.

49. Neeze Botermans left her infant bastard daughter in the care of a nurse, who left her alone by the fire. The child burned four fingers and was severely mutilated. The *scepenen* awarded 54 lb. par. SAG, G 6,1, f. 49v; Z 5,5, f. 18r.

50. SAG, Z 6,4, f. 15v. In a similar case, which may reflect the common practice of having children do chores around the house and yard, Hectorkin de Scouteete suffered an accidental injury while watching the pigs. Z 6,2, f. 20r.

51. SAG, Z 1,2, fos. 5r, 13r; Z 3,5, f. 3v.

52. SAG, G 6,3, f. 52v; G 2,1, f. 3v.

53. The youngest may have been considerably younger than his siblings. The guardian situated one of the runaways with Boudin de Moer to learn a trade in 1358, a surprising development in view of the mother's claim, and in 1360 an escutcheon was bought for the other runaway of 1357, suggesting that he was about to be emancipated. The third child was still under wardship in 1366. SAG, G 1a, f. 26r; G 1,2, f. 21r; G 2,1, f. 19r; G 2,2, f. 14r.

54. Kerstkin Van Vlachem accidentally injured Zoetin Van Zwalmen in 1364, but Zoetin did a pilgrimage for hitting her in retaliation. SAG, Z 3,5, f. 1v.

55. Liefkin de Moelneere was awarded no compensation for an injury received from the horse of Heinric de Neckere, since Liefkin had been chasing the animal and hit him with a stick. SAG, Z 3,5, f. 10v.

56. SAG, Z 5,3, f. 5r.

57. SAG, Z 5,4, f. 14r; Z 2,5, f. 11v; Z 2,2, f. 13v.

58. SAG, Z 2,5, f. 2v; Z 5,4, f. 18v; G 9,1, f. 57r; Z 4,1, f. 12v; Z 5,5, f. 3r.

59. SAG, G 2,5, f. 15v; G 3,1, f. 5v; G 2,2, f. 40r–v.

60. SAG, K 1, fos. 141v–142r, 108v; K 3,1, f. 9v.

61. SAG, G 8,1, f. 5r; G 9,2, f. 23r.

62. SAG, G 2,5, f. 42v.

63. The widow of Cornelis Uten Berghe made a substantial gift to her adult granddaughter when the girl married, superseding an earlier gift for alms and services, suggesting that the girl was illegitimate and hence unable to inherit directly from the paternal side; SAG, K 1,2, f. 13r; K 2,2, f. 38v.

64. SAG, K 11,2, f. 66v; K 7, f. 6v; K 10,1, f. 39v.

65. SAG, G 6,5, f. 11r.

66. Liliane Wynant, "Peiling naar de vermogensstruktuur te Gent op basis van de staten van goed 1380–1389," in *Studien betreffende de sociale strukturen te Brugge, Kortrijk en Gent in de 14e en 15e eeuw, Standen en Landen* 63 (Heule: Administratieve Uitegeverij N.V. U.S.A., 1973): 50.

67. SAG, G 1,3, f. 1r; G 2,1, f. 22r; G 1,5, f. 15r.

Chapter 8. The Legitimacy of Illegitimacy

1. SAG, G 7,3, f. 67v. This feature is common to most Flemish inheritance customs, both urban and rural. Le Roy Ladurie, "Family Structures" in Goody et al., *Family and Inheritance,* 67.

2. SAG, K 8,3, f. 25r; K 8,2, f. 31v; G 4,5, fos. 31v, 35r.

3. The same seems to have been true in seventeenth-century England. See Alan Macfarlane, "Illegitimacy and Illegitimates in English History," in Peter Laslett, Karla Oosterveen, and Richard M. Smith, eds., *Bastardy and Its Comparative History* (London: Edward Arnold, 1980), 75.

4. SAG, G 5,3, f. 40r; K 4,2, f. 33r; K 9,2, f. 45v; G 6,4, f. 33v; G 6,5, f. 8r; K 8,2, f. 16r.

5. Laslett, *Family Life,* 112–113, postulates low illegitimacy rates from the 1550s on the basis of parish records, which he admits are fragmentary. The number of casual references to bastardy at Ghent suggests that he may be erring on the side of generosity.

6. SAG, K 8,2, f. 1v, and *passim;* G 2,3, f. 36v.

7. SAG, K 1, f. 254r; G 1,4, f. 31r; G 3,3, f. 19v.

8. SAG, G 1,5, f. 15v; G 3,1, f. 10v.

9. SAG, K 13,1, f. 58v.

10. SAG, G 5,1, f. 31v.

11. SAG, G 5,3, f. 10v.

12. SAG, G 4,4, f. 47v.

13. SAG, K 3,1, f. 5v; G 1,3, f. 32r; G 4,3, f. 10v; G 4,4, f. 44v; G 6,2, fos. 42r, 45v, 55r; G 7,4, f. 48v; G 8,2, f. 60v; G 9,1, f. 19v.

14. SAG, K 7, f. 8r.

15. SAG, G 6,1, f. 21v; K 4,2, f. 11r; G 6,5, f. 23r; G 6,3, fos. 5r, 8r.

16. SAG, K 11,2, f. 60v; K 6,2, f. 8r.

17. SAG, G 4,4, f. 28v; G 6,4, f. 11v; G 3,1, f. 17v; G 3,3, f. 30v; G 3,4, fos. 38v, 47v; G 4,2, f. 32r; G 5,4, f. 35v.

18. SAG, G 3,4, f. 3v.

19. SAG, K 1, f. 141v; K 9,1, f. 12r.

20. SAG, G 1,1, f. 30r; G 1,4, f. 21r; K 8,3, f. 26r; K 13,1, f. 54v.

21. SAG, G 3,2, fos. 35r, 43v; G 3,5, f. 37r; K 8,2, f. 23v; G 8,3, fos. 1v, 37r; G 8,1, f. 75v.

22. SAG, G 6,1, f. 3v; K 2,2, f. 10v; G 3,1, f. 64r; G 3,2, f. 32r.

23. Together with his apparently legitimate brother Martin Van Axel, Lievin was involved in 1362 in warfare against the Van Drongen and Van Ponteraven, also prominent butcher families. Among other offenses Lievin and Martin had entered the meat hall armed and attacked their opponents with a gang of "strangers." Lievin Van Axel the bastard also did a pilgrimage for assault in 1366. That he did violence against rival butchers suggests that he was adopting his family's feuds as his own, not that he felt himself an outsider. SAG, G 1,1, fos. 28v, 35r; G 1,2, f. 29r; G 2,4, f. 25v; G 3,2, fos. 2v, 32v; Z 3,2, f. 12v; Z 4,1, f. 8r.

24. SAG, Z 3,4, f. 3v; G 2,1, f. 35v; G 2,3, f. 21v; K 1, f. 244r; G 3,2, f. 10v.

25. SAG, G 1,1, f. 9r; K 13,1, f. 58v; G 7,3, f. 35v.

26. SAG, K 8,2, f. 1r; K 8,1, f. 17v.

27. SAG, G 7,3, fos. 14r, 23r, 54r.

28. SAG, G 8,4, f. 54r; G 9,1, f. 61r.

29. SAG, K 5,2, f. 9v; G 5,3, fos. 26r, 32v; G 5,4, fos. 32v–33r; G 5,5, fos. 14v, 20v, 36v, 35r; G 6,1, f. 13r; G 6,3, fos. 49r, 53r; G 7,3, f. 37v; K 8,1, f. 7r; K 8,3, f. 34r; G 7,4, f. 76v; G 7,2, f. 15v.

30. RAG, St. Niklaas 118, fos. 88r–v, 92v, 94r, and original charter of Oct. 16, 1344; S 152, f. 9; S 155; S 157, f. 14v; S 159, f. 10v; SN rol 141.

31. SAG, K 9,1, f. 9v. Kateline Bruusch, in a document of 1377, which was only recorded in 1382, willed 6 lb. gr. to the three bastards of her husband, Willem Hudgeboud, of whom she was guardian. She was acquitted by her husband's heirs in 1382, showing that she was childless. SAG, G 7,2, fos. 16v, 19r, 17v, 35r.

32. SAG, G 7,4, f. 13r.; G 6,3, f. 10r.; K 8,2, f. 35v; K 8,3, fos. 24v, 37r; K 9,1, f. 23r.

33. SAG, G 3,4, f. 53r; G 1a, f. 7v.

34. SAG, K 12, fos. 62v, 44v; K 3,1, f. 3r; Z 4,5, f. 4v; Z 5,2, f. 12v; G 5,3, f. 47r; G 8,4, f. 74r; G 7,3, f. 67v; Archive of St. Jacob's Church, Ghent, charter of Dec. 9, 1367; 1232, f. 68r.

35. SAG, G 2,2, fos. 28v, 29r, 33 r–v.

36. SAG, K 8,2, f. 10v; K 1, f. 253v.

37. SAG, G 1,1, f. 47v; G 1,2, f. 28v; G 1,1, f. 52v; G 1,2, f. 15v; G 1,4, f. 34v; G 1,5, fos. 2v, 17r; G 3,1, fos. 24v, 55r; G 3,2, f. 4r; G 5,1, f. 52v; K 7, f. 15v; K 8,2, f. 2v.

38. SAG, K 2,2, 46v; K 6, f. 45v; G 6,3, fos. 11r, 20r; K 6,2, f. 18v; G 6,3, f. 28v; G 6,4, f. 6r; G 7,2, f. 12r: "because of the current crisis, as a result of which scarcely anyone has money on hand to use for payments."

39. SAG, K 7, f. 53v. This bequest was only paid in 1410, to the beneficiaries' descendants.

40. Heinric Martins, about to go abroad in 1383, surrendered to three trustees his rights on the estates of his parents for the benefit of his two bastards, but the trustees were to act on the advice of the children's mother. He extended his bequest in 1390, by which time the daugher had married. The case shows continued and perhaps growing interest and affection as the children grew older. SAG, G 7,3, f. 48v; K 12, f. 71v.

41. SAG, G 7,4, fos. 17v, 18r; K 9,1, f. 10r.

42. SAG, G 8,4, f. 43v; G 9,2, fos. 1v, 2r.

Chapter 9. Clans at Peace

1. Note the case of the two daughters of Jan Dienaert, both named Betkin. The girls had different mothers, but the confusion became compounded when one Betkin died and the other inherited her property. SAG, G 6,5, f. 22v; G 6,4, fos. 16v, 18r; G 6,1, fos. 17v, 8v; G 7,4, f. 64v.

2. For example, SAG, G 5,2, f. 47v. The terms designating in-laws were *zwegher, zwagher, zwaesnede,* and *zweer.*

3. SAG, K 5,2, f. 22r, and G 5,4, f. 3v, for two examples.

4. Jan Van Erdbuur is called the "brother" of Jan, Pieter, Gilkin, and Callekin Van Munte. He was the husband of Marie Van Munte. Compare SAG, G 3,5, f. 34r, with G 7,4, f. 56r.

5. SAG, G 2,2, f. 9v.

6. SAG, K 4,2, fos. 1v, 27v, 28r; Z 7,5, f. 17v; K 2,2, f. 9v; G 3,2, f. 29r; G 5,5, f. 42v; K 1, f. 226v; Ser. 190–1, f. 1 bis, 3 r–v. The Temmerman family owned three adjacent houses Tusschen Walle in the abbey village of St. Pieter, south of the central city; G 4,4, f. 12r; Gillis de Cousmakere owned two houses at the Crommen S and Pieter de Cousmakere an adjacent property; K 13,1, f. 88v.

7. See case involving the weaver Zeger Van den Roden, SAG, G 8,4, f. 16r.

8. SAG, K 1, fos. 10r, 108v.

9. SAG, Wenemaershospitaal 441, f. 86r–v. For similar cases, see RAG, charter of St: Michiel's church of Mar. 10, 1361; St. Niklaas 118, f. 92r–v.

10. ARA, BR 1384, f. 4; RAG, S 157, f. 9r; S 159, f. 5v.

11. SAG, K 13,1, fos. 33v, 57v.

12. SAG, G 4,5, f. 2v; K 1, fos. 234r, 245v.

13. SAG, K 1, f. 105v; K 2,2, fos. 36v, 10r; K 12, f. 19r; K 10,2, f. 17r.

14. SAG, G 5,3, f. 11v; K 5,5, f. 19r; K 6,2, f. 48v.

15. SAG, K 12, f. 66v; G 7,3, f. 54v; K 10,2, f. 110r; K 1, f. 45v.

16. SAG, K 5,1, f. 34v; K 12, fos. 51v, 79r.

17. SAG, K 1, f. 129r; G 4,1, f. 31r; Z 3,4, f. 2r.

18. SAG, Z 5,3, f. 4r, and above, cha. 7; K 8,3, fos. 2r, 6v; K 9,1, f. 31r.

19. SAG, G 3,2, f. 38v; G 8,1, f. 68v.

20. SAG, G 7,5, f. 53r.

21. SAG, K 13,1, f. 30r; G 8,1, f. 28r. The son's marriage had evidently been childless, and his estate would thus revert under the custom of Ghent to his parents, since both were still alive.

22. SAG, K 6,2, f. 29r. He apparently did not live long. The sister's husband was acquitted of her estate in 1385 by two other brothers, but Clais is not mentioned; G 8,1, f. 22r.

23. SAG, K 2,2, f. 24v; K 3,2, f. 18v. If one year's support for him would cost 4 lb. gr., he must have been an invalid needing constant care.

24. See Hans Van Werveke, *Gent. Schets van een sociale Geschiedenis* (Ghent: Rombaut-Fecheyr, 1947), 57; H. Van Werveke, "De Gentse Vleeschouwers onder het Oud Regime. Demografische studie over een gesloten en erfelijk ambachtsgild," HMGOG, n.s. 3 (1948): 3–31; and H. Van Werveke, "Het bevolkingscijfer van de stad Gent in de 14de eeuw. Een laatste woord?" in *Album Charles Verlinden* (Ghent: Story, 1975), 449–465.

25. See, for example, E. Van der Hallen, "Het Gentse Meerseniersambacht (1305–1540)," HMGOG, n.s. 31 (1977): 106–112. SAG, Ser. 160, no. 6, f. 21v, a reference of 1386 to the brewers. The restricted definition of "freedom" in the guild is found before 1385 only with the *wijnscroeders* and the carpenters; see SAG, Ser. 176, no. 1, f. 1r; Ser. 190–1, no. 1 bis, fos. 6r–8r.

26. SAG, WD f. 24r; G 8,1, f. 77v; Ser. 160, no. 6, fos. 10r, 14r, showing that Busscaert de Naen and his bastard, Philips Busscaert, were both brewers. For the other trades, see G 7,4, f. 44v; G 6,1, f. 24r; G 9,2, f. 28r; G 6,3, f. 28r; G 5,4, f. 29v; K 9,1, f. 12v; and the charter of 1436 of the boatmen, printed De Potter, *Gent,* 3: 8–9.

27. See, for example, SAG, G 3,2, 21r; G 2,3, f. 32v; and G 3,1, f. 37r, where the words are *eenich ambacht,* "any trade."

28. SAG, G 7,4, f. 82v; G 1a, f. 9v. A baker Jan Van Roden was injured by a butcher Jan Van Roden in 1353; and the baker had a dual matriculation in the guilds of bakers and of millers, each of which had its own organization; Z 1,3, f. 13r; Z 2,5, f. 8r; Z 1,3, f. 11v, where he is called Jan Van Roden "the miller and baker."

29. See, for example, the baker Jan Van Ghend and the grain measurer of that name; SAG, G 3,3, f. 2r. There are separate references to a tailor and a legging-maker Jan Van Roden, and it is impossible to determine whether they are the same man; G 7,3, f. 30v; K 5,2, f. 13v; G 9,1, f. 35v. The ability to change professions also extended to the textile trades. Reference is made in 1353 to a folder named Clais Rabau, in 1366 to a measurer of that name, and in 1372 to a dyer. The man's wife is named in each transaction and proves that only one person is involved. Rabau was

thus able to exercise three professions in nineteen years; G 1,4, f. 11r; G 4,2, f. 4v; K 4,1, f. 1v. Several boatmen were related to shipwrights; see K 11,2, f. 81v; G 2,5, f. 3r; G 3,1, f. 51r.

30. SAG, G 5,1, f. 18v. By 1377 the tailor's son was being taught haberdashery, G 6,3, f. 5v. Although these trades are close, they had separate guilds.

31. SAG, K 8,3, f. 20r; G 4,1, f. 26r; G 3,1, f. 79r; Z 1,4, f. 14r. The fruitmonger Boudin Van den Kerchove and the cordwainer Clais Van den Kerchove were kinsmen; Z 1,5, f. 1v. In 1390 the property of the children of Jan de Smet included a smithy, but the older boy was apprenticed as a bowmaker to his uncle at Bruges; G 9,2, f. 10v. This list could be extended.

32. SAG, G 9,1, f. 60v. One of his sureties is called a baker and the other was probably a boatman, for he had relatives who definitely practiced that profession.

33. SAG, G 5,1, f. 53v; G 7,2, 3 bis r; G 7,3, f. 4r; and especially G 7,4, f. 68r, where the words are "brewer and shearer."

34. The case of Jan Van den Hecke, called "int Scotkin." SAG, G 1,2, f. 1v; G 4,4, f. 38r; G 7,2, f. 19r; Z 2,2, f. 11r.

35. SAG, K 5,2, f. 5v; Z 1,2, f. 1v; Z 1,4, f. 11v; Z 2,3, f. 3v.

36. SAG, WD f. 29v; G 3,1, f. 15r; Ser. 160, no. 6, f. 15r. The carpenter was overdean of the small guilds for a lengthy period; Ser. 190–1, no. 1 bis, f. 5v; Ser. 400, 9, f. 243r.

37. SAG, G 2,1, f. 14v; G 5,3, f. 32v.

38. Van Werveke, "Vleeschouwers" 27–28; SAG, Ser. 160, no. 6, fos. 13v, 15r.

39. Van Werveke, *Gent*, 51–52. The statutes of the brewers and the list of masters of 1362 are printed in de Pauw, ed., *Cartulaire des Artevelde*, 589–93. All references are to my compilations from the *Neringboek der brouwers*, SAG, Ser. 160, no. 6, fos. 10r–18v, 25r–27v. The list of 1362 is entitled "The following persons are in the old book as having been free brewers since the Incarnation." This list contains a Lambrecht Van den Rijse. A Jan Van den Rijse, who is in neither this nor the list of 1363, is identified elsewhere as a brewer. He had died by Dec. 1361, leaving two sons who apparently did not become brewers, for they are not in the later lists. But the date of his death fixes the date of the first list as early 1362. Z 3,1, fos. 7v, 8v; G 3,2, fos. 11r, 28r. I hope to expand upon these conclusions in a separate publication concerning the brewers of Ghent.

40. The brewers furnished 208 militiamen in the muster of 1357, a figure considerably closer to that of the list of 1363 than to that of 1362. *Rek. Gent 1351–1364*, 296.

41. Since there is this much overlapping between the lists, we cannot maintain that the earlier one contained or was intended to contain only the names of deceased brewers as an explanation of the discrepancies.

42. SAG, Ser. 160, no. 6, fos. 20v–21r, 21v, 24r, 28r.

43. SAG, G 3,4, f. 36r; K 3,1, f. 20v; G 4,4, f. 69r; G 7,5, f. 20v; G 8,2, f. 61 bis r; G 7,5, f. 1v. Although he left a son, Mathijs, who had been emancipated on Sept. 17,

1387, and was still alive in 1393, the boy did not follow his father's profession, for he never appears in the guild lists of the brewers.

Chapter 10. Clans in Conflict

1. For example, SAG, G 2,5, f. 41r.

2. Goody, *Development of the Family,* 29–30; Flandrin, *Families in Former Times,* 74–92.

3. In 1369 and 1370 Betkin, daughter of Sanders Uten Wissele, inherited property from Kateline Mond, wife of Willem Van Pottersberghe and apparently her maternal half-sister. The heirs held a conclave to settle the estate at Van Pottersberghe's house around June 22, 1369, and all coins, which are listed individually, were to be repaid eventually to Betkin in their value as of that date. SAG, G 5,2, f. 24v.

4. SAG, K 12, f. 10v.

5. SAG, G 7,1, f. 35v; G 7,3, f. 62r.

6. SAG, K 10,1, f. 34r; K 2,1, f. 9r.

7. SAG, G 1,4, f. 5r; K 1,f. 164v; K 9,1, f. 18r; K 8,2, f. 16r.

8. Case cited Nicholas, "Crime and Punishment," 1146.

9. SAG, K 1, f. 151v; K 5,1, f. 37r.

10. SAG, K 11,1, fos. 86v, 87r, 89r.

11. SAG, G 8,4, f. 12v.

12. SAG, G 3,3, f. 22r.

13. SAG, G 6,2, f. 15v; K 1, f. 159r.

14. SAG, G 1, 5, f. 18v.

15. SAG, K 10,1, f. 8v.

16. SAG, G 1a, f. 39r; G 1,1, f. 14v. Mother and son evidently reached a more sensible arrangement soon afterward, for in 1352 she had bought half the house from him in dower, and they had agreed on a division of the chattels and debts; G 1,2, f. 48v.

17. SAG, K 13,1, f. 45v; K 1, fos. 136v, 176r.

18. SAG, G 5,2, f. 34r–v; G 5,4, f. 28v.

19. Dankaert was to pay Pieter the value of the land sold according to the appraisal of "good people." But the same good people, now defined as "common friends," were to decide what payment Pieter should make to Dankaert for the latter's expenses in taking him out eating and drinking. The evil genius had tried to lure the boy into bad business by showing him a good time, but the young man at least had to pay him back the cost of the fun. SAG, K 1, f. 118r.

20. SAG, G 7,4, f. 25v; G 8,2, f. 39v; G 8,3, fos. 7v, 11v.

21. SAG, G 6,3, f. 29v; G 6,1, f. 32v; G 8,3, f. 55r.

22. SAG, G 2,5, fos. 11r, 17v, 29r, 35v; G 7,4, f. 32v.

23. SAG, G 8,3, f. IV; G 8,4, f. IIr.

24. SAG, G 5,5, f. 38v.

25. SAG, G 4,3, f. 42r. This was a plague year; it is surprising that more contests of this sort did not arise. The magistrates did make this ruling contingent on the inability of Clais's heirs to prove that he had died first.

26. SAG, G 2,4, f. 30v; G 2,5, f. 8v; G 2,4, fos. 29v, 31r.

27. SAG, G 7,3, f. IIr; G 4,2, f. 48r; G 4,3, f. 2v; G 6,2, f. IV; G 3,4, f. 20r.

28. See in general Nicholas, "Crime and Punishment." Stone, *Family, Sex and Marriage*, 95: "The family that slayed together stayed together."

29. The knight Willem Van Campine as party leader paid 76 lb. gr. in 1365 for the death of Clais Van Reghensbrugghe. Included in this, however, was the death of Mayhu de Coc, a retainer of the Van Campine party, who had been executed. Willem Van Campine acknowledged that the blood price for his antagonist would have been higher had the latter's party not prosecuted de Coc and had him executed. He pledged to bring Mayhu's brother before the *scepenen* to swear to keep the peace. SAG, Z 3,5, f. 10r.

30. SAG, G 1,3, f. 3v.

31. SAG, K 10,1, f. 41v.

32. SAG, Z 3,1, f. 3v.

33. SAG, G 9,2, f. 66r.

34. SAG, Z 3,5, 5 bis r. For a refusal to contribute, see G 2,3, f. 38r.

35. SAG, Z 6,1, f. 2v; Z 4,3, f. 3r.

36. SAG, Z 5,5, f. 17r; Z 5,2, f. IIv; Z 6,1, f. 19r.

37. SAG, G 7,3, f. 37r. As one example of many, Heinric Van Doinse in 1382 bought the brewing implements of Gillis Van Doinse from the city for II lb. gr.; SAG, K 8,3, f. 16r. While the real estate was sold cheaply, there seems to have been more market for chattels—this is a very good price—perhaps because buyers would have less reason to fear that their titles would be challenged after the war.

38. SAG, G 5,1, f. 24r.

39. SAG, G 6,3, f. 53v; G 8,3, f. 17r. The father had remarried by Mar. 15, 1390, and was dead by Apr. 6, 1391; K 12, f. 39v; G 9,2, f. 34r.

40. SAG, G 4,4, f. 13r.

41. SAG, G 3,1, f. 62v; Z 6,3, f. 18v; Z 1,2, f. IIr.

42. The blood price of Jan Bierman was 24 lb. gr., of which the clan allowed 3 lb. gr. to go to the widow. After expenses for masses, costs of settlement, and other deductions, the oldest son received 9 lb. gr., while his younger brother took 4 lb., thus being exceptionally favored. The rest of the clan divided the remainder. SAG, Z 6,2, fos. 9v, 12v; Z 6,3, f. 12r.

43. SAG, Ser. 93 bis, no. 1, f. 192v. The Ghent system of four branches of a bilateral kin system corresponds to that of early modern Scotland. See Jenny Wormald, "Bloodfeud, Kindred and Government in Early Modern Scotland," *Past and Present* 87 (1980): 54–97; Goody, *Development of the Family*, 236.

44. SAG, K 1, f. 126v.

45. For example, in 1374 Simon Van Ravenscoet agreed to atone the wounds that he had inflicted upon Jacob Van der Linden. The arbitrators were two "common kinsmen" to be chosen by the injured party and two others who were his kinsmen but not Van Ravenscoet's, suggesting that the antagonists were probably cousins. SAG, Z 5,4, f. 8r. The ruling was only promulgated in 1376; Z 6,1, f. 10r.

46. SAG, Z 3,3, f. 10v; Z 6,5, f. 4v for the de Vlaminc homicide. For other cases involving Ghiselin de Vlaminc, see Z 4,3, f. 11v; Z 4,5, f. 17v; Z 5,1, f. 12v; K 4,2, f. 45v; Z 5,5, fos. 13v, 14r, 9r, 17r; Z 6,2, f. 14v; Z 6,4, f. 5r; Z 6,5, f. 4v. The period of the marital separation was quite active for him. Within a year of it he had sustained 34 lb. par. worth of injuries, another attack for which his assailant did a pilgrimage, and had himself been sent on a pilgrimage for his part in a tavern brawl.

47. SAG, Z 6,3, f. 18r; Z 6,2, f. 17r; Z 3,4, f. 15r.

48. SAG, Z 5,2, f. 13r; G 5,3, fos. 6v, 14–1.

Index

Index

DUE DATE

DATE DUE